BEHIND THE SCENES WITH BILLY GRAHAM

Stories from the 60-year Diary of

MAURICE ROWLANDSON

kevin mayhew

First published in 2007 by
KEVIN MAYHEW LTD
Buxhall, Stowmarket, Suffolk, IP14 3BW
E-mail: info@kevinmayhewltd.com
www.kevinmayhew.com

9 8 7 6 5 4 3 2 1 0

ISBN-10 184417 723 8
ISBN-13 978 184417 723 3
Catalogue No. 1500976

Cover design by Sara-Jane Came
Edited by Peter Dainty
Typeset by Richard Weaver

Printed and bound in Great Britain

DEDICATION

This book is dedicated to our six younger grandchildren – Matthew, Philip and Peter, the sons of JULIAN and FIONA; Rachel, Sarah and Cheryl, the daughters of JACKY and JEFF – and the two older grandchildren, Andrew and Timothy (the sons of GARY and DIANA) and their wives Katherine and Kate.

CONTENTS

ACKNOWLEDGEMENTS

I APPRECIATE Sir Cliff Richard's agreement that we could use his Foreword from *Life with Billy*. He says that what he wrote then, applies now! So he is happy for it to re-appear in this new book. I am also grateful to Canon Michael Saward for his Introduction to me as the writer. I could not think of anyone better to do this for, over the years, he has experienced all my foibles!

A special thank you to my Editor, Peter Dainty, who has guided me through chapter by chapter, correcting those anomalies and deleting the irrelevant! It has been a relationship – though distant (he is in Bury St Edmunds and I am in Swindon) – which I have enjoyed and appreciated.

Our only difference of opinion arose over whether to use a capital 'H' or a small 'h' when using the personal pronoun in reference to God and the Lord Jesus Christ. The publisher's practice is to use the small 'h'. I firmly stuck with my conviction that the small 'h' somewhat denigrates the Glory of God and the Trinity. I also believe it can lead to misunderstanding when a misplaced pronoun could look as though it referred to the writer rather than to God.

Thank you too to Audrey Parker who has gone through chapter by chapter, meticulously, before it went to Peter Dainty. She has ironed out some of my grammatical errors (and punctuation!) and has made some useful suggestions about the order of the paragraphs. Her long-suffering husband Norman says that now the book is finished, perhaps he'll get some cooked meals again! Audrey and her husband are members at the Freshbrook Evangelical Church in Swindon – a remarkable church of which my wife and I are also members. Our Pastor, David Earnshaw, has been a great encouragement to us, especially during the dark days of our eldest son's final illness.

Thank you too to Marilyn, my wife, who has put up with my mind being elsewhere most of the time. I have been concentrating on the story just written, or the story about to come. Now that it is all finished, perhaps we can get out and see the countryside together and find some nice little eating places! Maybe that will be some compensation.

I thank God for His goodness in maintaining the 'Thin Gold Line' throughout my life. Through tragedy and trauma He has been faithful to us as a family. That 'Thin Gold Line' passed through Billy Graham's ministry. His faithfulness to me and trusting me in the things he allowed me to do for him enabled me, in turn, 'to do great things for God'.

Finally, thank you too, to my trustworthy computer. Every word, every chapter, has been typed by my own fair hand. My custom-built computer, mostly assembled by my son Julian and organised by my local computer expert Sean Lewis, has kept running and survived without a 'crash'.

It is my hope that these stories will encourage others to launch out and follow God's leading in their lives. I pray that those who read these words will see how a whole lifetime can be used by God in service to Him.

FOREWORD

Sir Cliff Richard

I'VE POSED for a fair number of pictures in my time, but one of the strangest had to be on a Billy Graham crusade platform at Earls Court back in 1966. The photograph shows me looking surly and bored – behind me, grim-faced and every inch the bouncer, is Maurice Rowlandson.

What the 12,000-strong audience didn't know was that we were filming a scene for the Billy Graham movie *Two a Penny* and, at a given signal from director Jim Collier, who had wisely secreted himself away from public view, I had to slip into character. Unfortunately for me, 'character' meant yobbing it up as Jamie, a thoroughly cynical and nasty bit of work, who, according to the storyline, was only at the crusade under duress, and on the platform by animal cunning. I took the subsequent letters of censure as a tribute to my acting.

My respect for Dr Graham is no secret, so for me to read a book which gives a unique insight not only into the man himself, but also into the team and organisation that have surrounded him for so long, is fascinating. From the outset, the Billy Graham Association's professionalism and efficiency were impressive, often in contrast to some of the other well-meaning but ultra-casual Christian organisations I encountered in my early days as a 'celebrity Christian'.

Maurice Rowlandson of course was the Billy Graham 'face' in the UK. He was the one with whom we discussed projects and possibilities, and it was he, I suspect, who persuaded Dr Graham to invite me to give that much-publicised testimony at an earlier

Earls Court meeting. I can't imagine that Billy Graham, or anyone else in the American team, come to that, would ever have heard of Cliff Richard.

In many ways, that particular evening was a significant landmark for me. Certainly I had shared my Christian testimony before, but never on such a public platform. There was no going back after that night. The press ensured that my colours were well and truly nailed. I was a Billy Graham man; more important, I was Christ's man. Thanks, Maurice, for helping me make that clear!

INTRODUCTION TO MAURICE ROWLANDSON

Canon Michael Saward
Canon Emeritus of St Paul's Cathedral

THIRTEEN YEARS ago I reviewed a book by Maurice Rowlandson and called it 'easy, pleasant, and an enjoyable read.' Nothing changes. Maurice (or Maur-eeeece as the Americans insist on calling him) is much the same guy as he was when I first met him almost fifty years ago.

His personality and strengths remain his most attractive features and his occasional myopia is hardly likely to stop being evident in his declining years. He is an ardent Americanophile to his back teeth and seems incapable of understanding how and why his many fellow British Evangelicals (including me) continue to have elements of uneasiness about some aspects of mass evangelism.

Most of us would explicitly exempt Billy Graham from that uncertainty. His integrity is unquestionable, his amazing achievements are there for all to see and Maurice sets them out (and his relation to them) with clarity and honesty. Going back to the 1940s he tells his own story and how it has intertwined with that of Billy's ministry for sixty years.

He began working with Tom Rees (and I claim to be one of the very few who once fell asleep while Tom was preaching in the Royal Albert Hall!) and our paths first crossed in 1959 when I was a curate in Edgware and Maurice and his American wife Marilyn belonged to our church. I've stayed in their home and one of my daughters was, briefly, enamoured as a teenager with one of his sons. We've often disagreed (amicably) and enjoyed lunching together (at his expense whenever possible). He invited me (entirely properly) to share the Admiral's cabin on a Caribbean sailing ship for a couple of weeks and we very occasionally spoke to each other to prove that we were still friends.

He and Marilyn have three times faced deeply traumatic suffering in their family life and he does not flinch from describing what their Christian faith has meant in such circumstances.

Then, in Mission London 1989, to my amazement I was invited to introduce Billy Graham to the world's Press at the Westminster Conference Centre and I even have a photo to prove that I haven't been dreaming. Afterwards, I asked him to lunch with me at the Athenaeum but he declined as he was due to lunch with George Bush, senior. Not many people have been turned down in favour of the US President.

Maurice, fascinatingly, takes the occasional lid off the Graham organisation's doings, which was an eye-opener to me and while nothing would be of interest to the tabloids it certainly intrigued me to discover some of the things I had only guessed at.

So here is a most illuminating book by a most delightful character about a world-class Christian evangelist. I'm honoured to have been asked to write this Introduction and wish both the book and the worthy Maurice every blessing. You won't get a clearer picture of what Billy and Maurice have been up to since the end of the Second World War.

PROLOGUE: THE EARLY YEARS – Leading to Billy Graham and the 'Thin Gold Line'

MY CONVERSION at seven years of age was a direct answer to my parents' prayers. My father and mother were deeply involved in Spiritual activity at the time I was born.

Apart from his leadership of the Men's Bible Class at Enfield Baptist Church, my father ran a monthly meeting in the same town 'For the deepening of Spiritual Life'. This involved bringing significant speakers from all over the country – speakers rarely travelled from America on short visits in those days! As a result I met many famous preachers ranging from the great evangelist Gypsy Smith on whose knee I once sat. In his book *The Beauty of Jesus*, Gypsy wrote:

> A tiny chap [Maurice] used to accompany his father when the latter brought his car to take me to a meeting. He wasn't shy to be riding in a car with a gypsy and sat on my knee. We had only just left the house on our journey when he began to teach me a chorus which he liked, and soon four people in that car were singing something like this:
>
> The birds up in the treetops sing their song.
> The angels sound His praises all day long.
> The flowers in the garden lend their hue,
> so why shouldn't I, why shouldn't you
> praise Him too?

I also met and heard exceptional Bible teachers like the Revd J. Sidlow Baxter, and the great Scottish 'divine' Dr J. Douglas

Adam. His booming voice scared the living daylights out of me and it was not until many years later that I discovered he had a very soft heart.

I had an uncle, Reginald Harrod, who was married to my father's sister. He was the general secretary of the Japan Evangelistic Band which had been founded by Paget Wilkes. The Harrods too were a deeply spiritual couple and they brought a plethora of Japanese missionaries to our house – as well as several Japanese pastors – many of whom spoke at the 'Monthly Meetings'. I remember Juji Nakada – who taught me origami – and Pastor Segawa, who led me to the Lord. Then there were Mr and Mrs Archie Dyer, Mr and Mrs Henry Stark, Mr and Mrs James Cuthbertson, Mr and Mrs Cecil Wilkinson, Miss Irene Webster Smith who ministered to Japanese students (and later to American students) and Rose Bailey who had done so much for Japanese children through her 'Sunrise Band'. All of them believed deeply in Victorious Living as Christians. My father's other sister, Alice Peay, was another deeply spiritual member of the family and they all prayed for me right from the time of my birth.

The other half of my father's family, his brother, his wife and his children, moved in social circles and they were the monied side of the family. It was many years later – long after the death of my parents and that uncle – that some members of *his* family began to find the life that is to be found in Jesus Christ. For me, I always dreaded 'family meetings' which brought both sides of the family together, with my father and his two sisters continually 'preaching' to the other side of his family. As a young child I was most embarrassed and, in later years, my wife and I determined that, whenever we met with the whole family, we would not 'preach' to them. It was an indictment upon us later on when my uncle's grand-daughter came to Christ and she said to us, 'Why have you not told me about Christ before?'

Denominationally I was brought up a hybrid! My father did not believe in denominations, or in church membership. He saw both as man-made devices to keep members and statistics. His only criterion in any church worship was 'Is the Word being preached?' If it was, then that was where we worshipped. But if the minister started talking about the importance of church membership, or strayed from biblical exposition or, worse still, mentioned a 'Church Bazaar', my father would declare 'It's time for us to move on'. So in my boyhood we attended Methodist, Baptist, Church of England, Brethren, Congregational – and even the Salvation Army when their outstanding Bible teacher, Thomas Blower, was the rage of the day. During those peripatetic days we heard such great preachers as Dr Dinsdale T. Young (at Westminster Central Hall – Methodist) and the Revd G. Campbell Morgan (at Westminster Chapel – Congregational) who was later succeeded by the legendary Dr D. Martyn Lloyd-Jones. So I heard some great preachers when I was a boy.

Westminster Chapel was so full in those days that you could reserve a pew for your exclusive use. Your name appeared on a little brass plate at the entrance to the pew. Non pew-holders queued in the aisle for vacant seats, for the unoccupied pew-holders' seats were released five minutes before the service started. On occasion my father would telephone the church early on Sunday morning to say that we would not be there that day and that our seats could be released earlier.

But it was the Japan Evangelistic Band that proved to be one of the significant events in my life. Each year we attended their annual Convention at Slavanka in Bournemouth. There was not much for me to do. Children's play areas, or crèches, were unheard of in those days. So it was a delight to find a young Japanese Pastor – Pastor Segawa – who loved children and spent most of his time amusing me. He drew beautiful coloured pictures; he did origami as well and he told me stories of Jesus. Although he had come to Slavanka to spend his time at the Convention, most of his daytime hours were spent with me. One day he said 'Maurice! wouldn't you like to ask Jesus to come into your heart?' Gently he led me to do just that and on 23 August 1933 I became a Christian.

Even before I became a Christian I had an evangelistic zeal! I was born on 15 August 1925, and I can recall an incident when I was 3 and Bev Snowden, the little boy next door, came in to play one day. As we walked down our hall corridor we passed a large painting, 'The Tabernacle in the Wilderness'. My father was deeply into biblical typology and never tired of telling us what everything in the tabernacle meant. Bev drew my attention to the picture and asked, 'What is that all about?' I remembered that my father had some enlarged pictures of each part of the equipment in the tabernacle that helped him to explain what the various 'types' in the tabernacle meant. So I telephoned him. In those far-off days there was no dialling. I just had to tell the operator, 'Put me through to my daddy please.' The girls at the telephone exchange were so used to my voice that they knew what number I wanted! My father was at his office and I asked him where those pictures could be found. He told me to look in his desk drawer where I would find them. I had remembered my lessons well from my father's descriptions of what everything meant. At three years of age I preached my first evangelistic sermon and, in the next hour or so, Bev got the full works!

I was conscious through all of my school days that, as a Christian, I was 'different' from the other boys – and this led to some bullying. This was partly due to my frail condition during my school days. In 1931 I had contracted a mastoid problem and was operated on for the removal of the mastoid bone. Two days later the other ear flared up and a second operation was performed immediately. No sooner had I partly recovered from those operations when I contracted scarlet fever. In those days, both mastoiditis and scarlet fever were life-threatening problems. Scarlet fever was the 'MRSA' of those days and was often contracted when the patient was in hospital or nursing home. My condition stimulated prayer from all my father's many Christian friends. In his diary he wrote: 'Is our darling Maurice to be taken from us? God answered our prayers through the mastoid operations. Our many friends are praying with us now that he will survive the scarlet fever.' In later years he said, 'He was saved to serve.'

It was almost a full year before I had recovered enough to go back to school. By then I was exempted from football and all contact sports. Nor was I allowed to do anything, like swimming, which might expose me to infection. So the bullying was quite a problem. I knew that a Christian 'turned the other cheek' and I did not swear like the others did. However, eventually, God provided me with a good friend at school – Patrick Hodge – who took me under his wing and by his protection I was saved from a lot of bullying. I am sorry that I lost contact with him in later years. Maybe this book will bring us together again.

Each summer my father rented a house at Frinton-on-Sea so that my cousin Joyce Bell and I could attend the four-week Children's Special Service Mission (CSSM) on the beach. It was there that I first met people like Maurice Wood (years later to become the Bishop of Norwich) and Gordon Harman (who became the rector of Edgware Parish Church which we attended). They were members of the CSSM team ('Workers' they were called). All of them were students from Oxford or Cambridge, and a formidable bunch they were, dressed in their grey slacks, white shirts, college ties and gaudy blazers! A few years later – in my adult years – one of the team members contracted polio. As a result the entire team were put into quarantine and a parents' committee was formed to keep the mission going. Mr Randle Manwaring, who organised it, called to see me one day. 'You realise, don't you Maurice,' he said, 'that we will not be able to use you because you haven't been to Oxford or Cambridge!'

It was during the Frinton Mission when attending 'Keenites' as a boy that, sitting on the cliffs above the beach at Frinton, I learned from another CSSM worker, Frank Gray, the fundamentals of what it meant to be a Christian. Back at home throughout the rest of the year I attended the Crusaders' Bible Class every Sunday where the most wonderful leaders – Fred Cursons, Roy Cattell, Norman Smith and John (later Sir John) Laing – taught me many things about the Christian life. Every Friday was 'Bible Study' (held at our house) and it was there I first learned to pray aloud and came to understand what the Bible was all about.

Two things that Fred Cursons taught me as a boy have remained with me ever since. One was how to remember the order of the minor prophets in the Old Testament, and the order of the Epistles in the New Testament. For the minor prophets he said to remember 'HO JO AMOB JO MINA HAZEE HAZEE MA'. It is not some strange language, but the first sound of each of the minor prophets in order – Thus, HOsea; JOel; AMos; OBadiah etc. Since then, I have never forgotten the order! For the Epistles he said 'Remember GEPCAT – Galatians, Ephesians, Philippians, Colossians and Thessalonians.' How valuable that teaching was!

Another thing that he taught me was:

> Joshua, the son of Nun, and Caleb, the son of Jephunneh, were the only two who ever got through to the land of Milk and Honey!

I am eternally thankful for that, and other teaching, that came from Fred Cursons.

One important activity of the weekly Crusader Bible Class was the 'Text Comp'. The results of this competition built up points for the four teams into which the class was divided. Our leaders always devised something special for the winning team each quarter – maybe a day out on the Thames or a visit to the Zoo. The competition worked like this: at some point in the afternoon's meeting the leader would announce 'Now it's time for the Text Comp'. He would then call out the reference of a text and the first person to find it gained points for his team and then stood up and read it. Usually there were five or six texts each week and we quickly learned to find our way about the Bible. New members had their finger in the index to quickly find the right book and page. Older members knew the favourite text of each leader and often had their finger already in the place – fairly confident that sooner or later that verse would be included. It was an enormous help in learning the books of the Bible and it has stood me in good stead for the whole of my life. I know that many others benefited in the same way.

The war intervened and much united Christian witness and activity was put on hold. My father's business was 'blitzed' twice and prompted him to write a booklet *Blitzed but Blessed*. However, in 1944 a group of Christian leaders decided that the time had come to make a new impact for Christ on the City of London. They formed a committee (of which my father was a member) who decided to hold a series of 16 meetings at London's Royal Albert Hall in March and April of that year. They called it 'The Faith for our Times' campaign. The meetings were to be addressed by outstanding evangelists of the day including Lindsay Glegg, Dr Frederick T. Ellis, The Revd Theo M. Bamber, Mr Robert Laidlaw, Dr Alan Redpath and a young man called Tom Rees. I went to those meetings and was a steward. The style of the meetings was rather old-fashioned in concept. It was off-putting, for example, to find little old men who walked around the stalls and the boxes asking people, 'Are you saved, brother?' I did not feel that I could expose my young friends at Crusaders, Scouts or church to such an atmosphere.

On the last night of the campaign, Roy Cattell, who had just accepted an invitation to work with Tom Rees, came to our box in the Royal Albert Hall. He said to my father, 'I have brought a young man I want you to meet. His name is Tom Rees, and I believe he has a great future.' Until that moment none of us had met Tom Rees face to face. We had only seen and heard him from the platform. It was to prove to be yet another significant moment in my life.

A year later my father came home from a meeting of the 'Faith for our Times' Committee to say that they had been approached by Tom Rees asking them to sponsor a month-long series of meetings in London's Westminster Central Hall. He said that Tom Rees wanted to be the only speaker and that he planned to lead the meetings too. The committee was not impressed and declined the invitation. My father, Leonard Rowlandson, however said that he thought they had made a wrong decision. He saw a potential in the young evangelist that the others had not perceived. When Tom Rees heard of the committee's decision he decided, nonetheless, to go ahead with his plans, in faith and on his own. What happened then is another story.

From 1941 to 1944 I had been articled to the borough engineer and surveyor of the Wembley Borough Council. My father had decided that I should have a qualification before entering his business, then if ever the business failed, I would have something to fall back on. It was while I served this apprenticeship that I learned to drive. In 1942 I was 17 years of age and, although there was a scarcity of petrol and very few cars on the road, I applied for my driving licence. By so doing I avoided the need to take a 'test' because all tests were suspended during the war. One day in 1942, Mr Cecil Trapp, the borough engineer, put his head into the drawing office and asked, 'Has anyone in here got a driving licence?' I immediately replied to say that I had. He told me to get a car from the car pool in half an hour and to take him up to Edgware Road.

Although I had never driven a car before, I ordered the car immediately from the car pool. Then I used the next half-hour getting used to the feel of a car and driving up and down the extensive forecourt of the Wembley Town Hall! When Mr Trapp got into the car, I drove off – albeit in bottom gear for greater control – and erratically took him to Edgware Road. The roads were, mercifully, quite empty of traffic because of the war. He did ask me if I shouldn't change to a higher gear to which I replied, 'I'm new to this car, sir, and I have greater control in bottom gear until I get used to the car!' I must have done alright for, thereafter, whenever he needed to be taken anywhere he always asked for me. By the end of another two years I had become quite a competent driver!

In 1944 my father was taken ill and had to go to hospital. I had just finished my articles and had qualified as an incorporated surveyor. He asked me to move into his printing and stationery business and to run it in his absence. It was an example of God's perfect timing in my life. It was his dream and vision anyway, that I should succeed him and keep the business going. However, God had other plans!

Another activity that had been put into cold storage during the war was the annual Keswick Convention. It was not until 1946 that the meetings in Keswick resumed and my father decided that we should attend. July that year I attended my first-ever Keswick Convention. Little did I know then that 33 years later I would become the secretary of that selfsame Convention. It was at the evening Missionary Meeting on Friday, 19 July 1946, that I responded to the invitation that those who felt God calling them to serve Him should stand up – wherever, whenever and however He might lead. I was one of those who stood.

The following year God brought to fruition the commitment I had made at Keswick. On 9 January 1947 I had a telephone call from Tom Rees to ask me to join his team and to work with him, full time, at Hildenborough. My father was devastated! All his dreams of me coming into the business were shattered, but he realised that if this was the call of God to me, then he could not stand in the way. He put out a fleece. He advertised for someone to take my place (for in his weakness my contribution to the business had already become important). He said that he trusted God to find the right person. Within two days of the advertisement appearing he had had an application from a Mr Horace Dales. He was a Christian man – a Crusader – and had all the qualifications needed. I left for Hildenborough Hall on 17 January 1947 (Tom Rees had said he wanted me to start 'right away'). Three days later Horace Dales started working with my father and he remained there until he retired four decades later. He was, indeed, God's man for the job.

That confirmation gave comfort to my father as a response to his 'fleece'. He wrote in his diary 'Maurice left me to go to Hildenborough! To Dorothy and myself this is one of the saddest days of our lives and one of bitterest disappointment to me personally. Yet if this proves to be the plan of God's appointment for our dear Maurice, we shall rejoice. I fear it will take a long time for me to be reconciled that Maurice is not joining me in the business. However it may be that his going out will mean his coming back later, with a larger outlook on life and more fitted as the result of outside training to take on the management of Chas. Davy & Co. However, we must wait and see.'

That 'coming back' never did happen. Indeed that date in January proved to be the very beginning of the 'Thin Gold Line'. It stretched from January 1947 and seemed bound to end in Eternity. It was provided by God to give me the comfort and assurance of His guidance. As the story unfolded, I was to see His handiwork in the continuous forging of that 'Line'. With every new experience I became aware that He was there before me and after me. I learned to latch on to it and to trust Him for all that was to come. I didn't know at first that God had it all planned out for me. In everything I did throughout my life, He kept showing me how the 'Line' brought me back into association with Billy Graham and his ministry. Looking back from the perspective of more than 60 years I can see now that the 'Thin Gold Line' was unbroken. Because of that it must become a part of the theme of this story. Corrie Ten Boom said:

> My life is but a weaving betwixt God and me;
> I do not choose the colours, He worketh steadily.

Oft times He weaveth sorrow, and I in foolish pride
forget He sees the upper, and I the underside.
Not till the loom is silent and the shuttles cease to fly
will God unfold the pattern and explain the reason why,
for the dark threads are as needful in the Weaver's skilful hand
as the threads of gold and silver in the pattern He has planned.

Benjamine Malachi Franklin

She added, 'God has no problems – only plans', and that was true for me through all of life. How it all came together will have to wait until Chapter 2!

CHAPTER ONE

THE VENTURERS NORFOLK BROADS CRUISE

BEFORE BEGINNING with the 'main' story, we need to deal with the 'founding' of the Venturers Norfolk Broads Cruise. It pre-dated all the other Christian activities in which I became involved. I was just 20 years of age when I started the cruise. Little did I know then that it would last throughout the greater part of my life and become a major factor in all that I did. The cruise would bring to our family some of the happiest experiences of our lives. It also would bring many lifelong friends and colleagues. The 'Thin Gold Line' had not yet even begun and I did not know how God's hand and over-ruling would shape my entire life. He used the Venturers Norfolk Broads Cruise as part of that experience. Because it pre-dated all other events, the story of the cruise must be explored and recounted first.

It all began because I had read the 12 books by the children's author, Arthur Ransome. He would be quite surprised to know that he had been the inspiration for an innovative evangelistic programme. He was not in any way noted for his spirituality.

The plots of two of his twelve books unfold on the Norfolk Broads. Soon after reading *Coot Club* (in 1939) I wanted to sail on the Broads. That ambition was realised in 1940 when, under the auspices of the Varsity & Public Schools Camps (VPS), I was able to sail as a boy crew member with the Spinnakers Cruise. I had a wonderful skipper – John Inglesby, brother of the famous ballerina Mona Inglesby (who died in October 2006) – and it was a memorable experience from the very beginning. I couldn't wait to do it again. Unhappily the war intervened and holidays of that nature were denied for several years.

In 1945 the Broads appeared to be open again so I asked the VPS if the Spinnakers would be sailing this year. Their reply was a firm negative. 'The Broads are not yet open' they said. I was pretty sure they were wrong because the Broads boat people had just sent me a catalogue of available boats. I assumed they would not have done that if the Broads were not yet open. So I booked six yachts and a motor cruiser – in faith for April 1946 – and set about finding enough boys to fill them. I had a few who would come from my Scout Troop and from the Crusader Class. But forty-eight in all would be needed. The fees for that year (to cover all the costs) were £4.15s plus 5/- for fares from London (note: in 2006, for the same holiday, the fees were £210)!

As the VPS would not be sailing I approached the headquarters of the Children's Special Service Mission (CSSM) – who ran the VPS – to ask if my new cruise could be regarded as a VPS Cruise. Mr Hubbard, the general secretary, welcomed me enthusiastically and gave me carte blanche to advertise for participants. Because we were the first cruise to venture out after the war, I decided that we should be called the 'Venturers' – and so it has been ever since.

A week later I had a letter from Mr Hubbard giving me the names of two potential Skippers for my cruise – Mr Henry W. Hole, and Mr John B. Woodward. I wrote immediately to both of them. Mr Hole said 'yes': Mr Woodward was, at that moment, growing peanuts in Africa but said that when he returned he would be happy to come – as indeed he did some two years later.

Two weeks later came another letter from Mr Hubbard to say that he had acted precipitately and that he had spoken without authority. Some members of his council had seen my advertisement for boys and Mr Hubbard was in 'hot water' for speaking out of turn. He had to withdraw his agreement with me and said that we could *not* be a VPS Cruise. So we became an 'independent' cruise and have remained so ever since.

The most important outcome of our three weeks as a 'VPS Cruise' was the way in which God had used that event to introduce me to Henry Hole who became my closest friend, mentor, advisor and counsellor for the rest of his life. It was also the first contact I had with John Woodward. He sailed with us for many years as a very competent skipper and a past master when it came to dealing with boys. His aristocratic manner and precise instructions became a watchword on the cruise. To have a milk bottle on the breakfast table he called 'squalor' and he would never allow any table to be set without a tablecloth! He was one of the 'characters' on the cruise.

I saw the Venturers as an evangelistic effort. We would teach sailing and engender a healthy respect for water during the day. Each morning we would have a brief devotional time around the breakfast table and in the evening our Padre would end the day bringing a message from Scripture – including some gentle evangelism. This paid off and, as the years went by, many dozens of boys (and later girls too) came to accept the Lord Jesus Christ as their Saviour.

One of our skippers in the early years was Mr A. Morgan Derham, the editorial secretary of the CSSM. He was so inspired by what we were doing that he sought our permission to start his own cruise along similar lines. Thus the 'Otters' came into being – and later he expanded to start the 'Kestrels', the 'Mallards' and the 'Harriers'. As Morgan introduced new ideas into the sailing activities, the 'Otters' became the first cruise to include girls also. The 'Mallards' and the 'Harriers' extended the activity into the summer. Others too were inspired to set sail on the Broads. In the peak years there were some 28 organised Christian Cruises sailing in Norfolk in the month of April. By the millennium more than 30,000 youngsters had sailed on those cruises and countless hundreds had come to faith in the Lord Jesus Christ.

Sixty, and more, years later the Venturers were still going strong and were numbered amongst the few remaining organised Christian cruises. They still had every intention of carrying on into the foreseeable future. By the early 2000s there were sons and daughters, grandsons and granddaughters and even a great-grandson amongst those who came. More important was that by then every one of the skippers had been a boy or girl on the cruise in years gone by. Some even dated their conversion to the time when they came as a boy or a girl on the cruise. They had now returned to render their services to the cruise having, by now, gone through intensive training.

One of the boys, who had 'grown up' to become first a skipper on the cruise and later succeeded me as Honorary Secretary was Tim Smith. He wrote to express his feelings:

> I have not, to my shame, offered my personal thanks to you for your past leadership of the Venturers. I have found your enthusiastic and pro-active concern for all matters related to the cruise to be a great source of inspiration. I am confident that your attention to detail and continuous focus on the spiritual objectives of the cruise have left their mark on those of us who now carry on the good work. It is my hope that a small part of your leadership over my thirty-something years of Venturing will 'rub off' on me as I endeavour to serve the Lord on cruise affairs in the coming years.

In 1947 Henry Hole became the commodore of the cruise and was an exceptional leader. He inspired those who worked with him to give of their best. He demanded and expected total loyalty amongst the officers and a high level of discipline from all the youngsters who sailed on the cruise. All of this produced such a high standard that it was formally recognised nationally when he received the award of an MBE from Her Majesty the Queen 'For services to the Venturers Cruise.' When he retired shortly before his death, he was succeeded by his son-in-law, John Spradbery and upon *his* retirement several years later, the new commodore was Julian Rowlandson – son of the founder. So it had gone the full circle.

Throughout its life the Venturers Cruise maintained evangelism as its goal. It also had a very high standard of sail-training. So many Venturers have been inspired to acquire their own ships – from small dinghies to large seagoing yachts – that the Cruise has shaped and changed the lives of those who came into contact with it both physically and spiritually. One of these was Tony Charles who first came as a 13-year-old boy. He has told his story for posterity:

> The Venturers Cruise was, without any shadow of a doubt, the formative event of my life. It is a remarkable organisation which owes its existence to the dream of Maurice Rowlandson when he was a young man. Now the cruise is still going 60 years later

after the dream was made reality. I have just retired as vice commodore some 45 years after I first went as a boy of 13 with very mixed feelings.

I too had a dream to sail a real yacht and live out adventures I had read about in my story books. Next door but one to me lived a family who had an outboard motor in their garage. I reasoned, 'If they have an outboard motor, they must have a boat'! It so happened that Maurice lived in that house, and he had been sizing up the small boy who lived at No. 13 as a potential Venturer. After I had spoken to him I only had one problem. They seemed to be a 'churchy' lot. I supposed I could put up with the religious bit for the sake of sailing. Church, you see, was not part of our family life.

When I got to the cruise my problem surfaced. These churchy people were indeed different. The problem was that they were differently different! Their Christianity was clearly a part of their everyday life – and yet they still had fun!

I had thought that I was a Christian, but when I went on that first cruise I really had no idea what becoming a Christian meant. By the end of the week, however, I had asked Jesus into my life and I knew that that would mean changes.

God spoke to me progressively over that week. No one pressurised me. The Venturers Cruise has always held its two objectives as important – to introduce people to a love of sailing and to the love of God.

Mine was only one of many similar stories of people who have found God on the cruise. The fellowship with Venturers people has meant a lot to me through all of my life. None of that story would have happened had it not been for that outboard motor in Maurice's garage.

Inevitably traditions grew up within the cruise. They became the hallmark of the cruise itself. For example, the narrow decks of a Norfolk Broads yacht often meant that a boy or a girl missed their footing and fell overboard. Any such were honoured at the evening singsong by being awarded 'Ye ancient Order of ye Wette Pantes!' Then everyone joined in to sing:

Happy bathday to you, happy bathday to you,
happy bathday dear Venturer, happy bathday to you.
He(she) was only blowing bubbles. Bubbles in the Broads
. . . S P L A S H!

Alongside the fun songs there are happy memories of a skipper quartet singing hymns and choruses around the piano. Henry Hole (who had been a member of a Gospel Song Team) was joined by Dr Vincent (John) Edmunds, John Woodward (at the piano) and myself to sing:

> We shall see His lovely face, some bright golden morning.
> When the clouds have rifted and the shades have flown.
> Sorrow will be turned to joy; heartaches gone for ever.
> No more night . . . only light, when we see His face.

They are precious memories of very happy times.

In the early days a sailing regatta (or race) took place each year as the big boats raced against each other. This eventually led to a disastrous year when many of the boats were damaged and Henry Hole ruled that, in future, this would not happen again. Instead he planned a daily dinghy (small boat) race in which the dinghy from each yacht would sail around a couple of marker buoys and the whole fleet. On each round a different member of the crew from each yacht would take the helm (under instruction from his or her first mate). This became a major feature of the cruise. Under sheer pressure of being 'on the helm' all the youngsters learned how to sail a small boat on their own. Then, one year, there was a very light wind and some dinghies were stranded away from their own big boat. It was then that we discovered that many of the youngsters did not know how to row a boat. That problem was solved by adding a 'rowing regatta' to the programme each day. The youngsters soon learned how to row too. That pattern of a dual regatta each day has been maintained as a feature of the cruise programme ever since.

A system of awards was established early on. Each yacht crew was marked on the cleanliness and smartness of their boat; knowledge of knots and of sailing; and points awarded for their success in the regattas. At the end of the week the crew of the winning ship each received a superb bosun's knife – which often became their prized possession. Other awards were added as the years went by and the boat owners donated an 'overall' shield for the winners, and separate shields for the best boys' and girls' boats. To determine the winner we devised a complicated system of 'points' which were translated into 'marks'. This system meant that there was no 'runaway winner' and the result was always very close. In the 1980s, Henry Hole introduced the 'Venturers VC' – the Wry-necked Shackle. This was awarded for any special initiative, courage or bravery which came to the notice of Commodore Henry Hole. The awards ceremony on the last night of each cruise remains a highlight of the week.

My later involvement with Billy Graham – still a long way in the future – was to have an unexpected effect upon one aspect of the cruise. Soon after I joined the London office of the Billy Graham Evangelistic Association we started working on the distribution of the new magazine *Decision*. The first edition came from America 'in bulk' – already printed – and in an enormous wooden crate (looking a bit like a coffin). We set about distributing the magazine to the 27,000 plus on the mailing list.

That 'coffin' was to have a remarkable history! On the Venturers Cruise we had just decided upon a programme of central catering. A team of three stewardesses would prepare the meals, centrally, on the motor cruiser and then distribute the cooked food to the eight yachts. To do this we had to purchase a whole lot of new cooking equipment and baking trays. At the end of the cruise all this had to be stored somewhere and that 'coffin-like' box came to mind. I took it with me to Norfolk the following April and it proved to be exactly the right size for all our equipment.

I then negotiated with the management of the Herbert Woods Boatyard in Potter Heigham to store the box in their sail loft. They readily agreed to do this. Little did we know then that the box would continue in storage there for the next 45-50 years. Each year we would retrieve it, unpack it and, after using the cooking equipment on the cruise, repack it back into the box and take it up into the sail loft. Herbert Woods have served us faithfully – even moving the box to a new sail loft when the original one was demolished and rebuilt. Furthermore, they have never charged the Venturers Cruise a penny for this magnificent service. The next issue of *Decision* magazine was printed in England, so we never had another box like that. It was a one-off! The Lord knew our needs exactly and had His plans already in place!

From our sailing activities we were spared from events which could have resulted in serious accidents. We did have some problems but, happily, they were very rare. One year, when the yachts were sailing on Wroxham Broad, Mark Smith had an unpleasant experience. He had first come on the cruise as a 12-year-old boy and was, by now, understudying me as honorary secretary. He was in charge of a yacht with six crew and they were having a great sail. Suddenly, when running with the wind, it changed direction slightly and Mark was involved in an unexpected and uncontrolled gybe. That happens when the sail whips rapidly from one side of the boat to the other with great power as the wind gets on the wrong side of the sail. Unfortunately as this happened Mark had the rope twisted around his ankle. In an instant he was catapulted overboard in a flying arc and was virtually 'surfing' behind the fast-moving yacht. With great presence of mind his first mate rose to the occasion. He brought the boat under control and came back to the rescue of his skipper. For that action he received the Venturers' highest award for initiative and bravery – the Wry-necked Shackle! What could have been a nasty accident was averted by the quick thinking and correct action of his well-trained first mate. That evening we thanked God for his watchfulness over us.

The cruise itself received a special award in October 1994. The Broads Society makes an award of the Lady Mayhew Trophy to any organisation which, in their opinion, has contributed in an outstanding way to the introduction of young people to the Norfolk Broads. They saw the Venturers Cruise as well-deserving for this award.

There was a year when the cruise had been moored in Thurne Dyke and had used the little Methodist Chapel there as the location for the evening singsong and devotional time. The people at Thurne Dyke Methodist Chapel had themselves honoured all the Broads Christian cruises by installing a magnificent stained glass window in their new chapel. The window depicted a Broads yacht sailing up the river. That particular year the padre had given a very moving evangelistic address and one felt that the atmosphere was ripe for an appeal. As the padre finished, the commodore stood up and said that we had forgotten to sing 'Happy Bathday to you' to some of those who had fallen overboard during the day. It totally broke the atmosphere and, as the skippers returned to the motor cruiser for their bedtime coffee, they expressed surprise to each other that the commodore had done such a disruptive thing. The commodore himself was unrepentant and said that he felt that the evening had been far too tense and needed bringing down to earth.

A year later, at the same location, a young 17-year-old sidled up to the commodore. 'Commy,' he asked 'do you remember being here last year when the padre gave a talk about accepting Christ, and you asked us to sing "Happy Bathday" afterwards?' The commodore acknowledged that he did remember it. The young lad went on to say that it was on that night that he had accepted the Lord Jesus Christ as his Saviour. He suddenly saw that it was possible to be a Christian, and still be a normal person. That singing of the 'Bathday' song had been the instrument that God had used to win his heart. That lad later became a missionary and spent his life in Africa working amongst Ethiopians where he brought the Gospel to them. Ultimately he died there, still in harness and serving his Lord.

In 1955 the cruise received one of the 2000 plus landline relays from the Billy Graham Crusade in Glasgow. As I was the organiser of those relays, it had been a simple matter to include the little Norfolk hamlet of Repps as one of the receiving centres. The relay went into the tiny Methodist Chapel in the village on the night that the cruise moored at Potter Heigham Bridge. Earlier in the day I checked that all was well with the arrangements and was amazed to find a queue already waiting outside the tiny chapel. As there were only sufficient seats inside for the 60 plus members of our crews, it was unlikely that any of those waiting outside would ever get in. The Post Office engineers said that they would rig up a loudspeaker outside. In the event there were more people listening outside than there were inside the chapel.

Because we felt it might be inappropriate to include Mr Graham's appeal 'to come to the front' we had decided to fade out the broadcast at that point. As it happened, he did not give his usual approach to the 'appeal' so we missed the moment and the broadcast went right on to the end. We were astonished when four or five boys, accompanied by half-a-dozen or so members of the public pushed their way in from outside to come to stand in front of the small black box containing the loudspeakers. From those who responded, two became missionaries (one in Africa and one in South America) and others remained active Christians for the rest of their lives. It was an effective form of evangelism that the cruise was able to use on that occasion. Amongst boys who sailed on the cruise, two grew up to become Lord Mayors (one of London and one of Norwich). Seven became headmasters of schools. Several achieved high rank in the Royal Navy and many of them became leaders in a variety of business and professional fields.

There was something special about being a Venturer. Although we only met once a year, for one week in April and had no other unifying activity which kept us together, there was a unique relationship between all the officers, and between the officers and the youngsters. Whenever a major activity took place in the Christian world, more often that not it was a team of Venturers officers who formed the backbone of the organisation. For example, all of those who organised and controlled the stewards for the great Billy Graham Crusade at Earls Court in 1966 were Venturers officers. They knew each other's mind and worked together as a unit. They could always be relied upon and they thoroughly trusted each other.

For me there was evidence that the Venturers Cruise was part of God's will. Part of that evidence was the willingness of each of my employers over the years to allow me to organise the cruise from within their work. Whether it was Tom Rees, Colin Kerr, the Evangelical Alliance or the Billy Graham Evangelistic Association, none of them had ever demurred at the time I spent to organise the cruise. Nor, indeed, had they ever objected to the week in April when I attended the cruise itself. I could not have done this so effectively had they not given me their full support. Had I been required to do the organisation in my own spare time the cruise might never have lasted beyond a year or two. My commitment to my various Christian works was total. When you are involved in a vocational ministry of that nature, only time left over is 'your own' – except that there *is* no time left over! So if the cruise could not have been organised within the working hours it might never have happened.

Writer John May was on a private holiday, with friends, on the Norfolk Broads. While there he saw the Venturers fleet and, when he got the opportunity, he asked questions about it. He had been impressed with their sailing abilities. Later he discovered that this was mostly due to the dedication of all the officers, and to the high degree of discipline engendered by the commodore. As a result he devoted a whole chapter to the Venturers in his book *The Norfolk Broads Holiday Book and Pocket Pilot.* He said:

> The Venturers rules did not dampen anybody's enthusiasm. Indeed a touch of yachtsmanlike discipline seemed more than ever a good idea. Even setting sail in the morning was well organised as the commodore gave each boat in turn its orders to sail, so that they should not jam the river. Throughout each day all the boys and girls kept one another up to scratch.

From 1946 until the early 1990s there was very little change in the style and organisation of the cruise. Then along came the European Union with a whole mass of new regulations. Since the 1970s the cruise had already adopted the requirement to wear lifejackets. Now, in the 1990s along came the need for skippers to have their competence certificated; the stewardesses needed certificates to say that they had been trained in hygiene and all officers, including the junior first mates had to be approved by the Criminal Records Bureau – or 'CRB'd' as it became known. All these changes have meant an increased load to the honorary secretary and the commodore but they have had to be done.

I firmly believe that this activity was something that God inspired me to start. These years of activity have been a blessing to many and it has all been to His Glory. When I started the cruise in 1946 I intended that it should be for just that one year. But at the end, everyone said, 'Let's do it again next year.' And we are still doing it more than 60 years later!

We are now ready to move on to the beginning of the 'Thin Gold Line' which started with my involvement with Tom Rees.

CHAPTER TWO

TOM REES

Tom Rees! His was a name to conjure with in the late 1940s and early 1950s. Britain's first post-war evangelist, he became in many ways a 'John the Baptist' for Billy Graham. Due to the war, Britain had been deprived of effective evangelism for more than five years. The first post-war efforts still followed an old-fashioned pattern which was not right for the culture of the day. London would not have been ready for Billy Graham had not Tom Rees 'paved the way' with his outstandingly relevant campaigns from 1945 onwards.

My closer involvement with him started very early in 1947. In the summer of 1946, when I had taken a group of young people to a Holiday Conference at Hildenborough Hall, I had sat down with Tom Rees in his study and told him all about my experience at Keswick. He simply said that he would 'pray about it'.

The imperative telephone call on 9 January 1947 was the result and it had an atmosphere of urgency about it. He said that he wanted me to join him as a personal assistant on 17 January. The events which led up to that move have already been described in the Prologue.

Throughout September 1945 I had been an enthusiastic participant in Tom Rees's youth rallies in the Central Hall, Westminster. I had worked as a steward at every meeting, and night by night the hall was packed to capacity with young people. When Tom Rees asked those 'under 30 years of age' to wave their programmes in the air it seemed that most of the hall was in that age group. Tom Rees himself had *his* programme in the air for, at the time, he too was less than 30 years of age!

He led the meetings as song-leader; soloist; Scripture reader and speaker. It was a remarkable experience. Any one who was there would still be able to hear his resonant voice saying; 'Sing it – London' and we did! If Tom Rees did nothing else, he taught post-war young people to sing again.

If we didn't start on the first note, he would stop us and make us start again. If we dragged the music he would stop us and demonstrate – in his beautiful Welsh baritone voice – how it should be sung, and up to tempo. Sometimes, after a verse of 'What a Friend we have in Jesus' he would interject and say – 'now listen to this' and he would sing a solo:

> Said a robin to the sparrow, 'I would really like to know,
> why it is these human beings, rush about and worry so.'
> Said the sparrow to the robin, 'I just think that it must be,
> that they have no Heavenly Father, such as cares for you and me.'

and then it was back to the rest of the hymn.

At other times he introduced us to new hymns, or to new tunes. I have a vivid memory of the night he introduced us to the tune 'Limpsfield' for the hymn 'We have heard the joyful sound, Jesus Saves'. He demonstrated to us in staccato fashion how the old tune sounded: 'We have heard . . . the joyful sound . . . Jesus saves . . . Jesus saves.' And then he went on to show how much better and smoother the new tune was. We were soon singing it with great gusto – and indeed, it has become the 'norm' in any church using that hymn today. It was Tom Rees who first introduced it.

Although he led the meetings himself, he had a team backing him up. Joyce Silcox was his beautiful soprano soloist and Heather Brown (later Olford) was his pianist. My own crusader leader, Roy Cattell was the man in charge of the administration, and Oliver Gilbart-Smith was in charge of the stewarding. I had known him for many years for, as a young boy attending Westminster Chapel with my parents to hear the Revd G. Campbell Morgan, Oliver Gilbart-Smith was always on stewarding duty up in the gallery. He was also a crusader leader and he had seen my badge. Week after week he always gave me a cheery wave from the balcony. So it was lovely to work with him now that I was 'grown up' and had become part of his stewarding team.

When it came to the Scripture reading, you were never asked to *read* the Scripture: the invitation was always to *recite* the Scripture. The first time he asked me to do this it was from Ecclesiastes 12. I was expected to memorise the passage and recite it word-perfect. It was quite an ordeal for me to stand on the platform of the Westminster Central Hall or – even more terrifying – the Royal Albert Hall before some 8000 people. In those days it was before health and safety regulations restricted the numbers. Those recitations were simply a reflection of Tom Rees's own conviction that the memorisation of Scripture was important. He himself had memorised most of the New Testament and had reached 1Timothy when he died in a New York hotel room with his Bible open on his knees at that Epistle.

He was strict about the 'appeal' too. He never used the traditional method – the method that called for 'all heads bowed; all eyes closed; no one can see you except God and me. If you want to accept Christ, put your hand up. I'll see it and pray for you.' Those who raised their hands did not know what was to follow the prayer! The evangelist would then say, 'Now we will sing a hymn, and I want all those who put up their hands to come and stand at the front, where we will give them a booklet.' Tom Rees regarded that method as dishonest because there had been an improper disclosure in the raising of hands. Instead, as he concluded his message, he asked people there and then to come to the front as an 'outward and visible sign' that they were seeking Christ. Years later, on the first night of the Harringay Crusade, Billy Graham used the traditional method. Tom Rees was sitting on the platform and afterwards shared with Billy Graham his view that the traditional method was dishonest. Billy asked him why and Tom Rees explained. Thereafter, starting the next night, Billy Graham adopted Tom Rees's method and has never used any other method since.

The last night of the September 1945 series was held in the Royal Albert Hall – little knowing that, later on, it would become the venue for every meeting. A special guest on that occasion was the famed evangelist, Gypsy Smith – probably his last appearance on a London platform. In the prologue I have recounted how I had met him once before when I was 5 years old.

When the Central Hall meetings concluded I received a beautifully illuminated and engraved card, written in Tom Rees's own handwriting which said 'How Good is the God we adore. Thank you, Maurice Rowlandson, for your faithfulness during the past month. It is deeply appreciated. Tom Rees.' It takes a great man to take the trouble to acknowledge the help given by 'small fry' like me. Note! It was not a duplicated or a printed letter but a personally handwritten note. That impressed me greatly. This man *appreciated* me!

Following the month-long series at Westminster Central Hall in September 1945, Tom Rees promised the largely youth audience that he would 'do it again' the next year. He also promised that he would open a Holiday Centre where the same atmosphere as Westminster Central Hall would prevail. The story of that ministry will follow later.

He booked the Westminster Central Hall once more for September 1946, but before the contract was signed the United Nations had requisitioned the hall as the location to launch their agenda and plans. The UN authorities apologised profusely to Tom Rees and promised him that they would pay the bill for 'any other hall in London' that Tom could reserve.

Never slow to grasp an opportunity Tom Rees contacted the Royal Albert Hall and found that it would be available for 30 Saturday nights: between March 1947 and April 1947 and again from December 1947 to April 1948. He booked the lot – and sent the bill to the United Nations! Altogether between then and 1953, Tom Rees held more than 50 rallies in the Royal Albert Hall which he came to call 'my little Mission Hall in Knightsbridge.'

To fill the Royal Albert Hall for two series with a total of 30 consecutive nights, with some 8000 people a night, was a big undertaking. So he devised a series of special nights – one of which, on 22 March 1947, was assigned to me. Tom Rees had this vision of a vast concourse of youth, assembling at the Marble Arch and marching through London's West End to the Royal

Albert Hall. He stuck his neck out by giving the whole job of organising it to me. Up until then he had had no real experience of my abilities. For him it was a great step of faith.

I had only two months to bring together the support of innumerable youth organisations; police arrangements; permission to use the Royal Park where we established a 'saluting base' and special arrangements with the management at the Royal Albert Hall. The last was the most difficult because in those days – as now – admission to the hall was by ticket only to a numbered and reserved seat. For 'Youth on the March' (as we called it) I managed to persuade them simply to open the front doors and allow all the young people to march straight in to take whichever seats were vacant. The management didn't like it – but in the event they did a good job.

Surprisingly, although the notice was fairly short, most youth organisations supported us with large contingents – including several bands – and the assembly at Marble Arch as well as the march itself went off without a hitch. Colonel Orde Dobbie (son of the great defender of Malta, Lieutenant General Sir William Dobbie) took the salute at 'the Cockpit' in Hyde Park and the entire march was accommodated within the Royal Albert Hall without difficulty. Tom Rees had invited Stephen Olford to speak that night, and he appealed immensely to the young people. All in all, it was a great night – my first success and an occasion to demonstrate to Tom Rees my organising abilities!

I continued to help at the Royal Albert Hall where my main responsibility was to stand in the platform corridor leading to the orchestra's room, and to keep my eye on Tom Rees at the podium. He devised a series of hand signals (behind his back) which communicated to me some need that he had. From that position I was able to respond quickly to what he needed. I soon learned the importance of concentration. Only once, when I allowed my attention to wander, did I miss an important signal and later (when we got back to Hildenborough Hall) Mr Rees asked me what had gone wrong. I learned my lesson well and, in future, always kept my eyes open. I learned that, when you are given a job to do, that job is paramount and all other distractions must be put aside to allow concentration on the job in hand.

When the Royal Albert Hall series ended Tom Rees invited me to stay on with him and become the estate manager of Hildenborough Hall – Britain's first Christian Holiday Bible Conference Centre. My task was to supervise the overall maintenance of the building and grounds and it was a job I loved. I remained on the staff of Hildenborough Hall until 15 May 1948. By then, the first vestiges of the 'Thin Gold Line' had begun to manifest themselves.

The summer of 1947 was a busy one at Hildenborough with groups of around 100 different guests each week coming to stay in conference. Some of the most outstanding Bible teachers came week by week to lead the conference. I had the privilege of getting to know so many of them – knowledge which would stand me in good stead in future years.

Once the summer season was over we continued with week-end conferences for all except the month of November (which was the staff holiday month). Some of us young people on the staff played an April Fool joke on Tom's wife, Jean. She was responsible for all the private conferences which took place in the autumn, winter and spring. For her it was an immense joy to keep the Hall filled during those months. It all helped to 'balance the books'. One day, late in March 1948, we wrote a spurious letter from a fictional Christian Organisation, booking the entire Hall for a full week mid-November. We posted the letter to arrive with the morning mail on 1 April. Jean Rees, as always, opened the mail and . . . when she came across our fictitious booking her delight knew no bounds. Suddenly she realised that it was for the middle of November – the holiday month for all the staff. She spent the morning telling all the staff that their holiday dates would have to be changed. She told us that we just couldn't turn down a booking like that! Everybody agreed of course. They were all 'in' on the joke. We sprung the trap at 12 noon and it took Jean a long time to forgive us. We had a lot of Christian fun at Hildenborough!

Although I have mostly referred to Tom Rees by his full name or as Mr Rees, privately, and in his own office, we called him 'Tom'. But in public and in any formal situation he was always 'Mr Rees' – or latterly 'The Boss'! I once heard him remonstrate with a younger member of staff who was bringing in a high-ranking Government official to visit Mr Rees. This young lad knocked on the study door and said, 'Tom, may I bring in Mr X to see you.' He was afterwards called in and given clear instructions that, in future, the director would always be 'Mr Rees'.

During the week-end conferences that we ourselves ran, many of us on the staff were involved in speaking, leading Bible studies and taking part on a Brains Trust panel. It was the latter which made me realise that I needed some Bible training. My knowledge of theology was not great, and I didn't know a great deal about doctrine either!

Tom Rees's secretary at the time was Heather Brown (who was later to marry Stephen Olford). Heather was sponsored to go to the Moody Bible Institute in Chicago where she had a wonderful time. She wrote back to us at Hildenborough and told us all the good things about it. This prompted me to give real consideration to go to Moody myself. I felt I could get the training I needed there. My colleague at Hildenborough – the conference centre pianist – was a Scotsman called Lex Smith. He too felt the same way as I did so I sent off for the brochure and application forms for both of us. All went well until I reached the insurmountable stumbling block of cost. At that time the British Government would only allow a person to take £25 out of the country on overseas trips. I made enquiry of the Treasury and discovered that no machinery yet existed to allow overseas college or university fees to be paid in addition to the allowance. So the idea of going to Moody had to be put on the back burner.

On 18 February 1947 a group of us on the staff at Hildenborough obtained Tom Rees's permission to use some of our precious petrol ration to drive to Lewisham for an American 'Youth for Christ' rally. Canon Tom Livermore who had been a speaker at a weekend conference at Hildenborough had told us all about it. American input into evangelism was still quite rare post-war and it seemed like an attractive opportunity to discover what was going on, on the other side of the Atlantic. The only American influence during the war itself (and immediately afterwards) had been the US Forces Gospel Song Team under the leadership of Hal Shaw. They had given regular concerts in Westminster Chapel and we rarely missed an opportunity to hear them. They were a ray of sunshine in an otherwise dark war-time vista.

So we were glad to accept Canon Livermore's invitation to go to Lewisham Parish Church to meet 'these Americans'. It was on that day that the 'Thin Gold Line' really started, for the keynote speaker at that rally was a young American, in purple slacks and a bright yellow tie, called Billy Graham. Undoubtedly he was dynamic and we were deeply impressed by him.

A few days later, Tom Livermore brought him to Hildenborough to meet Tom Rees. Unhappily it was on a day when I was away on engagements in London so, on that day, I did not meet him. We did discover, however, that with two or three of his American colleagues (years later to become 'his Team') he had spent a solid six months in the UK. He had travelled from one end of the country to the other. He had spoken in small chapels; he had stayed in many private homes. It was the winter of the fuel strike with no electricity and no coal. Billy Graham and his colleagues slept in their overcoats to try and keep warm. Years later he told us that in 80 per cent of the homes in which he stayed, severe war-time rationing meant that their staple diet became tomato soup followed by sausages and mash! The important thing however, was that God used that six-month period as a time of training for Billy Graham. When years later he came back for the Harringay Crusade, he *knew the mind* of the British. He understood their culture and he had shared some of their hardships with them.

The winter of 1947/8 saw the continuation of the Royal Albert Hall rallies – now under the slogan '***Britain's*** *Youth for Christ*'. These had been a remarkable series of meetings. Saturday after Saturday saw the Royal Albert Hall packed out and Evangelism became news. There are many who look back over the years with great thankfulness for the vision and ministry of Tom Rees. It was just what was needed for post-war evangelism. We were jealous to protect the wonderful success that God had given him throughout this evangelistic series.

So, as a staff – although not Tom Rees himself – we were unhappy to read that there would be some meetings in London under the banner '***British*** *Youth for Christ*'. We felt that, with a name like that – so close to ours – it was a little 'near to the bone'. When we learned later that it would be run by an American Team, we were even more disturbed. In spite of that five of us piled into one of the cars to drive up to Westminster Chapel. With me there were Lex Smith, Mary Amies, Eleanor Lax, and Jean Rees who drove. As we were about to pull out of the driveway, Tom Rees appeared at the side of the car. Knocking loudly on the roof he made Jean wind down her window. 'Now listen,' he said, 'you lot are going up to London with quite the wrong attitude. You're critical, whereas you should be praying for the speaker. His name is Billy Graham, and God could use him in a very special way.'

Duly admonished we went on our way. As we reached Lewisham, Jean Rees said, 'Why don't we pray for Billy and the meeting?' Still driving, she started to pray and I sneaked a look at her, greatly relieved to find that her eyes were open! She prayed fervently, and so did the rest of us. By the time we arrived at Westminster Chapel I think we were all in a good frame of mind!

The service was led by Stratton Shufelt who was the musical director of the Moody Memorial Church in Chicago where Dr Harry H. Ironside was the pastor. With him, and taking part, were Chuck Templeton and Torrey Johnson from America's Youth for Christ (virtually, at the time, Billy Graham's employer). There was also the musical quartet called Couriers for Christ. It was a good and lively meeting and we were all impressed by it. Then along came the main speaker (more soberly dressed on this occasion!) – Billy Graham. He was a powerful speaker. But, in the middle of his address, the 'Thin Gold Line' made its presence felt once again.

Billy Graham told us that he was president (principal) of the Northwestern College and Bible School in Minneapolis, Minnesota. He also told us that the Lord had laid a great burden on his heart for the young people of Britain. During the six months that he had lived in the UK he had seen for himself that, as a result of the war, so many young people had been deprived of spiritual leadership. He went on to say that he wanted to make it possible for ten young men from Britain to go to Minneapolis. There, at his expense, he would provide a special 18-month training course. It would prepare them to come back well-equipped to work amongst young people in Britain. All they had to do was to pay their way to America. Everything else would be 'on him'.

I looked at Lex and Lex looked at me. He nudged me and, in his Scottish accent said, 'Och mon. That's us!' The 'Thin Gold

Line' had started to move. Immediately the meeting was over, Lex and I went behind the platform to speak to Billy Graham. It was the first time I had ever spoken to him face to face. We told him we wanted to be two of the ten. He wrote our names on the back of an old manilla envelope which, literally, he screwed up and put back in his pocket. Lex turned to me and remarked that that was the last we would ever hear of that. But it wasn't! A few months later came a letter from Dr O. E. Sanden, the dean of Northwestern, to say that Billy Graham, the president, had given him our names. He wanted to be assured that we were both genuine and suitable, so he had arranged for us both to be interviewed by Dr Eric Hutchings, a British evangelist associated with British Youth for Christ, and by Tom Livermore who, by now, was the British president of Youth for Christ. Both these men were well known to me because they had been speakers at Hildenborough Hall. Lex too knew them for the same reason. Hutchings and Livermore must have been satisfied with us because they authenticated us both.

A few days later I received a confirmation that I should arrive in Minneapolis on 16 August to acclimatise myself to a different way of life in America and be ready to start my academic studies at Northwestern on 15 September. By then I would have found my accommodation and taken part in the 'freshman orientation' week.

CHAPTER THREE

NORTHWESTERN COLLEGE AND MINNEAPOLIS

I ARRIVED in Minneapolis at 6.20pm on Monday, 16 August 1948. The day before, en route to Minneapolis, I had stopped at Buffalo, New York. It was Sunday, so I went to Cazenovia Park Baptist Church to worship – my first visit to an American church. The first hymn was 'Oh worship the King' and the organist played the first five notes (with one finger). It was the introduction to the tune I knew so well . . . only the remainder of the melody was completely strange to me! I learned for the first time that, for many of our well-known hymns, the Americans often had different tunes. As the service started, they passed around a 'sign-up' clip-board on which there was space for a visitor to say where they were from and to where they were going. I dutifully filled it in.

My main purpose on this visit to Buffalo was to see the great Niagara Falls – which I saw for the first time on my twenty-third birthday. The next day from Buffalo I took the *20th Century Express* train to Chicago and from thence to Minneapolis on the *400 Express* (which did the 400 miles in 400 minutes)!

From Minneapolis train station I took a taxi. I told the driver to take me to a hotel in the City which was not too expensive. He took me to the Curtis Hotel which, at the time, was about the equivalent to the Ritz in London! So much for the help of taxi drivers!

Bearing in mind that I had only been allowed to take £25 out of the country under the Government regulations which applied at the time, I had very little of that left after two days in New York and a day in Buffalo. There was certainly not enough to pay a hotel bill the size of that at the Curtis Hotel!

My father had, however, discovered a clause in the UK finance Bill which allowed dependants who lived in America to receive an annual allowance from the UK. This amounted to around $250 per month – but it had to be done by direct transfer to a bank in Minneapolis. My father had activated that transfer a week before I left. So I had confidence that there would be $250 awaiting me at a bank downtown.

Early the next morning I went to the bank, but they had never heard of me! I was praying about the situation – for I was in dire straits – when my eye alighted upon a neon sign in a shop window. It said 'Loans on your signature only'. It seemed to be the answer to my prayer so I entered the shop. The clerk, who served me, quickly told me that the sign did not mean what it said! Some security would be needed. He said that I had to learn that the Americans were hard-hearted people. I told him that I didn't believe that because they had been so good to us during the war by sending CARE packages of food. I explained that I was an Englishman who had just arrived in Minneapolis. As soon as my transferred money arrived from England I would have adequate funds. I told him that, in England, words meant what they said and I expected him to live up to the offer. I added, 'There's a well-known phrase, "an Englishman's word is his bond" – and that is my only available security.' This seemed to impress him and he went back into the office to talk to his colleague.

When he emerged it was to tell me that they would loan me $250 interest free for two days but that, if I didn't return to pay it back by then, they would have the police after me! At any rate, I walked out of the shop with $250 – more than enough to pay the Curtis Bill. From there I walked up to Northwestern Schools – five minutes away – and checked in with the bursar, a man called Jerry Beavan. Two days later my money had arrived from England and I went and repaid the loan!

They had been expecting me at the College and said that they had arranged for me to be accommodated at the Medicine Lake Camp Grounds. I would stay there until my accommodation at the College became available. That week at Medicine Lake was a wonderful introduction to life in America. I was quickly integrated into the life of the camp. I joined the choir which sang at the evening meetings. I played new (American) games like volley ball. I enjoyed the 'lake-echo sing' when half of the camp went out in boats on the lake, with candles, in the dark. The other half stayed on the shore. Those in the boats would sing a chorus (of their choice). We on the shore would echo it, and then sing a chorus of our choice – which they then echoed. It was a very moving experience.

I learned at breakfast time that the small cereal boxes were so made that you opened the long side and poured the milk right into the box! It saved dishes – but it was another new experience. We slept in a log cabin in which there were six bunk beds. The cabin had an earthen floor. Each evening we had some great Bible teaching.

Dr Harry S. Stam, brother of the martyred missionaries John and Betty Stam, adopted me and took me out in the car with him whenever he went into Minneapolis. It was a relationship that started then, and lasted until he died many years later.

On the Sunday, the Revd Herb Hazzard (one of the professors at Northwestern College) invited me to travel with him to Brainerd, Minnesota. He was taking services at a church there and asked me to bring a greeting from England at the morning service and to give my testimony at the evening service. We left Medicine Lake Camp at 6.30am and did not arrive back until 3am on Monday morning. It was a journey of 400 miles and we drove home in a gigantic storm.

On my last night at Medicine Lake it was announced that there would be a special speaker at the evening meeting. Billy Graham had just returned from Europe and he would be coming to speak! I was thrilled for it was the first time I had met him since Westminster Chapel, and now I was able to greet him as my college president (principal). He told me how glad he was that I was there and he certainly gave me the impression that he had remembered me! Later I was to discover that he had a remarkable memory and often did remember those people who had met him in unusual circumstances.

I was sorry to leave the camp when Jerry Beavan collected me and took me back to check in to my accommodation at the Fireside Dormitory of Northwestern College. 'Mother Carey' was the strict and notorious house-mother who ruled her dorm with both love and discipline. I moved all my things in and unpacked. Afterwards I returned to the college to visit their employment bureau. It was the 'norm' in American academic life to find a job to 'pay your way'. In my case, I needed to earn money to pay my fare home eventually. American student life was geared to employment. Classes started at 7am and ended by 12 noon. The afternoon was then free to do a job and, in the evening, you did your homework assignments.

Before I left the college to seek employment, they gave me a letter which had arrived for me. It was from Dr J. Palmer Muntz the pastor of the Cazenovia Baptist Church in Buffalo. He urged me to attend church in Minneapolis when I arrived, and he recommended the First Baptist Church. I was astonished and impressed by this 'follow up' from the clipboard I had signed in the Buffalo church. As it happened, I discovered that the First Baptist Church, whose pastor Dr Curtis B. Akenson was to become a lifelong friend of mine, was the 'home church' of Northwestern College. Dr Akenson had also had a letter from Dr Muntz asking him to 'follow me up'.

The employment bureau of the college sent me out on a wild-goose chase. The five possible jobs they sent me to turned out to be unsuitable for a student from overseas. I was a little despondent as I went back to the employment bureau to try and find another possibility. While I was waiting to be served, I picked up a leaflet from the table. It was headed 'Our students in your home'. It described how students from Northwestern would live in an American home and do all the housework – including cleaning, dusting, cooking, washing up, clothes washing and ironing. As I read it, I thought to myself 'any old fool could do that if they set their mind to it'. So, when my turn came I asked about it. The young lady said, 'I think I have just the place that would suit you.'

She sent me to 42 Park Lane, the home of a Mrs Sargent and her daughter Geraldine. As Mrs Sargent interviewed me something 'clicked' and she very quickly said that she would be happy to employ me. One of the great bonuses was that I would live in her lovely home (right on the shore of Cedar Lake), and have my own room. This meant that I had to go back to Fireside dorm and repack all my things. Mother Carey was not especially pleased to see me go.

For me it was clear that the Lord was in it. I had a wonderful home and a superb employer. She taught me to clean, cook, wash, iron and serve meals. I was virtually her 'English butler'. Above all it enabled me to live within an American home with an American family and I loved every minute of it. Mrs Sargent figured in much of my life over the next few years, ultimately taking the place of my elderly parents when I went back to Minneapolis to get married.

College life started properly on 20 September when Billy Graham welcomed all the students – especially the students from Britain – at the opening Chapel of the semester. He told the student body that he had invited Dr T. W. Wilson to join him as Vice-President and that, from then on, all our contacts would be with him in the first instance. I met T. W. Wilson (whom we affectionately called simply TW from then on) a few days later. I could not have known then that, as the years went by, he would become my mentor and one of the biggest influences on my life – but at that time he was just a part of the 'Thin Gold Line'!

After Chapel Mr Graham invited the ten of us from England to his office where he gave us each an individual welcome and told us that, whenever he was at the College, we were welcome to talk with him. In the event we hardly ever saw him because he was away on Youth for Christ Missions for most of the time.

During freshman orientation the previous week, there had been many activities which had helped to introduce us to college life. All of the professors were introduced; our potential courses were outlined; we were given a tour of the brand-new school buildings ('college' is called 'school' in America, and the colloquial name for the students is 'kids'); and, rather surprising to Lex and me, was a detailed lecture on personal hygiene! We discovered that the Americans were very conscious of 'BO' (body odour)!

One evening there was to be a 'freshmen's concert' and we were all invited to make a contribution. Lex Smith turned to me and said, 'Hey Maurice! You and I must be first to volunteer. We can't let the Brits down!' So we did and, at the evening concert, Lex was first on. He wore his kilt which was a great attraction to the American audience. He then recited a hilarious poem by Robbie Burns. As he finished there was very little applause.

I followed it with a fun song that had been taught to me by Tom Rees:

A mother was bathing her baby one night –
'twas the youngest of eight and a terrible sight.
The mother was tired, and the baby was thin,
'twas only a skellington covered in skin.
The mother turned round for the soap off the rack;
she was only a moment but when she turned back
her baby was gone, and in anguish she cried,
'Oh where is my baby?' and an angel replied:
'Your baby has gone down the plug hole,
your baby has gone down the plug.
The poor little thing was so scraggy and thin
It ought to've been bathed in a jug!
Your baby is really quite happy and
won't need a bath never more.
Your baby has gone down the plug hole;
not lost, but gone before!'

In the past, in England, this song had often been received with tumultuous applause but on this occasion there was a little polite hand-clapping and that was all! After our two items the concert went on for another two hours and *every* other item was deeply spiritual – either a reading from the Bible, a testimony or a moving spiritual poem! Lex and I were devastated! We shouldn't have offered to go on first! It took a long time for us to live that down!

Our first activity as a student body was to fulfil a plan devised by the school's business manager, Mr George M. Wilson. When the new building had been opened early in September, he had had a quote to move the school library from First Baptist Church to the new building – eight blocks away. The quote was for $13,000. On the first day of school, George Wilson had every one of the 1000 plus students go to the library and collect an armful of books. They would then walk up the road to the new building where a carefully indexed shelf would be ready to receive them. We then returned for another armful of books until the entire library was moved – at no cost! It was the first time I learned of George Wilson's expertise in both organisation and in saving money. When he later became the business manager of the Billy Graham Evangelistic Association he virtually became my 'boss' – but that's jumping ahead in the story!

The classes were both intensive and excellent. Dean Edwin J. Hartill taught us hermeneutics and he was an outstanding professor. He 'called the roll' at the beginning of each class by walking into the room and calling out 'one'. Every student had a number – Dean Hartill being number one – and we simply reeled off the numbers. When a number was missing the line stopped and a note was made of the absent student. It was from his classes that I learned most of the things of value to me which would be so helpful in my future life and ministry.

It was he who taught me not to be a timewaster when it came to speaking. In *Life with Billy* I recall how he said that if I spoke to one person for one minute and said nothing worthwhile, I had wasted two minutes – one of theirs and one of mine. Likewise if I spoke to 500 people for one minute and said nothing of note, then I had wasted 501 minutes! Years later I was to remember that when Billy Graham addressed 110,000 people at the Wembley Stadium and made every minute count! A thought like that concentrates the mind!

The other most helpful classes were the speech class and the etiquette class – the latter under the tuition of Mrs W. B. Riley – a tall, broad-shouldered, imposing grey-haired matron with flashing eyes. Everyone was afraid of her! Her late husband, Dr W. B. Riley had been the founder of Northwestern and on his death bed had invited – almost commanded – Billy Graham to succeed him.

There was an occasion in Morning Chapel when Dr T. W. Wilson had needed to remonstrate with the students over some 'griping' about an insignificant problem. Both Billy Graham as president, and he as vice-president, were often away from the school. On this occasion the griping had occurred while they were away.

In order to try and introduce the subject he described how he and Billy Graham had been in Florida where they had been taken to a fair-ground. There was a stand which declared that visitors could see 'the cat with three eyes'. He told how he and Billy Graham had gone in to see this wonder. 'There was the old grey cat,' he said. 'Two of its eyes were closed but the third eye was open, taking in everything that was going on.' He went on to say that he and Mr Graham were rather like that old grey cat. Two eyes (he and Mr Graham) were closed but the old grey cat's third eye was open taking in everything that was going on. His analogy was good as far as he and Mr Graham were concerned, but the student body dissolved into laughter as they equated Mrs W. B. Riley with the third eye of the old grey cat!

During my time at Northwestern Dr Billy Graham urged the founding of a full-time Christian Radio Station. He appointed Mr Loren Bridges to be the director of the station, and many students were given the opportunity to assist in the setting up of the station. I was one of those involved and it awakened in me a lifelong interest in Christian Radio. All American radio stations are known by a four letter code (which is just the name of the station and does not relate to anything else). The school's radio station was called KTIS and was exclusively devoted to Christian music, messages, teaching and interviews. I worked there for several months before becoming involved, more deeply, in KEYD – the Christian radio station operated by the Christian Business Men's Committee at Hospitality House. This station was more aligned with a commercial Station but with Christian interests. We did not play exclusively Christian music and we carried advertisements. But there was a strict watch on the content of the advertisements. The philosophy of KEYD was good programming to the extent that we would attract listeners. We would follow a popular programme with a Gospel message. In its own way it was very successful. We enlisted the services of one of the key 'newscasters' in Minneapolis. His coverage of the news was the best in the twin cities of Minneapolis/St Paul, and he won us a lot of listeners.

My main job with the station was at weekends, when I was on 'continuity'. That meant announcing the name of the radio station every half hour: 'This is KEYD 1440 on your dial. Your friendly family station Minneapolis/St Paul. Stay tuned for good listening.' That announcement became etched on my memory for ever!

KEYD had a unique way of attracting new listeners. Every hour, on the hour, they would dial a number – at random – from the telephone directory. There was one simple question 'What was the last record we played?' The record had always been a Gospel record. If the person we phoned could name it, they received a cheque for $1. If not, the $1 was added to the next hour with $2 then on offer. And so on! As listeners could rarely name the record, it was not unusual for the prize to reach even four-figure proportions. By then it had become headline news in the local newspapers, and *everyone* listened alertly to the programme in the hope of being the successful winner!

KTIS also had a good news programme and concluded each news broadcast with the comment 'Now here is today's Good News . . .' followed by a brief reading from Scripture. KTIS is still 'on the air' more than 50 years later and still follows the same general pattern. Many of its current personnel still remain as my good friends today. KEYD came to an end when the Christian Business Men's Committee withdrew their support in the mid 1970s.

One highlight of my time at Northwestern was 7 March 1949 when a letter came from Tom Rees. He said that he would be coming to Minneapolis for a few days. He hoped to be able to see us all. I went to see T. W. Wilson and told him of the visit. His immediate response was to invite Mr Rees to speak at Chapel for four days that week. We were delighted and it was lovely to welcome Mr Rees amongst us.

Now Tom Rees was not a person who liked a 'handle' attached to his name. He was always simply 'Tom Rees'. When T. W. Wilson introduced him the first morning he welcomed 'Dr Tom Rees'. Afterwards Mr Rees took him aside and said, 'No "Dr", TW. Just plain "Tom Rees" will do.' Day two the introduction was 'The Revd Tom Rees'. Once again he told TW to 'keep it simple'. Day three it was 'Brother Tom Rees' and on day four 'Evangelist Tom Rees'. Our dear American friends just could not get used to someone without a pedigree! We never did get the plain 'Tom Rees'.

Mr Rees took four of us out to dinner one evening. During the meal he looked at me and said, 'Maurice! Whatever you do when you eventually come back to England, don't ever think about starting a Bible Holiday Conference Centre! It's too much of a headache.' It was hard not to tell him that on 26 October 1948, back at home in England, my father had seen and negotiated the purchase of a property in Frinton-on-Sea. It was on the seafront and was called Kelvin Lodge. He thought it would be an ideal place for me to establish and run as a Bible Holiday Conference Centre when I got back. I think my father also saw it as an 'insurance' to guarantee my return to England when I had finished at Northwestern. But the Lord had other plans. The 'Thin Gold Line' was still running, and it did not run through Kelvin Lodge.

Four months later I realised that, much as I loved working for Mrs Sargent and living at her home, I was simply not earning enough money to pay my fare home when the time came. I hesitated about leaving to find a new job when, unexpectedly, the catalyst came. One day my job at Mrs Sargent's was to paint the garden furniture. If there is one job I do not enjoy, it is painting. It made my mind up for me so, with great reluctance, I searched for another job. Once again the Lord was leading me. Near where I boarded the bus back to Park Lane was a glass door to a building on the corner of 9th Street and Hennepin Avenue. Written on the door were the words 'Hospitality House Christian Center'. I think my immediate reaction was that Hildenborough Hall and Hospitality House both contained HH! On the spur of the moment I went up the stairs and asked if there were any jobs available.

Miss Verna Peterson spoke with me and with regret in her voice said, 'I'm sorry. We have no vacancies.' I turned away and started down the stairs. Halfway down, Verna called me back. 'Just a moment,' she said. 'I will have a word with our director, Mr George England.' Five minutes later she returned to say that, because I was an Englishman, there might be a way in which they could use me. We agreed terms and on 29 November 1948

I started work at Hospitality House. On my first day Verna Peterson said, 'Your first job will be to paint the office where you will be working!' I think the Lord was teaching me a lesson!

I think Verna Peterson had her eye on the publicity that could be gained from my employment at the Centre. Certainly the Minneapolis Star and Tribune came out with a report of my arrival with the heading: 'England comes to Minneapolis to see England!' The article went on to say that 'England wanted England to come to England but because of pressing duties England couldn't go. So naturally England has come over to see England!' It was rather 'corny' but it made a story and was the precursor of more than a dozen articles about me during the next nine months. George England believed that 'all publicity is good publicity' and he exploited every opportunity he had to get as much as he could out of my story for the work of Hospitality House.

When I returned to Mrs Sargent's and told her I had a new job, she immediately asked, 'Where will you live?' I told her that I supposed I would have to go back to the school dorm at Fireside Hall. I was totally surprised when she replied, 'We would like you to stay on in your room here.' Her kindness and generosity meant such a great deal to me and I lived at No. 42 Park Lane for all my extended time in America.

In many ways the training and experience I got at Hospitality House far exceeded the training I got at Northwestern College. Hospitality House gave me practical experience in so many ways. Film evangelism, youth work, speaking, and sheer administration were all skills I learned there. My job included every part of the Hospitality House work.

It was an incredible building. If it was in London its equivalent location would be in Leicester Square. In the basement there was a Christian Bookstore. On the ground floor there were the studios of the Christian Radio Station already referred to. On the first floor we ran a restaurant where, on a Sunday, we would serve 500 plus diners at lunchtime. (Sunday is regarded as 'Mother's day off' so everyone goes out to eat after church.) Of the restaurant, George England used to say: 'In this restaurant you are more conspicuous if you don't say grace, than if you do!' Also on the first floor were the offices; a library; a resource file of Christian talent in the Twin Cities of Minneapolis/St Paul; a Chaplain in the Juvenile Courts and our film department.

On the second floor there was the Youth Centre proper with a snack bar serving hamburgers, cokes and milk shakes, together with a juke box playing Gospel records. There was an extensive games room with a wide assortment of table and floor games and where, every Sunday night, nearly 1000 young people from churches of all denominations and from all over Minneapolis would congregate for an 'after-church sing' which I ran for my entire time at Hospitality House. On the roof of the building there was a 30 x 60 foot neon sign with a Scripture text which shone high over the city.

We served many Christian groups for meals in one of the four private dining rooms that we had. There was a narrow door from one of those rooms into the kitchen. On one occasion I had just made a remark to the cooks and was coming through the narrow door with my head turned towards them. At the same moment one of the waitresses was coming through the door and into the kitchen with a tray full of dirty dishes. Inevitably we collided and tray, dirty dishes and waitress all went flying. It was the first time I really became aware of Marilyn Sandberg (one of my waitresses). A month later, concerned about this lonely Englishman who would be spending Christmas alone, Marilyn persuaded her parents to invite me to her home for Christmas. Thus we started a courtship. After my return from America our courtship carried on by correspondence. On 9 July 1949 Marilyn telephoned me from America (at two in the morning because she had not yet discovered the 6-hour difference between the time in Minneapolis and the time in England). Her answer was 'Yes' and she wanted to fix the date. Three months later, on 14 October 1949, we were married in Minneapolis. Marilyn says, 'We have been meeting over dirty dishes ever since!'

One day at chapel Billy Graham was the speaker and he was telling us about a meeting he had had the previous week. He described the meeting as 'packed and jammed into the building', It so happened that Lex Smith and I had attended that meeting, and we knew that this was just not true. There had been many empty seats. Lex Smith's sense of Scottish honesty made him exclaim to me, 'Maurice! That's just not true. We must go and see him.' I backed him up, for Tom Rees had always taught me that accuracy in such things was of extreme importance. Too often we saw exaggeration in Christian work and it needed to be nipped in the bud.

We made an appointment with the president's secretary and later the same day we went into the president's office. He greeted us warmly and after some preliminary chit-chat he asked us what we wanted to see him about. Lex launched in without hesitation. 'Mr Graham,' he said, 'we were at that meeting you talked about in chapel, and we know the church was not filled. Yet you described it as "packed and jammed into the building". That was just not right. The Lord will not continue to bless your ministry if you exaggerate like that!' Billy Graham was taken aback and appeared to be repentant. As he looked back at us he confessed, 'You are so right. I needed someone to say that to me and the Lord has sent you to me. I will be more careful in the future.' It is my experience that he has been ever since. Indeed, as the years have gone by his insistence upon accuracy in figures has been impeccable. Lex was right when he said that Billy Graham had tears in his eyes as he was confronted by this accusation. He appeared to be overwhelmed that anyone should have had the courage to refute him in this way. God may have used the occasion to help him in his entire ministry.

There were many special experiences during my time at the College. One of these was a visit from the great evangelical historian, Dr J. Edwin Orr. He was a quietly spoken man, but had great authority and power. He spoke at chapel for five mornings in a row and the student body was greatly affected. On the final day he challenged the students about their lifestyle. No sooner had he finished speaking, and before T. W. Wilson could close the meeting, a student stood up and started praying out loud. He poured out his heart to God and sought cleansing in his life. No sooner had he stopped than another student also started praying.

That started a flow of spontaneous prayer that went on throughout the day and late into the evening. At noon, T. W.

Wilson broke in to say that all classes had been cancelled for the day and that chapel would remain in session. They didn't even break for food. The prayer time went on and on in an unemotional but truly realistic manner in which we all sensed the power and presence of God. It was such an experience, and I have never since been in a prayer meeting where God's power was so evidenced. It was a moving and memorable time.

As the end of my time at Northwestern approached I made an appointment to see the vice-president. Billy Graham was away at the time, but it was important to know how my time of study could be consolidated into some form of recognition. At the start Mr Graham had said that 'some form of diploma' would be given to us, but nothing further had been said. When I spoke to T. W. Wilson about it he was flummoxed! Mr Graham had said nothing to him. However, as a non-accredited college there was nothing to stop them formulating some sort of academic recognition of their own.

A day or so later TW called me back into his office. 'We have decided,' he said, 'to originate a form of recognition which can be given to all the special students from the UK. We will award you an ABK – Acquired Biblical Knowledge! And so it was to be. The award was not ready in time for the graduation ceremony in the Minneapolis Auditorium, so it was sent on to me by mail afterwards. In the event, it meant really nothing. But it was nice to have! The degree entitled me to wear Northwestern's scarf and hood and I was proud to have that in my possession. It needs to be recorded that, of the ten British students who had accepted Mr Graham's invitation to study at Northwestern, only two ever returned – Leslie Edgell and myself. The other eight remained in America for the rest of their lives. Justifiably, the college sought a refund of the fees they had been excused!

As the 'Thin Gold Line' progressed through my life, it is interesting to note that both Jerry Beavan (the first person I ever met in Minneapolis) and George M. Wilson, were to become full-time members of the Billy Graham Team and, as time went by, dear friends and close colleagues of mine in that work.

I left Minneapolis with a greater accolade from the director of Hospitality House than I did from Northwestern. Accompanied by all my colleagues on the staff George England came to see me off at the train station as I returned to England. They had presented me with two magnificently framed pictures – one of which, Salman's 'Head of Christ', I presented to Hildenborough Hall when I returned to England. The other, 'What Happened to Your Hand?', still hangs in a pride of place in our home. As I left Minneapolis I put all thoughts of Billy Graham out of my mind. I was now anxious to get home to fulfil my dream of starting a 'Hildenborough Hall by the sea'. But God had other plans!

CHAPTER FOUR

HILDENBOROUGH, KELVIN LODGE AND THE CAMPAIGNERS –

The Start of the Billy Graham Years

MY FIRST visit to Hildenborough Hall was as a guest in August 1946. I had taken four young people from my church. Stephen Olford was the speaker at that week's conference and all four of those young people found the Lord Jesus Christ as their Saviour.

Later they wrote this poem in my autograph book which I included in *Life with Billy*:

There was a young fellow called Steve
Who lives to give souls their reprieve
He led us to Jesus
And He'll never leave us
And that we all firmly believe.

All four of them went on to live effective and meaningful lives as Christians.

It was also during that week that I had asked for a private interview with Tom Rees. I told him all that had happened at the Keswick Convention. Then I told him that I was sure that God was calling me to be an evangelist. 'Great! Maurice!' he replied, and added, 'How many people have you brought to the Lord today?' When he saw my obvious hesitation he added, 'This week? . . . This month?' I hung my head, crestfallen! 'No,' he said, 'God has not called you to be an evangelist. He's called you to be an administrator: your gift is to help people like me to be a good evangelist.' He told me to develop my gifts and to concentrate upon that side of my ministry. It was the most valuable advice he could have given me and he was a part of the 'Thin Gold Line'.

On 4 June 1949 I returned to England after my time in Minneapolis and I saw Kelvin Lodge for the first time. It was the property that my father had found. He knew of my love for Hildenborough Hall in Kent and of the successful ministry it had. But *that* Hall was in the heart of Kent. I believed that changing attitudes would demand more access to the coast. Those two factors combined had led my father to talk to his brother – a wealthy man – and to persuade him that it would be an 'investment for Eternity' to purchase Kelvin Lodge. My uncle was not renowned for his interest in spiritual things but he had great affection for his brother and for me as his nephew. These two factors persuaded him to acquiesce to his brother's idea.

Although I didn't know it at the time, my years in America, and also my earlier time with Tom Rees, had been a 'training ground' that prepared me to work, later on, with Billy Graham. Tom was a perfectionist in everything. Whatever we did for him had to be done to the highest degree of competence – for we were doing 'as unto the Lord'. He constantly reminded us of 1 Corinthians 14:40: 'Let all things be done decently and in order.' So if the foundations laid down in the Prologue and in these opening chapters seem rather extensive, they are necessary to support the building to follow.

Amongst the things I had learned at Hildenborough was complete trust in God. Tom Rees demonstrated it in everything he did. He 'prayed in' money when it was needed. He was adventurous for God and he taught me the importance of that trust. One Monday morning I came into the main entrance hall just after breakfast. Tom Rees passed me on the way to the office. 'How are you today?' he cheerily asked me. I replied with a shrug of the shoulders, 'I'm OK thank you, Tom. You know, it's Monday morning anyway!' He turned on his heel and exclaimed, 'Don't ever let me hear you say that again! Remember "This is the day that the Lord has made. We will rejoice and be glad in it!"' I learned the lesson well and I never have had that 'Monday morning feeling' again!

On another occasion when Tom Rees was away, he left his brother Dick Rees in charge of the Hall. Early in 1947 my accommodation at Hildenborough Hall was at the Gate House (formerly the stables), a quarter of a mile away, down the drive. I was on 'wake-up duty' which involved arriving in the office at five minutes to seven. Precisely at 7am the xylophone sounded over the Hall's loudspeaker system, followed by a cheerful 'Good morning' greeting and a text for the day. We then played some good, lively, Christian music to get all our guests moving.

One morning my alarm did not go off. I awoke at three minutes to seven. I threw on my clothes and ran down the drive at full tilt. As I got within fifty yards of the house, I heard the xylophone, the greeting and the music. As I came into the main entrance Dick Rees was coming out of the office. All he said was, 'You know, Maurice, the Lord is a good alarm clock. Tell Him and you'll be up on time.' But the look he gave me spoke volumes! Once more, I learned my lesson. Yes! Hildenborough Hall was a good training ground.

Now I planned to bring all the best features of Hildenborough Hall to Kelvin Lodge at Frinton. I wanted to follow a very similar programme to theirs. I still had in mind what Tom Rees had said to me in Minneapolis, so I wrote and told him all of my plans. He replied giving me God's blessing on all I planned to do.

Then disaster struck! We discovered that because, in effect, we were changing a private house into a conference centre it was, in the eyes of the planners, a 'change of use'. Planning permission would be required and notices had to be prepared and displayed. The council told us that they had had 67 objections. Under the planning regulations at the time, this meant that our case had to be made before an arbitrator whose decision would be final.

It was in mid-1949 that my earlier confrontation with the waitress at Hospitality House in Minneapolis had developed to the point at which we were now engaged. My father thought that Marilyn Sandberg should come to England for a period of eight weeks before we were married. He felt that she needed to know that she could cope with England as well as with me! So she had arrived as the arbitration was about to take place.

She arrived on 8 September 1949 and I went to London Airport to meet her. We travelled down to Frinton by train. In lovely hot summer weather my father came in his car to meet us at Frinton Station. Meeting his future daughter-in-law for the first time was a difficult thing for him to do anyway, so he tried to make conversation in the car. Looking over his shoulder at us, sitting in the back of his car, he asked, 'Marilyn, do you bathe?' For him a summertime swim in the sea was a big thing. What he didn't know was that, to an American, 'Do you bathe' meant 'Do you take a bath!' Marilyn wondered why he was so interested in her hygiene! There was some explaining to do and I learned that I would be doing a lot of translating!

Marilyn survived those eight weeks and the two of us returned to Minneapolis to get married. Hanging over us was the result of the arbitration waiting to be declared. We did not know the answer before we left.

The local Frinton paper *The East Essex Gazette* had carried a somewhat cynical letter about the proposal which went:

It simply isn't Frinton, it really can't be done
A Xylophone to start the day of consecrated fun!
Marilyn and Maurice, we all agree with you
That if we don't reach Heaven we won't know what to do.
But why should we have pep talks to help us on our way?
Remember, this is Frinton and NOT the USA!
Grand choruses and laughter to break the evening still
(No baccy, beer or bebop – which seems a bitter pill!)
'Will our redemption be complete?
Shall we secure a forward seat?
Shall we be sure to land in Heaven?
If we pay eight instead of seven?'

(Constance Wells, Crown Hotel, Thorpe)

The last line referred to the fact that a room with seaview cost one guinea (£1.1s) more than the back rooms!

The whole project was also headline news in many of the national newspapers. Anything which 'disturbed' Frinton was headline news – especially the *Daily Express* which declared 'Consecrated Fun Centre Boss writes a stiff note of protest'. That article told how Tom Rees took serious objections over our plans and had complained accordingly. As it happened, Tom Rees was with us on the day the headline appeared and he offered to go home and write the letter, so that the headline was true! We had a good laugh over this sensational and inaccurate reporting!

When we went back to America to get married, my parents, for health reasons, could not travel across the Atlantic. Instead my friend and former employer, Mrs Sargent, stood in the wedding reception line to welcome our guests in their place. It was a wonderful thing she did.

We had a lovely late night wedding – as was the custom. To our surprise, Dr C. T. Cook (who was the editor of the newspaper *The Christian* in England) happened to be in Minneapolis on that day, and he heard about our wedding and came to it. We were delighted to see him there.

There were those in Minneapolis who felt that I should be ordained to the work and ministry that I was going to do. It was not unusual in America to be dedicated in that way so, a few days before the wedding, I went through a ceremony of ordination at the First Baptist Church in Minneapolis and eventually returned to England as 'The Rev Maurice Rowlandson'. I later discovered that no denomination in the UK would recognise an American ordination so a year or two later I dropped the title and have not used it since – except . . . on my driving licence!

When I came back to England I needed a new driving licence and 'The Rev' got included upon it. A few years later, with four small children in the car, I was driving to the Farnborough Air Show. The traffic was horrendous and moving very slowly. I was unaware that I had driven through a red light until there was a knock on the car roof and a police officer was standing there. I wound down my window to talk to him and he drew attention to my misdemeanour. In his Irish accent he said, 'I'm sorry, Sir, but everybody is ignoring the lights today and we are prosecuting everyone. Can I have your licence please?' I handed my licence to him. He took one look at it and saw 'The Rev' as he glanced at the children in the back of the car. He handed it back saying, 'I'm sorry, *Father*. Please drive on!' I think he probably thought it was a Sunday School outing!

For many reasons, after our wedding on 14 October 1949, Marilyn and I would have wished to stay on in America for an extended period. But we had in mind the work we believed we were called to do at Kelvin Lodge. Still no word had come from England about the result of the arbitration so we were anxious to get back as soon as possible. We took the view that 'no news was good news'.

We spent our honeymoon aboard the *Queen Elizabeth*. Before we left Minneapolis we had packed all our wedding gifts in a large trunk. We fully expected it to arrive in New York before we boarded the ship. But, up to the time we went on board it had still not arrived. I had to make arrangements with shippers to forward it on when finally it came.

We went aboard the *Queen Elizabeth* at 4pm and she was due to sail at midnight. However, at 2am the telephone in our cabin rang and the purser told us that a trunk had just arrived on board and that two stevedores would bring it to our cabin. When I expressed surprise about the lateness of the hour, the purser told me that the ship's departure had been delayed. As a result our trunk had arrived just in time. My only problem was that I had changed all my American dollars and had only twenty-five cents left in my pocket to 'tip' these two burly stevedores who arrived at our cabin to deliver the trunk. We were treated to some of the fruitiest New York expletives as a result.

After we had sailed we had the roughest crossing the ship ever made. At the peak, the waves were 75ft high! Years later, in the early 2000s, the *QE2* also had a rough crossing which was described as the 'roughest-ever crossing, since the original *Queen Elizabeth* was hit by 75ft waves in 1949'! And we had been on board! As the ship rolled in the hefty seas, that wretched trunk slid from side to side in the cabin keeping us awake all night!

On arrival back in England, my father greeted us with the disturbing news that the arbitration had gone against us. We would not be able to open Kelvin Lodge as we wished. My first reaction was with some anger that my father had not told us before we left

America. He had known ten days earlier and if we had known the result we would have stayed in America longer. We had no other immediate need to return to England. However, I had to accept that 'God has no problems, only plans' and waited to see in which direction He would lead.

As a footnote, it is interesting to note that five years later I had a telephone call from Tom Rees to invite me to have tea with him. He then told me that he, and his wife Jean, had been looking for a new location for Hildenborough Hall. In a remarkable way they had been led to the Esplanade Hotel at Frinton-on-Sea. It was available to them on a seven-year lease. Because it was already a hotel, no 'change of use' permission was required to use it as a conference centre. However, Tom Rees wanted to be sure that it would not hurt Marilyn and me if he proceeded with his plans to move to Frinton. We were delighted to hear the news and gave him every support. Incidentally, many of the original 67 objectors against our plans later became our close friends and were embarrassed that they had objected to us many years earlier. However we were able to reassure them that it was all 'within the will of God' and that we bore no ill-will against them. Tom Rees had a highly successful seven years at Frinton and many people were blessed through his ministry there.

As for me, for nine months after the arbitrator's decision, I was in 'purdah'! Nothing came along. I spent the time writing a book – my first. It was written for children and was called *Unexpected Adventure* and was published by Pickering and Inglis. Then, just after our first son was born in August 1950, I received an invitation from Prebendary Colin C. Kerr – founder of the Youth Movement, the Campaigners. Tom Rees had mentioned my name to him and he wrote to ask if I would accept a dual role as Boys' Administration Chief and Chaplain to the Campaigners Movement.

I went up to London to see him. He said, 'This post will not be a gold mine. We will be able to pay you £300 a year!' But even that was better than nothing so I accepted the offer and spent the next two years working with him.

During that time he taught me many things, but one thing I learned especially from him: he said that, if he told me something exceedingly confidential, he was telling me because I was his close friend whom he trusted and he knew I would respect his confidence. At the same time, he said, he had to recognise that I too had a close friend whom I trusted who was someone I knew would respect *my* confidence. It was a very different thing from asking, 'Did you hear about . . . ?' That was gossip. The sort of confidence he was talking about was often shared because it was accompanied by a request for prayer. I learned that true confidential information is shared with no one else at all.

In the many years that I worked with Tom Rees there were often times that he told me something 'in confidence' and asked me to keep the information to myself. Only later did I discover that he had told the same thing to many of my friends, also warning them to 'keep it to themselves'. Sometimes it was many weeks later before we all found out that each of us had known for some time, but none of us had talked about it!

On 9 September 1952, towards the end of my time at Campaigners I received a message from Tom Rees to say that his staff accountant, Elizabeth Smith, would be going into hospital for an extended period. He wanted to know if I would take over that part of her work for the next four to five months. I shared the need with Colin Kerr, and he readily agreed to release me for one day a week so that I could go to do the work at Hildenborough.

Three times in the following years (between 1960 and 1970) I was called back into service for Hildenborough. One of these I accepted. But for the other two – although they were both close to my heart – I had declined. I did not feel that the Lord was leading me in those directions. However, I did accept his invitation in 1960 when he devised a series of ten Sunday Evening Services to be held in the Palace Theatre in London's West End. I had a call from him in June 1960 asking me to be the organiser of those ten services. It was a great challenge and I was glad to be able to accept the invitation. We had ten magnificent Sunday evening services supported by the London Emmanuel Choir. My friend and colleague, Gordon Stowell, designed a special 'stage set'. It was one of those times when Tom Rees had told me to 'tell no one else' before it was all cut and dried. I discovered over the next few weeks that everybody knew about it anyway and they were all praying about it!

The second time I was called back was a year later (in 1961) when he planned a nationwide evangelistic crusade in Canada. He dearly wanted me to organise the event, but my commitments with the Evangelical Alliance at the time were such that I could not take off the twelve weeks needed.

The third occasion was in 1970, shortly after Tom Rees had died in New York: I had a message from Jean Rees asking me to call and see her. She was still reeling from the sudden death of her husband. Nonetheless she had the future to think about. It was something of a surprise to me when she said, 'We want you and Marilyn to take over Hildenborough Hall (now in Sevenoaks) and run it, and the evangelistic work, like Tom did.'

I was not sure whether or not the 'Thin Gold Line' was running through this offer and I felt I had to 'test the water'. I told her that I would only be prepared to consider it if the trustees would disband, and allow me to run Hildenborough as Tom Rees had – on an executive basis without a committee. There *was* a picture hanging in Hildenborough Hall of 'the Hildenborough Committee in session'. Eight people were sitting around a table. One was speaking; another was making notes; still another appeared to be asleep and a fourth was listening intently, and so on. Every one of the eight, by trick photography, was a picture of Tom Rees himself. I saw that 'committee of one' as the reason behind his success, and I would only have been prepared to do it the same way.

My 'test' was not acceptable to the trustees, and I turned down the offer. As on every other occasion when some by-path meadow (to use a Bunyan phrase) opened up, my decision turned out to be exactly right because there were new initiatives from Billy Graham just around the corner. To take a side track would have been contrary to the Will of God.

As far as my time at the Campaigners was concerned, one day, at the end of August 1952, I came home after a day at the office and said to my wife, Marilyn, 'This work at Campaigners is not "me". I have become less and less happy in it. I am going to write to Roy Cattell at the World's Evangelical Alliance (WEA) to see if he might have a vacancy there.'

That Tuesday evening I wrote the letter and went out and posted it. On Wednesday morning there came a letter from Roy

Cattell to say, 'If ever you are thinking of leaving Campaigners would you let me know because I have a post here at the WEA which would be just right for you.'

On Thursday morning I received a letter from Tom Rees which said 'Why don't you write to Roy Cattell at the World's Evangelical Alliance and see if he has an opening that would suit you?'

The 'Thin Gold Line' had started to work overtime! It all rapidly came together and on 12 September I left the Campaigners (although they asked me to remain a member of their governing council) and on 29 September 1952 I started working with Roy Cattell at the WEA.

Shortly before my appointment I had had an interview with Lieutenant General Sir Arthur Smith who was chairman of the World's Evangelical Alliance. He was a brusque, formidable person in interview and he terrified the living daylights out of me! In his 'military voice' he said: 'Rowlandson, you've had many jobs in your short life. You've worked with your father's company, with Tom Rees, Hospitality House and Campaigners. How do we know that you'll stay with us?' I replied to say that every change I had made was because the Lord had led me in that direction. I said that I felt he had now led me to the WEA and I told Sir Arthur my evidence. Until the Lord showed me a different direction, I said, this was where I would stay. The General said, 'I like that answer, Rowlandson. OK you can come to us.' A few years later, the answer that I had given to Sir Arthur Smith was crucial to keeping my job with the Evangelical Alliance. Roy Cattell, in confirming my appointment, also acknowledged that I could continue with my commitment to help Tom Rees at Hildenborough.

In March 1952, the WEA sponsored a meeting at Church House Westminster for some 700 Christian leaders. The occasion was to hear an address by the young American evangelist, Billy Graham. At the time there was no thought at all that the WEA would necessarily be invited to organise a crusade with Billy Graham. However, Mr John Cordle, the treasurer of the WEA, had other ideas.

Humanly speaking, without John Cordle there may never have been a Harringay Crusade. At the time he was a Member of

Parliament for a Bournemouth constituency, so he carried some 'clout'. It was he who had 'discovered' Billy Graham in America way back in 1946, and it was he who had now persuaded Roy Cattell that the WEA should become involved. Roy had accepted the challenge. Shortly after I joined the WEA Roy called a meeting to form an exploratory committee. Their brief would be to investigate whether or not it would be feasible to organise a crusade.

Out of that exploratory meeting came a decision to send every clergyman and minister throughout the British Isles a printed copy of Billy Graham's address at Church House. In that address Billy Graham had outlined with clarity and in great detail the whole concept of his evangelistic work – the meetings and their content; his message; the 'appeal'; the follow-up and the prayer commitment. My first job with the WEA was to make a transcript of that address and to obtain quotes for it to be printed. It was eventually published under the title *The Work of an Evangelist* and copies were mailed to tens of thousands of clergy and ministers throughout the UK. It set the scene for a possible crusade in London and I found myself once again back in the orbit of Billy Graham. Once more the 'Thin Gold Line' had reconnected with me and I found myself in the very centre of the activity with Billy Graham.

From the very beginning of my time in Christian work I had considered it important to be engaged in some form of secular activity to 'keep my feet on the ground'. I needed to be constantly reminded that there was a world out there that needed Christ, and my involvement in Christian work must allow for contacts in that sphere. I first decided to join the Civil Defence. It seemed to me in those dangerous days that this was a service to the community which would be useful. At the same time it would bring me into contact with those outside the church. I joined the Search and Rescue department and we attended training for two hours a week. I had done this for several years and gained my certification as a qualified Rescue Team person along with my First Aid certificate.

Therefore on 8 October 1952 when there was a horrendous train crash at the Harrow and Wealdstone railway station, I presented myself (along with other members of our rescue team) ready to be of service. In the briefest of terms we were told 'to get lost'!

I couldn't believe it! Here we were a team of ready-trained men and women who knew what to do – probably more so than some of the other people – and yet our help was being refused. I promptly resigned from the Civil Defence. The same day I saw an advertisement in the newspaper asking for volunteers to join the Royal Naval Volunteer Reserve (RNVR). That sounded attractive and I applied to join – but I didn't think I would be accepted. During the latter part of the war I had tried to get into the Royal Navy, but my history of a double mastoid operation did not make it possible. However, I now found I was confronted by a Welsh doctor who needed to clear me for joining the RNVR. His office was on the 14th floor of the Queen Elizabeth's Mansions, and there was no lift! When I arrived at the doctor's office he took one look at me and said, 'You're still breathing? OK, you're in!' And that was the sole medical examination I had! So my application was accepted and that phase of my life is another story!

Meanwhile each morning in the WEA offices, Roy Cattell and I would meet to discuss and pray over the day's activities. He gave me my 'marching orders' for the day and kept me very busy. Very soon the matter of forming a special committee came to the fore. It was to be under the auspices of the World's Evangelical Alliance – who had, by now, decided to drop 'World's' from the title and to become simply the 'Evangelical Alliance' (EA). The brief of this new committee would be to plan and organise a Greater London Crusade with Billy Graham.

Roy instructed me to write to all the prospective committee members and to secure their agreement to serve. Every one of those we invited accepted and, at the first meeting of the committee, I became an ex officio member. I soon found that my major task was one of 'translation'. Many times members of the American Team* made a statement in committee which (from my experience in America) I understood, but the committee was in danger of misunderstanding. Conversely I sometimes had to explain to Jerry Beavan, and members of the American Team, what the British committee meant by what they had said. Such 'translation' avoided many possible occasions of conflict.

* The use of Team/American Team throughout this book refers to the team working with Billy Graham (the Billy Graham Team).

Billy Graham had sent Jerry Beavan to be a liaison between himself and the British committee. Without Jerry's expertise, enthusiasm and enlightenment we would have had a very difficult time. Generally the committee made decisions on the basis of 'Why should we do that?' The American attitude always was 'Why not?' – a question that Jerry Beavan often asked. He was also a past-master at diplomacy and he demonstrated it on many occasions.

The most famous must be the statement in the Billy Graham Calendar (circulated from Minneapolis) which said: 'What Hitler's bombs could not do, socialism, with its accompanying evils, shortly accomplished.' This statement, published in many British newspapers, provoked an immediate reaction. *The Daily Herald* banner headline read 'Apologise Billy – or stay away'. In the House of Commons a Labour Member of Parliament said it was a direct and highly personal insult to the Labour Party. Questions were asked in the House whose Members debated whether or not Mr Graham should even be allowed to land in England.

There was a somewhat ironic twist to this furore because the British press, which had hardly mentioned the coming of Billy Graham for a crusade, nevertheless made a lot of publicity out of this story. It was headline and front-page news in many newspapers, giving us exposure that we could never have bought, engineered nor paid for. Nonetheless it was at first an immediate concern for the new crusade committee under their chairman, Major General D. J. Wilson Haffenden ('Haffy' to everyone). He had accepted our invitation to be the chairman.

Jerry Beavan read all the newspaper reports about the statement in the Billy Graham Calendar. He sat in my office biting his finger nails. Suddenly he looked up. 'Once again it's a translation problem for you,' he said. 'You should know that in America the word "socialism" means "secularism". In any case,' he concluded, 'note that, on the calendar, the word is spelt with a small "s". Had we meant the Labour Party we would have spelt Socialism with a capital S.' He issued a press release to this end, and the furore died down overnight. But we had had our share of publicity from the event. The devil had overstretched himself and it was a masterly demonstration of Jerry's abilities led by the Holy Spirit.

CHAPTER FIVE

THE GREATER LONDON CRUSADE (1 March to 12 May '54)

1

FROM THE very beginning 'Haffy', as chairman, never took a vote at a meeting of the Greater London Crusade committee. Everything was decided by a clear consensus and unanimity. Even committing large sums of money – as was inevitable – went through at the blink of an eyelid. In my experience I had never 'sat in' on a committee like it. There was debate on many items, but when it came to the decision there were no dissenters. It boded well for God's blessing on the event itself.

After the initial circulation of Billy Graham's address in *The Work of an Evangelist,* and the formation of the main committee, I set to work with Roy Cattell on many of the practical details. The most important question was, 'Where should the crusade be held?' That presented us with our biggest dilemma.

Traditionally the Royal Albert Hall had been the largest venue ever to house a Christian event post-war. But, by now, restrictions had already reduced its capacity. Earls Court, on the other hand, was unavailable for an extended period. We looked at several other locations, but for one reason or another, each was unsuitable. Then along came Mr R. G. Le Tourneau from Texas. He had designed an aluminium 'tabernacle' built of concentric circles and capable of seating 14,000 people. We sought planning permission from the London County Council to erect the temporary building on the banks of the Thames but planning permission was refused. So we approached the Wembley Stadium. Their manager was enormously impressed and interested in it and, for the publicity it would generate for Wembley. He readily agreed for it to be erected on one of their car park sites. I still have a sample plate and bolt from that proposed tabernacle.

Jerry Beavan, always the entrepreneur, produced an expensive oversized brochure designed to raise money for the venture from wealthy American industrialists. Meanwhile, the Bishop of Barking (the only Anglican Bishop to back the crusade plans) flew to Texas to confirm, to his own satisfaction, that the construction would work. While he was there the whole structure collapsed and the Bishop made the historic remark, 'I say, I don't think it is going to work!'

So Roy Cattell and I were thrown back to further research. It was then that a slightly smaller arena – the Harringay Arena – came into our sights. It was owned and operated by the Greyhound Racing Association and we were both invited to the directors' dining room at the White City Stadium to proceed with the negotiations. In my diary I recorded that it was a 'superlative lunch'! The directors of the Greyhound Racing Association fed well and the four-course meal was served by waitresses in uniform under the watchful eye of a head waiter. After lunch our negotiations were concluded and completed and we were given a *three-page* agreement. Roy and I signed the agreement on behalf of the committee and committed them to expenditure in excess of £30,000. It was the only document we ever had for our use of Harringay – in contrast to the *250-page* agreement with the Earls Court Arena 13 years later! The latter raised innumerable problems throughout our use of Earls Court whereas there was never a single problem that arose from our agreement with Harringay.

So Harringay it was! At the initial opening of the crusade five months later, the arena seated about 13,000 people. By the end of the crusade we were getting rather more than 15,000 in! There were no 'health and safety' regulations in those days. The management of the arena found that our crowd was orderly and disciplined. As they discovered this they allowed us, bit by bit, to get extra people in. First it was to allow a person to sit on each step. Then they allowed one at each end of each step. Later they allowed a line of people to stand behind the main seating area – and later they allowed two lines. All of these extras allowed the total capacity to creep up.

Soon after the Harringay agreement was signed, donations started pouring into the London Office. Amongst the donors was an ancient Chelsea Pensioner who came in – quite often – to give us 'the Lord's ten per cent of his football pool winnings'! This raised a great discussion about whether this was 'tainted money' and if we were right to accept it for the Lord's work. Jerry Beavan replied that 'all the money is the Lord's. Some of it is in the wrong hands, and we must get it back'! I pointed out to Jerry that, no sooner had we got it back, than we paid it to the Greyhound Racing Association for the rent of Harringay!

Jerry Beavan presented a plan to the committee to publicise the crusade. His conception was that there would be large bill-boards all over London, backed up by travelling advertisements on the side of each bus. Innumerable posters would be used in the underground and there would be newspaper advertisements. The message would be simple – HEAR BILLY GRAHAM. He pointed out that Billy Graham always had two criteria for a successful crusade – prayer and publicity.

When the astonished committee heard about the cost of such an advertising campaign they realised that it would have used up all and more of the committee's proposed entire budget! Jerry therefore came back with the proposal that £50,000 of the cost should be borne by the American Team, with such a refund as might be possible at the end of the crusade.

It was remarkably successful. Everyone across the whole city was talking about the crusade by the time it happened. Unexpectedly, of course, we had the headline news which arose from the questions in Parliament about Billy Graham's 'political' views.

Four other factors helped in preparation for the crusade. The first was the series of London-wide counsellor training classes. These were four weeks of intensive training to prepare those who would be counsellors and advisers at the crusade itself. The classes involved a team of men under the leadership of Dawson Trotman and his associates Charlie Riggs and Lorne Sanny. All three of them were associated with the Navigators Ministry which had been founded by Dawson. Thousands attended these classes and were sorted, in the end, into the two categories of counsellors and advisers. Every one of them was interviewed by a team of ministers before being awarded their suitable badge. It was not an unusual experience for some as they attended the classes to find the Lord Jesus Christ as their Saviour.

The second factor was a fortnightly series of evangelistic rallies in London's Royal Albert Hall. Once again Tom Rees had returned there and he used the occasions to 'talk up' the crusade. Early in March 1952 he was approached by Roy Cattell to ask if he would extend an invitation to Billy Graham to speak at one of the rallies.

Just at that time the BBC had asked Tom Rees to allow a broadcast of the *Songs of Praise* programme direct from the Royal Albert Hall. Mr Rees thought that on this special occasion he could combine an invitation to Billy Graham to be the special speaker. Jerry Beavan attended the Royal Albert Hall on Saturday 8 March and was very impressed with the quality of the meeting and the way in which Tom Rees led it. He felt it would be exactly the sort of meeting at which Billy Graham could be introduced to London. In effect, when Mr Graham spoke on 16 March 1952 it was his first major introduction to the people of London.

As plans for the crusade proceeded, later on Mr Rees encouraged his own choir, stewards and 'personal workers' to become fully involved in the meetings. Generously he passed all his mailing lists to the crusade committee.

Early in January 1953, Mr Rees had brought a young bass-baritone singer from Texas to form and train a choir for the Royal Albert Hall series. Frank Boggs immediately commended himself to everybody. He had such an outgoing personality that everybody loved him. Marilyn and I joined 'The Hildenborough Singers' as the choir became known. They were such an unusual group that the BBC showed an interest in them and wanted Frank Boggs to train them to a high standard. He did a very good job but, in the end, the choir was just not good enough to broadcast to the standard that the BBC wanted and the programmes were never broadcast.

All of us, nevertheless, became deeply involved in the plans for the Greater London Crusade and, during the Royal Albert Hall series, the coming Harringay Crusade was at the forefront of our minds.

A third factor which made a huge impact during the months of preparation was the introduction of 'Operation Andrew'. Devised by Jean Rees, the Operation Andrew programme took note that 'The first thing Andrew did was to find his brother Simon and tell him, "We have found the Messiah" [that is, the Christ]' – John 1:41. Jean proposed that we should adopt Operation Andrew in the crusade planning. It was a scheme by which an individual used a special card as a reminder and motivator to pray for unchurched friends and relatives who needed Christ. The scheme was so successful that it was adopted by the Billy Graham Team. He was so impressed with it that he decided that he and his team would start using it right away. They continued to do so as a major factor in all his crusades and missions ever since.

Finally, a major film programme was launched. The decision was taken at a Greater London Crusade Committee held on Bank Holiday Monday in August (in those days, the first Monday in August). So imperative had the need become, that the Bank Holiday was ignored in favour of getting the job done.

Two major feature films had been made by World Wide Pictures – the film 'arm' of the Billy Graham Evangelistic Association. The first, *Mr Texas*, was not deemed to be suitable to introduce Billy Graham to a UK audience, but the second, *Oil Town USA*, was warmly received and acclaimed. We 'tried it out' on a series of nightly showings in the private Gaumont British Film cinema in Wardour Street. We were overwhelmed by the success of those showings. In this we were helped by the personal appearance of cowboy Redd Harper – a star in the film – who came and gave his testimony night by night. After the film show each night we would go to Lyons Corner House in Tottenham Court Road for supper. There, with his guitar, Redd became quite notorious! There was some spontaneous evangelism in the café night after night – to the great delight of the waitresses ('Nippies' as they were called)!

Not only was the film an excellent story and a good film in its own right, it also served to introduce Billy Graham to the British public in the context of a crusade. It also had a strong evangelistic message and from the time it was first shown there were those who found the Lord Jesus Christ as their Saviour at every showing.

It was not, however, all plain sailing. The Evangelical Alliance received a few letters of complaint about the film. These were the days when many Christian people did not go to the cinema and when make-up was totally taboo in some Christian circles. Many Christian people had never seen *any* film in their lives before. Some of them never understood the technicalities of making a film. One day we received a letter in which the (lady) writer said: 'Thank you for showing us a wonderful film. But, do you think that, next time you show it, you could ask the young actresses to use a little less make-up!'

Nevertheless we took the decision to use the film as a major promotion vehicle for the crusade and it was a highly successful programme. Three film teams were established – one under Nigel Cooke of International Films; one under the leadership of The Revd C. Alan Stephens (a Baptist minister), and a third which I myself led.

Every night from early October to 21 February 1954 (with a short break over the Christmas period) *Oil Town USA* was shown in dozens of locations all over the London area and beyond. By January we were being asked to use larger venues which necessitated the purchase of an arc projector. This back-breaking piece of equipment (with three very heavy components) was assigned to my team and we spent many laborious hours carrying it up to the highest point in each hall that we used – usually up a spiral iron staircase!

One problem we had was that the film was on two reels. There were two obvious – but impractical – solutions. We could either use two projectors, switching from one to the other at the halfway point, or we could put the whole film on one enormous reel. Gaumont British (the makers of the projectors we used) made two extension arms for us. These enabled us to put the entire film on to one very large reel. We soon found, however, that the strain on the film was too great and it continually tore.

So Cannon Payne and I 'invented' a solution. We prepared the end of the first reel with a short 'tail' which we scraped ready for 'splicing' with film cement. Then we prepared the beginning of the second reel in a similar fashion. As the end of the first reel approached we unwound the last few feet by hand and draped it over the back of the machine. We then removed the empty reel and replaced it with the full reel two. A rapid splicing of the two 'tails' meant that it fed through the projector with only a short black gap. As the join came through we broke the join, removed the full take-up reel from the projector and replaced it with an empty reel to take up the film as it came through the projector. This system needed team work to be effective, but we used it for many showings without a problem. It was pretty nerve-wracking however!

When Mr Graham was invited to return a year later in 1955 for a second crusade, it was important for the film preparation to continue. This started again in September 1954 and carried right on until the end of April.

There is no doubt that these four factors, coupled with the intensive advertising campaign, started to awaken curiosity amongst the people of London and in the Home Counties.

At a meeting of the Greater London Crusade Committee on 8 February 1954, two major decisions were taken. The one that affected me most was my appointment as chief steward at Harringay. I immediately involved my closest friends as deputy chief stewards and together we devised our 'plan of action'. Henry Hole became my immediate deputy and he was backed up by David Rennie, Heini Sheldon, Cannon Payne, George Andrews, Percy Sprowson and John Baldwin. It was a cast-iron team and we worked together for the whole 12 weeks of the crusade.

An interesting telephone conversation took place shortly before Mr Graham arrived in Britain. Sir John Laing, the famous builder (who had been my Crusader Bible Class leader during the war years) telephoned to ask me a question. 'Where will Billy Graham be staying when he comes to London?' he asked. I replied to say that we were still looking for the most appropriate hotel – one which would have all the facilities we needed, plus adequate security – and that a decision had not yet been taken. He went on to ask, 'Will he be staying at the Hilton Hotel?' I was quickly able to reassure him on that point because the London Committee had felt that it would not give the right image if he used that hotel. Strangely enough, Mr Graham had a special card which gave him free accommodation at all Hilton Hotels worldwide. Therefore, to have put him there would have been economically sound but we feared that the 'image' would be wrong.

Having received my assurance that the Hilton Hotel would not be used, Sir John said that he would be sending a substantial gift to the funds of the crusade. It was indicative of the stringent life-style that Sir John himself exercised, living in a very humble home in North West London. In the event we used the Stratford Court Hotel in Oxford Street which, although not the most convenient location, was able to provide all that we needed and was able to give us very advantageous rates.

Prior to the opening night, a series of special events had taken place. The first of these was the arrival of Mr Graham at Waterloo Station. He had come from America on the liner *The United States*. One reporter (who had boarded the liner at Le Havre, wanted to know why Mr Graham had travelled in apparent luxury while Christ had ridden into Jerusalem on a donkey. Grady Wilson (Mr Graham's aide) promptly replied, 'Show me a donkey that can cross the Atlantic and I'll put Mr Graham on it!'

Most of the Christian press had carried the date and time of Mr Graham's arrival at Waterloo. I had gone to the station earlier in the day to try and persuade the station master to bring the train into a wider platform. I had failed dismally. He pointed out to me that, even for film stars, there never was more than a handful of people. I was still in his office an hour before the train was due to arrive. By then there was already an immense crowd at the entrance to the platform at which the train had been announced to arrive. In those days it was necessary to buy a 'platform ticket' to access the platform and the machine was working overtime!

Suddenly the station master realised that he had been wrong. As I stood at his elbow he picked up the direct line to the signal box, and ordered a change of platform for the train. The new platform was announced on the station loudspeakers and there was a sudden stampede as the entire hymn-singing crowd of more than 4000 people surged towards the wider platform 10. The station master was heard to remark, 'If these are Christians, it's time we let out the lions!'

As Billy and Ruth Graham alighted from the train, Roy Cattell, Jerry Beavan and I met them. As the crowd pressed around them, the two tall men (Roy and Jerry) shouldered their way through and allowed Billy and Ruth to progress towards the waiting cars. I got lost somewhere in the mêlée! The station, meanwhile, echoed with the vibrant hymn singing of the waiting crowd. It was a great occasion which remained in the memories of those who were there.

The next day, at the Harringay Arena, the first choir practice was led by Cliff Barrows (the Team member who MC'd the meetings and trained and led the choir). It had all begun! The enthusiasm of the choir members was matched by the excitement of Cliff Barrows as he taught them the special way in which they would be singing the hymns – especially 'Blessed Assurance' which became the 'theme song' of the crusade. On Friday 26 February at the Café Royal there was a great welcome lunch with 920 clergy and ministers as invited guests. The meal was a gift from a wealthy supporter who was most anxious that Mr Graham should have a proper welcome. The same night we held our first stewards' rehearsal at the Arena. We explained the different responsibilities of each group of stewards, the aisle captains, the group captains and the area captains. We told them how they would report to the deputy chief stewards who, in turn, were responsible to me as chief steward. The wives of my deputy team worked in the stewards' assignment room, instructing each steward where to go. They soon became territorially involved and, night after night, the stewards would ask for 'the same assignment please'!

As far as admission to the arena was concerned, Henry Hole was most outspoken against Jerry Beavan's declared intention of issuing almost half as many more tickets as there were seats in the arena. But Jerry would not be shifted. He took the position that 'we always did it' and that, because the tickets were free, many of them would not be used. Henry lost the argument and for the first three nights of the crusade we almost lost Henry Hole as crowds outside the arena were unable to get in! At first the people outside were inclined to be belligerent ('I've got a ticket: you've got to let me in!') But Jerry Beavan pacified both Henry and the crowd outside and, by the time events had settled down, we had no further problem. However, during the first three nights of the crusade, many hundreds of people came who just could not get into the arena. When Billy Graham heard that there were many hundreds outside, he responded by climbing out through a window, standing on the parapet over the main entrance, and giving a welcome and short address to those outside. It was a deeply appreciated gesture by the overflow crowd.

As we have seen, the Harringay Arena accommodated approximately 13,000 people when we opened on 1 March 1954. Apart from the first three nights (described above) we always got everybody in – in spite of the excessive number of tickets issued. Each night thereafter at Harringay, it seemed that exactly the right number of people came to fill the arena. As the management allowed us to put extra people in, so the number of people coming grew. The Lord over-ruled in this vital matter and we were always able to accommodate the number of people who came.

That is, of course, except on several of the Saturdays! The first Saturday, by 2.30pm, there was a queue outside the Harringay Arena long enough to fill the arena. When Billy Graham heard about it he told us to 'open the doors' and let them in. Then he led the first of three meetings that day. At 3pm the hall was full: outside another queue was forming. By 5.30pm we were able to fill the hall a second time and, undaunted, Billy Graham preached for a second time. The proper Saturday evening meeting at 7.45pm was again completely full and Mr Graham completed the marathon of three services on the Saturday. This happened on more than one occasion.

The second major decision taken at the committee meeting (on 8 February) before the crusade commenced was to warn Mr Graham against using the atomic bomb as an illustration in his sermons. The committee felt very strongly about this. They felt that it would not be appropriate in Britain for him to use this topic in his sermons. They recognised that it was relevant in America, but they did not think it to be so in Britain. The decision was communicated to Mr Graham and he said that he 'noted what the committee had said'. Nonetheless they all recognised that he would need to be led by the Holy Spirit in the things he said.

In the event, on 1 March 1954 (the very day that the Greater London Crusade started), the Americans announced that they had detonated their first hydrogen bomb on the Bikini Atoll. It was therefore, the most natural thing in the world for Mr Graham to incorporate something about it in his sermon that evening. The committee understood and accepted his decision. The Lord had a way of over-ruling!

On 27 February we had held a Dedication meeting at which Mr Graham spoke for the first time. The arena was well-filled with choir, stewards, counsellors, advisers and all their families. It was an evening of great expectation. Sunday followed, with the crusade itself starting on Monday, 1 March. It had all started to come together. Before it had finished twelve weeks later, it had become a way of life.

CHAPTER SIX

THE GREATER LONDON CRUSADE (1 March to 12 May '54)

2

A FEATURE of the Greater London Crusade was the total commitment that everyone gave to this great event. Stewards, counsellors, choir, staff and committee were there night after night. As has already been said, it became a 'way of life'. No one would have wanted to miss out on even a moment of the crusade.

My own responsibilities were three-fold. First was the organisation and operation of the stewarding team. From the time that the stewards arrived in the assignment room to the time when the building was finally empty each night, every one of them was dedicated to the task.

My second responsibility was to Roy Cattell with whom I worked very closely throughout the preparations and at the crusade itself. In modern parlance I was his 'gofer'. I stood ready to do whatever he needed to be done in order to keep the wheels turning smoothly.

Third, I had a responsibility to the Billy Graham Team. I was under the direction of Jerry Beavan and Willis Haymaker for that. Willis had been a campaign manager for many of the old-time evangelists, and was a tower of strength to us in all that we did. We called him 'Sunshine' because you 'only make hay when the sun shines!' Actually the nickname also reflected his constantly cheerful and smiling face. He was a great encourager!

Whenever there was a special need for Mr Graham or the other Platform Team Members (Cliff Barrows, George Beverly Shea,

Tedd Smith, Paul Mickleson, Dawson Trotman, and later after Dawson's death, Charlie Riggs), Jerry would call upon me, and any work for him took precedence over all my other commitments. It was a question of getting your priorities right!

The commitment shown by the stewards was matched also by the team of counsellors and the choir members. All of those involved watched in amazement as they saw the arena totally filled night after night.

From the first night – and on every night for the 12 weeks – the choir opened the evening by singing Cliff Barrows' version of the hymn 'Blessed assurance, Jesus is mine'. In his arrangement Cliff Barrows had the last line of the chorus drawn out and emphasised:

'This . . . is . . . my . . . story, this is my song, praising my Saviour . . . ALL . . . THE . . . DAY . . . LONG!'

For many years afterwards it seemed odd not to follow the same style in one's own church!

For the first three nights, the committee had agreed that there would be no offering or other appeal for money. They hoped that this would dispel the press criticism that 'they are only in it for the money'. It was a successful ploy and none of the headlines carried that criticism. It did, however, give us three days to work out our strategy and plan how best to organise the collection with the minimum of disruption and fuss. Thus Thursday, 4 March, was the first night that we took up an offering.

We had devised a scheme whereby under the end seat of each row a numbered ice cream tub would be placed in position. At the appropriate moment the person sitting in that seat would be instructed, from the platform, to 'reach under your seat' and pass the tub along the row. At the end of each row, the stewards would collect the tubs and deliver them to their 'aisle captains'. These would, in turn, be collected by the group captains and taken to the 'collection room' where each numbered tub would be checked off by a deputy chief steward. In that way we could be assured that every tub had been collected.

That first Thursday night, the team of chief stewards set about counting the collection. They finished at 4am! Night by night there would be some £13,000 to £15,000 in the collection – most of it in coins. So we borrowed a coin counting machine which enabled us to finish by 2am.

David Rennie, who was the chief executive of a large business company, remarked, 'We'll never survive doing this for 12 weeks on end.' He proposed a radical solution which, to everybody's surprise, actually worked. He arranged with the crusade's bank manager each morning to receive some 30 sealed bags containing coins, to be counted by his staff. This left us to deal only with paper money and cheques. Thereafter for the remaining eleven weeks of the crusade we would simply tip all the coins into large canvas bags supplied by the bank. We tied them up with string and sealed them with a lead seal the bank had given to us. The bags were then carried out and placed into the boot of my car in the car park. The next morning I drove to our bank in Southampton Row and, *by myself*, carried those 30 bags of coins (and about three bags of notes and cheques) into the bank. I had no security guard! Nor was there anyone else to help me. For eleven weeks that procedure went on and we never had a moment's problem. By the time of the Earls Court Crusade, eleven years later, we could not do that. We had to use Securicor with armed guards and a fully protected van.

Night after night Mr Graham ended his address with an invitation. 'I'm going to ask you to get up out of your seats and come and stand here at the front.' We stood back during those first few nights at Harringay and watched with amazement as, from every part of the arena, people streamed forward to the front. Billy Graham himself would stand back from the podium with his arms folded and his head bowed. He put no pressure upon them. He just allowed them to come as, in the background, Cliff Barrows led the choir in singing 'Just as I am without one plea but that Thy blood was shed for me'.

As they came forward each person was accompanied by a counsellor of the same sex and, as far as possible, of the same age as the 'enquirer'. It did not take long for the newspapers to claim that there had been 'X' number of 'converts'. The Team took great pains always to refer to those that came forward as 'enquirers'. Billy Graham himself always said that God alone knew the response of everyone's heart. Some would truly have come to Christ as a result of the evangelist's preaching – many did – but there were others who came to rededicate their lives to Christ, or simply for counselling in a problem. There were, inevitably, a few who came out of sheer curiosity – or to get a closer look at the evangelist.

In talking at a press conference prior to the start of the crusade Billy Graham was asked, 'How many people do you expect to convert?' He immediately replied, 'I hope none! It is my hope that anyone who responds to the message may be converted through the power of the Holy Spirit in their lives.'

The Press went on to ask, 'Do you think that the enormous expense of this crusade is justified?' Mr Graham replied that if just one person came to Christ it would all be worth it. He often referred to the Parable of the Sower, and described how just 25 per cent of the seed fell on 'good ground'. Nonetheless, subsequent evidence has shown that a great many more than 25 per cent in fact committed their lives to Christ. Some years later, Dr Stanley High (a researcher from *The Reader's Digest*) visited England. He came into my office to get some detailed information as he sought to find those who had come to Christ at Harringay. He confessed to me that he was a sceptic. After he had spent some weeks in the UK he returned to my office to tell me that he 'didn't want to believe what he had discovered'. He said that, in his research, it seemed that some 72 per cent were 'still involved in religion'. I told him that many of those would tell him that it was not 'religion' that they were involved in, but a personal relationship with Jesus Christ. I understand that some years later his own opinion had changed and he became a member of the committee which organised a crusade in New York.

Another demonstration of the effectiveness of Mr Graham's ministry at Harringay was a group of 23 ordinands who, 11 years later were seated on the platform at the Earls Court Crusade. They were then training for the Ministry. All of them had dated their conversion from the Harringay Crusade.

Many individual stories have been written. Mr Ernest Shippam was the head of a food company whose 'fish paste' products could be found on many a teatime table across the UK. At the time of

Harringay he was an alcoholic whose family dreaded to have him around the home. He was one of those who came to Christ during the Harringay Crusade and his testimony to the efficacy and power of the Holy Spirit to change his life was widely known. He became a much-sought-after speaker at Christian gatherings until the time of his death many years later.

Another was a military man – Major Richard Carr-Gomm. His life was so 'turned inside out' that he was given a deep concern for people in need around him. He founded the Abbeyfield Society as a result of his faith in the Lord Jesus Christ. When that society grew too big for him to handle he founded a similar society called the Carr-Gomm Society which fulfilled his concern and dream to make his faith known in a ministry to those who needed accommodation and help.

A third was a London actress named Joan Winmill who had appeared on the London Stage in a lead role in Douglas Hume's play *The Chiltern Hundreds*. She had had a lonely life that had been full of problems. In spite of her success, and the fact that she had been a girl-friend of the famous Bobby Kennedy from America, she had reached such a low point in her life that she was now seriously considering suicide.

At that time in her life a Mr John Mercer, a London insurance broker who had made all the necessary arrangements for the crusade's insurances, had befriended her. He offered her a ticket for the VIP section of Harringay (the area that the team of stewards referred to as 'The Plush' because they were the only upholstered seats in the arena). Joan accepted the ticket and came to the crusade. She was so overwhelmed by the evangelist's message that when he gave the invitation 'get up out of your seat and come and stand at the front' she was one of those who responded.

It has always been amazing how God prepares the way for such as Joan. For when she came to the front, in a remarkable way, her counsellor turned out to be Ruth Graham. Who better could there have been to fulfil such a responsibility? Joan's life was totally turned around.

Before the end of the crusade she was invited to take part in a feature film which centred upon the crusade. *Souls in Conflict* was to become one of the most effective evangelistic films that the

Billy Graham Evangelistic Association ever made. In some way it told Joan's actual story, as well as the stories of two others whose lives were affected by Billy Graham's ministry.

Many thousands responded over the twelve weeks and these three dramatic stories are but a few of the many more that could be told. Indeed, 50 years later, in my own experience, I am constantly meeting people who are anxious to tell me that it was at Harringay that they became Christians. They tell *me*, of course, because they know of my connection with Billy Graham. They would not necessarily be telling anyone else in a similar way.

Some years later, in 1969, I was asked to give a talk to a Central London Mensa Group (the High-IQ group) on the topic of 'the Ministry of Billy Graham'. In my address I remarked that I rarely went out to speak like this without someone standing up at 'question time' afterwards to say that it was at Harringay they had found Christ. I went on to imply that I hardly expected that to happen in such a group. When it came to the question time, one man was immediately on his feet to say, 'Mr Rowlandson can keep his record, because I came to Christ at Harringay 15 years ago!' It was a great testimony to the group.

Then, in 2001, the publishers Hodder & Stoughton commissioned me to research the stories of some 30 people whose lives had been changed through Mr Graham's ministry (both at Harringay and at other crusades and missions and through films and *Decision* magazine). The book *I'm Going to Ask You . . .* was the outcome of that research.

Throughout the Harringay Crusade there was great press interest. During the days just before the crusade there had been that flurry of press interest because of the Calendar incident (see page 73). For the opening few days of the crusade there was some curiosity, but that soon died down. That is, except for two major antagonists – William Hickey of the *Daily Express* and William Conner (known as Cassandra) of the *Daily Mirror*.

William Hickey was the first to agree to meet Mr Graham. He later said, 'He is not a man you can be rude to – a voice inside you tells you that this is a man of integrity.' When Billy Graham left him after the interview William Hickey wished him Godspeed, and said he was stunned to realise that his eyes were 'scalding with tears'.

Billy Graham wrote to his other critic and asked William Connor to meet him. Mr Graham had thought that Cassandra's articles, although acerbic, 'were two of the most cleverly written' that he had ever read. With a sense of irony Connor agreed to meet Billy Graham in a pub called The Baptist's Head. After a fascinating time together, William Connor declared, 'That bloke means everything he says.' Thereafter his articles became more sympathetic, and he and Mr Graham remained friends until 'Bill' Connor died.

There were many other doors which opened to Billy Graham throughout the Harringay Crusade. There were those in the top echelons of society who wanted to meet him and, although unwilling at first to go to Harringay, they invited Mr Graham to come and visit them. Many of them later came to the arena itself to see the evangelist in action. To list the names of those whose friendship he enjoyed would put those who did not come from such exalted positions at a disadvantage. It never mattered to Billy Graham whether his visitor was from the highest of social circles or a blue-collared worker from the factory. He welcomed them all with equal interest and a concern for their souls. His most ardent supporter from the House of Lords was Lord Luke who never wavered in his support for Mr Graham throughout his life. He always held him in highest esteem and opened many otherwise closed doors for Billy Graham to enter.

Both the hierarchy of the Church of England, and the heads of several Nonconformist denominations were not too welcoming. The Reverend Frank Martin, a journalist writing in the *Sunday Graphic* during the first two weeks of the crusade, declared (what he saw as the 'line' of British Churches): 'Billy Graham's line just won't do . . . the whole thing is too . . . immature.' Yet eleven weeks later, writing again in the same paper, he said, 'Thank you Billy. You've done us a power of good. Come again soon!'

Such a change in attitude was seen in much of the national press too. They could not ignore the hymn-singing crowds on the underground and buses, as they returned home from Harringay.

And the evidence of changed lives even 'won over' the Archbishop of Canterbury (Geoffrey Fisher) who agreed to sit on the platform at the closing meeting in the Wembley Stadium.

Another who was impressed by the advent of the Wembley meeting was Sir Winston Churchill. He had resolutely refused to meet Billy Graham throughout the crusade but the Wembley meeting aroused his curiosity. Two days after the Wembley meeting, Mr Graham was welcomed into Downing Street where he had a brief conversation with the great Prime Minister. Churchill had urged that the details of their conversation should remain private, but his aides later said that he had been impressed with the young American. Billy Graham himself said, 'I felt like I had shaken hands with Mr History.'

My own experience of Mr Graham thoughout the crusade was of a man who was deeply interested in me. Almost daily he asked me to come into his room at Harringay and he always received me warmly. He constantly wanted to know how things were going with me and my family and quite often he asked me to join in the prayer time they had before going on to the platform.

He was especially interested in one tragic circumstance when we found that one of our stewards had been stealing from the collection. He had been discovered by another steward and we had had to call the police. They questioned him and searched him without any evidence. Then, just as they were about to leave, one of the policemen ran his hand along the bottom of the steward's jacket. He obviously felt something there because he ripped off the jacket and tore away the lining. Out fell a dozen marked £1 notes and the steward was arrested. It transpired that he had a specially sewn pocket at the top of his jacket into which he had 'posted' the notes. When Billy Graham heard about it, he urged Major General Wilson Haffenden and me to go to the court hearing and plead leniency for the steward. We did so, and he was given a conditional discharge. But, of course, we were one steward less for the rest of the crusade. Mr Graham's personal concern and interest in the situation – in spite of his commitments and busy life – deeply impressed me.

On the last day of the crusade I was called into Mr Graham's office where he presented me with a gold watch. On the back was engraved 'With love from the Billy Graham Team'. He also gave both Marilyn and me red leather-covered Bibles in which he had written 'God bless you and thank you for your faithfulness. Phil. 1:6.' As he gave the Bibles to us he told us that the colour of the Bibles was to remind us that the 'Bible should be read!'

There were 'extra-curricular events' that became part of the Harringay Crusade. One Saturday there was a visit from Roy Rogers and his wife Dale Evans, with their horse Trigger. They came to a special children's rally which was held next door to the Harringay Arena, in the Harringay Stadium. The huge stadium was totally filled with children and their parents as they listened to Roy and Dale tell about their faith and encouraging children to trust in the Lord Jesus Christ.

Another two events were mass evangelistic open air meetings – one in Trafalgar Square and one in Hyde Park on Easter Saturday. Both occasions were well publicised and there were very large crowds at both as Billy Graham proclaimed the Gospel – with an appeal – at each of these events. Many counsellors and stewards were there in this additional commitment to their duties at the Harringay Arena.

Understandably, for the last four nights at Harringay, we could have filled the arena twice or more. Many more people arrived – with tickets of course – than we could possibly accommodate. At the last minute, the Harringay authorities allowed us to let the overflow crowd into the Harringay Stadium next door where a sound relay was installed. It was the best we could do!

On 11 May 1954 Harringay itself came to an end – but not before we realised that the big challenge would be upon us the next day. The crusade was to conclude on the final Saturday with a massive rally in the Wembley Stadium. As always, more tickets were issued than there were seats and it quickly became clear that many more people would be coming – from all over the country by special trains and buses – than we could possibly accommodate. A last-minute decision was taken by the Crusade Committee to have an overflow meeting at the White City Stadium on the Saturday afternoon. They bore in mind that, on many of the Saturdays at Harringay, there had been a queue outside from early in the afternoon. On each occasion that happened, Mr Graham told us to open the doors and let the people in. We fully expected that there would be enough people coming to White City on Saturday afternoon to allow a meeting to be held there, and still enough people would come to Wembley in the evening. We advertised the extra meeting well.

And so it happened. White City was completely filled with 60,000 plus people for the afternoon meeting. Logistically it was a nightmare for we had to transfer the entire operation from White City – choir, stewards, counsellors and team and, of course, Mr Graham himself – to Wembley some five miles away. We had a police escort for Mr Graham to make sure he got there safely.

In spite of the afternoon crowd Wembley was completely filled half an hour before the advertised time of the evening meeting. To our surprise the Wembley Authorities agreed to open the gates to the turf. Unbelievably nearly 11,000 people were let in to stand on the 'sacred turf' in front of the platform. At 111,000 this turned out to be the largest crowd that Wembley had ever – or would ever – accommodate. There certainly had never been a crowd that big before and, because of safety restrictions which were introduced shortly afterwards, there never would be again.

It was a great concluding meeting, during which it was announced that Mr Graham would return for another week-long crusade at the Wembley Stadium a year later in 1955.

Shortly after the crusade ended I had a letter from Billy Graham. It was the first one I ever had from him and I treasured it greatly. He had signed it personally and it was dated 24 May 1954 – the Monday immediately following the meetings at White City and Wembley Stadium. I was to receive many more letters from him as the years went by.

In this letter he wrote:

> I want to thank you for the splendid way in which you have directed the work of the stewards at Harringay and for the many additional responsibilities which you have graciously accepted with regards to the film ministry and other phases of our work here in Great Britain. Your faithfulness has been an inspiration. Thank you kindly.

Many other histories and stories have been written about the Harringay Crusade. To repeat them all here would be superfluous. (To the reader who wants much more detail, the full story can be found in *London Hears Billy Graham*: *The Harringay Story* and in the books by John Pollock on the Billy Graham story) – as well as in Mr Graham's autobiography *Just as I Am* and in my own book *Life with Billy* – See Bibliography, page 279.

CHAPTER SEVEN

LANDLINE RELAYS AND GLASGOW

WITH THE 1955 Wembley Crusade in the offing, we continued with the showings of the film *Oil Town USA* – except we now had a wider area to cover. The reason for this started with the vision of Bob Benninghof – a radio engineer from CBS radio in the USA. He had been seconded to London to broadcast the radio programme *The Hour of Decision* from the Harringay Arena. This involved one recording each week – which left him a lot of time to 'twiddle his thumbs'.

His interest in radio and telephony work led him to discover that there was, in the UK, a network of landlines which had been laid down during the recent war to provide security communications across the whole country. Bob contemplated using these landlines to carry a programme from the Harringay Arena to other parts of London and the Home Counties. An experiment was launched at the Trocadero Cinema at the Elephant and Castle in London, south of the Thames. Such was the interest in Mr Graham's ministry following the Harringay Crusade that we believed a landline relay to the Trocadero cinema could attract crowds – as indeed it did.

Word rapidly spread and other centres in the Home Counties asked if they could have a landline relay as well. By the early part of May 1954 some 175 cities across the UK were receiving the Harringay Crusade by landline.

This programme was so successful that the Evangelical Alliance contemplated making a deliberate effort to develop the system. They realised it could carry the Glasgow Crusade (planned in the spring of 1955) by landlines to any place that would like to have it. The EA estimated that, upon their experience in 1954, there could be as many as 500 relays. I was appointed to organise the programme and to plan the logistics.

There were three considerations: first was the need to train counsellors. The second was to centralise the publicity and the third was to estimate the cost and to cover our expenses.

The first need was solved by arranging for Lorne Sanny to come and put his four lectures on to tape. He would come from the Navigators HQ in Colorado Springs. We knew him well for he had been one of the trainers in 1954. These tapes, together with the training materials (and ultimately the follow-up materials) would be available for use at each location across the country.

In the event Lorne Sanny flew in to London from America and, when I met him at London Airport, he had no voice! He had a bad attack of Laryngitis. We had booked a studio in London for two days later and we had invited 25 students from the London Bible College to participate as a live audience. There would be four sessions through the day each one lasting around one and a half hours. It was a marathon for Lorne!

On the morning of the recording Lorne was no better. His voice was not even husky. It was just a whisper – but we prayed, and had been praying, since he arrived. When we arrived at the studio I was very apprehensive that the whole thing would have to be put off. However, when it came to the voice check, Lorne Sanny spoke in his normal voice – and so it remained throughout that long day. When I picked him up in the evening the laryngitis had returned and he could scarcely whisper. God had seen him – and us – through! We had recorded six hours of magnificent training tapes.

We also tackled the matter of different styles of publicity appearing in various parts of the country. We decided that everything would be designed centrally. Then we would distribute it on a nation-wide basis. We prepared posters, leaflets, prayer cards, Operation Andrew cards and letters for each centre to use.

The biggest factor with which we had to contend was to determine our costs, and the amount of the contribution required from each centre. We carefully calculated the printing costs of the publicity; the costs of making and producing the counsellor training tapes in bulk; the cost of printing the follow-up material. On top of all this was the cost of each individual landline rental which needed to include the provision of suitable public address equipment for the size of each hall. Finally, we added something to cover our own administration costs.

We originally based the overall cost per centre upon an estimated 500 relay centres. On my suggestion, we agreed to allow for a 10 per cent increase on our estimated take-up and we therefore based our costs upon 550.

Next we worked out a 'per head package deal'. Everything would be included. A small centre with – say – 250 seats would pay 250 times the basic cost: a large centre with 2500 seats would pay ten times that amount. Everything would be arranged and sent from our London headquarters. Each area needed only to book a hall or church of an adequate size and to provide the electricity. A larger hall would require bigger equipment. So the idea of working on a 'per person' calculation seemed to be best.

We designed an application form which we sent to every enquiry. The form provided all the details that we needed. It enabled us to prepare the right numbers of tapes, publicity material, follow-up material and the equipment needed for a successful relay.

We had an unexpected problem. Instead of the 500/550 centres we had estimated, we had in excess of 2000 centres wanting the relays! As a result – and because our budgeting had been based upon just 550 relays – we ended the day with a profit of nearly £13,000! As it happened, that was the Lord's provision for us in a very special need – but more of that later!

As I said earlier, I booked one of the relays to be used on that year's Venturers Cruise in Norfolk. I therefore had some personal experience from the recipient's end of the arrangements.

Shortly before the relays took place, the Post Office Telephones (who were the agency who operated the landlines) sent me a diagrammatic map with a dot marking each relay centre. It had been on my wall for two days when my secretary looked up and said, 'Have you noticed that the outline of the country is not on the map? It just shows where the relays are.'

I looked carefully and she was right! There were so many dots on the map that the outline of the country was quite clear without being drawn in! It was a remarkable coverage and indicated the enormous interest in the ministry of Billy Graham that had been generated from the Harringay Crusade. Our 'package deal' system worked well. Nonetheless, for the final ten days before the landline crusade started, most of my colleagues at the London office were working long hours, often beyond 10pm at night (sometimes even through the night), in order to get the 2000 plus packages made up and ready to go out.

Eventually we reached a situation when the Post Office said that they could accept no more bookings. For them there was a lot of paper work, as well as engineering plans for each centre. They could not see how any more could be handled.

Because of the explosive growth of centres there were even more centres that, at the last minute, wanted to be included. From the 'cut off date' we had to say 'no'. This raised a problem with the Post Office who complained to me that they were receiving both abusive calls – and even the offer of 'bribes' – to be connected after the cut-off date. However, they stuck to their guns and supported us in the decision that had been agreed. It was, however, a bad witness to the Post Office Telephone staff as supposedly Christian people were resorting to these back-handed tactics.

I had to apologise to the Post Office staff (with whom I had become quite friendly) and told them that we deplored such things happening.

My wife and I went to Glasgow for the opening night of the relay mission. By then, the Glasgow Crusade had already been running for ten days and we had completed all the logistical arrangements for the local centres. Up in Glasgow I first met the Post Office engineers who, before that, had only been voices at the other end of the telephone. It was a wonderfully cooperative effort and we appreciated everything that they did to make this landline crusade so effective.

Today I am constantly hearing of people who responded to Mr Graham's invitation as they came forward and stood in front of an inanimate black box, there to be joined by a trained Counsellor who told them how to accept the Lord Jesus Christ as their Saviour.

It was a remarkable thing to do, but so many did it and it changed their lives. It all happened because Bob Benninghof was 'twiddling his thumbs' one day.

As the Glasgow Crusade finished, and the landline series came to an end, Mr Graham went on a brief tour of other Scottish cities before returning to London for the week-long Wembley Crusade.

At Wembley it was the first time that the team of stewards had been interconnected by walkie-talkie radio. So vast was the stadium that it was impossible for us to maintain contact with each other as we had done at Harringay. There were many occasions when an urgent message needed to be passed on. In those days the small hand-held walkie-talkies of today had not yet made an appearance. Instead, each of the chief stewards wore a cumbersome and awkward backpack, with a tall aerial sticking out well above their heads. Jerry Beaven, the Billy Graham Team liaison officer, referred to those chief stewards as 'the men from Mars'. The Friday night was special to Heini Sheldon, one of my deputy chief stewards. He used the walkie-talkie to announce to his colleagues his engagement to Miss Sheila Keeble. She was one of our stewards' assignment team.

Billy Graham was tired by the time he arrived in London for the Wembley Crusade – but he had enormous resilience. After a couple of days' rest he was ready to go. He was buoyed up too by the wonderful response to the publicity for Wembley. The only problem at the stadium was that it *rained!* On all but one night the rain poured down. Mr Graham often preached from underneath an umbrella. It did not restrict him in any way from making his usual 'appeal' at the end of his address.

Remarkably as soon as he did so, people moved out from the relative dryness of their undercover – yet open air – seats to walk across the sodden turf to stand in front of the platform. Counsellors resorted to putting plastic bags over their shoes, and brought plastic bags with which to cover their Bibles. Some of them also carried extra plastic bags to give to enquirers to put over their shoes! The rain poured down but it did not deter anyone from coming forward, nor yet from allowing the counsellors to do a proper job.

More than 50 years later, elderly ladies and gentlemen – with great pride – still show you their rain-spotted Bibles. 'This is the Bible I used during Wembley in the rain,' they would say.

The planning for the Wembley Crusade had not been the same as for Harringay. Indeed the very ambience of the crusade committee was different. 'Haffy' had stood aside to allow the chairmanship to pass to Bishop Hugh Gough. It was significant that, at the first Wembley committee, the new chairman took a vote and one member of the committee produced a pipe to smoke! Those of us who had been 'in' on the crusade from the very beginning noticed the difference! But in spite of that there are many that look back upon 'Wembley in the rain' as the time they responded to the evangelist's call to start their Christian life. Billy Graham was preaching as powerfully as ever.

One evening was a special evening for us all because, in the Royal Box we were able to welcome the Duchess of Kent. The day after Wembley concluded, Mr Graham was invited to preach to the Queen Mother at All Saints' Church, Windsor Great Park, and afterwards he and Ruth Graham were invited to have lunch with Her Majesty the Queen at Windsor Castle. It was the forerunner of many similar invitations in future years.

As Wembley finished, the Evangelical Alliance was in deep trouble. Financially all of their resources had been used up on several projects including the Festival of Britain exhibition; opening the Alliance Club Hostel for overseas students; founding the new magazine *Crusade*; the emergence of the Christian Holiday Crusade at Filey and, of course, expenditure for the Harringay and Wembley Crusades. These programmes had used up all their remaining resources. Roy Cattell, who was aware of the severe financial problems, had brought three top businessmen on to the finance committee of the EA to try and sort out their affairs. Ironically one of the first things that George Goyder, Tony Kimpton and Peter Hemery did was to ask Roy Cattell to resign. In their opinion, the financial collapse had been his fault and they could see no way for him to remain.

For those of us behind the scenes they had reached a sad conclusion. Roy *had* overspent the original budget to a considerable extent. Yet he had done so under the encouragement of Jerry Beavan. Strangely they focused their decision upon one small and simple factor in Roy Cattell's expense account. They noted that, every day, for the past three years, he had taken a Christian leader to lunch at a local hotel. He did so simply to encourage their support for Billy Graham, and to share with them everything that the London Committee planned to do. To him it was simply an exercise in public relations and it was highly successful. Yet, on his expense account, the cost of those lunches had not been inconsiderable. The businessmen felt that this was an inappropriate item of expense and – in their opinion – demonstrated a serious error of judgement by Roy Cattell. They felt that he had to go.

At about the same time, there were moves afoot to bring together the financially flush work of the Movement for World Evangelisation (MWE), and the cash-strapped work of the Evangelical Alliance (EA). The team of three businessmen felt that it was superfluous to have two organisations doing many similar things, and that a merger could save money overall.

The 'marriage' of the organisations was postponed, however, until the Roy Cattell matter was sorted out. I left London in the middle of these problems to go to Minneapolis. During the final week at Harringay, Billy Graham had invited me to spend three months working at the head office of the Billy Graham Evangelistic Association (BGEA) in Minneapolis. I would be under the general direction of Mr George M. Wilson. George had been the business manager of Northwestern College when I was there so he was already known to me. He had been the mastermind behind the 'great library move' when the new college buildings had been opened.

By now, Billy Graham had passed on the presidency of the college to Paul Maddox – a former chief of chaplains for the American Command in Europe. Throughout most of the Harringay Crusade, Paul had been an aide to Mr Graham at the arena. He supported Mr Graham's invitation to me and said that I would enjoy working in Minneapolis for that period.

When Mr Graham resigned from Northwestern College, he had taken both Jerry Beavan and George Wilson with him. Both of these men became key figures in the BGEA, Jerry Beavan until 1961 and George Wilson for the remainder of his life. He died in office in 1999. George became the chief executive officer of the Minneapolis Headquarters, and it was to him I reported when I arrived at the offices in Minneapolis on 28 July 1955.

It was an interesting three months. George Wilson put me to work in the mail despatch department, working incredible machines which stuffed leaflets, letters, reply envelopes and reply slips into mailing envelopes at a rate of knots! It was all done by suction, and our chief challenge was to keep the hoppers full of the various papers. We had to ensure that there was always something there for the suction to pick up and to stuff into the envelopes. The hoppers ran out *very* quickly!

George Wilson was a great believer in using capital assets to the full. He firmly believed that God gave those assets to be used and not wasted. Hence he kept the Minneapolis headquarters running for 24-hours a day (with three separate staffs – 8am to 4pm, 4pm to midnight, and midnight to 8am) six days a week. He often jokingly said to Billy Graham that, if he would allow him to employ Seventh Day Adventists, he'd keep the offices working seven days a week! It was an impressive operation. I counted it a great privilege to be allowed to be part of the 4pm to midnight shift for that three-month period. I learned from George Wilson many ways to get things done efficiently.

While I was in Minneapolis I received three important snippets of news. They came to me from my 'mentor' Mr Peter Hemery who was one of the three businessmen brought in to rescue the Evangelical Alliance. Peter Hemery was the father of David Hemery who had won a gold medal as a hurdler at the Olympic Games.

In his letter Peter first told me that Roy Cattell had now resigned but that no decision had yet been taken about his successor. Secondly he told me that the 'marriage' between the MWE and the EA was now appearing unlikely. Finally he told me that the accounts for the landline relays had now been completed and that there would be a surplus of around £13,000. He said that, in all probability, that sum would rescue the work of the Evangelical Alliance.

Our time in Minneapolis had awakened a desire in my heart to stay alongside the work and ministry of Billy Graham. However, it appeared unlikely to happen because there was no immediate thought of a further ministry within the BGEA for me. Little did I know then that the 'Thin Gold Line' was already setting up the next phase of my ministry in association with Billy Graham.

When I returned to England in October, and to my work at the Evangelical Alliance, I found everything in a state of flux. My two senior colleagues, Jack Dain who was the overseas secretary of the alliance, and Timothy Dudley-Smith who had been appointed as editor of the new magazine *Crusade* which had been started by the EA, were concerned about the future leadership of the EA. (Later, both of them became bishops: Timothy Dudley-Smith as Bishop of Thetford and Jack Dain as a bishop in Australia.) They expressed a concern about working under the Revd Ben Peake if the 'marriage' with MWE went ahead. They asked me to join them in writing an 'open letter' to the chairman of the EA Council. They said,

> We would respectfully ask the Council to prayerfully reconsider the whole matter of the merger between the EA and the MWE. It is our conviction that there can be no blessing without harmony, unity and mutual confidence which, in our opinion, are lacking at present. We are sad to say that those of us who have no confidence in the merger would have to withdraw.

The signatories to the open letter made it clear that, in their opinion, Ben Peake was not in possession of the qualities which would be needed to lead the Evangelical Alliance. The council was in a dilemma. There seemed to be no easy solution to the problem. They considered three possible ways forward:

1. To discontinue the merger between the two societies
2. To accept the resignation of the three senior EA staff, or
3. To find another person of the Lord's choice to lead the EA

In their deliberations the council accepted that the merger should not go ahead. It was agreed that the Christian Holiday Crusade at Butlin's Filey camp, although initially the brainchild of the EA, should now be given to the MWE as a gesture of goodwill.

Meanwhile the chairman, Lieutenant General Sir Arthur Smith, undertook it upon himself to interview each of the three signatories to the open letter. He saw each of us individually. When it came to my turn he realised that I was the most junior of the three and most eligible to be dismissed. He asked me, 'Rowlandson, can you give me any reason why you should not cease working with the Evangelical Alliance at this time?'

In my reply I reminded him of his question to me when I had been appointed. He had asked, 'How do we know you will stay with us?' and I had replied to say: 'I will stay until the Lord shows me it is time to leave.' Sir Arthur was flummoxed! He accepted my reasons and assured me that I would remain on the staff of the EA 'until the Lord shows you otherwise'! In the event, all three senior members of the EA's staff retained their jobs.

So the council moved on to prayer, asking that God would reveal His will in the choice of a successor to head up the EA's work. As they prayed, and in that selfsame council meeting, it became clear to one and all that the Lord was leading them to the Revd Gilbert W. Kirby who was himself one of the council members. Later in the day, as that meeting ended, the EA entered the next important phase of its ministry – on its own, with its senior staff intact, and with a new general secretary in the person of Gilbert Kirby.

I little knew then that the 'Thin Gold Line' had been passing through all of those deliberations and that my own survival was all part of the Lord's plan to have me in position and ready for the next phase of ministry.

CHAPTER EIGHT

FILM EVANGELISM

ONE OF the EA council members at the time of the recent upheavals, and the commencement of the new era, was Mr Oliver Stott.

He was immensely supportive of the film ministry of the Billy Graham Evangelistic Association. He also had a burden to bring the Gospel to prisoners. He sought a way to bring these two factors together. Living near to Portsmouth, he contacted the chaplain of Portsmouth Prison and offered to bring a film – *Oil Town USA** – to show to the inmates. The response was positive and afterwards Oliver Stott asked me to spend a day with him at his home near Southampton.

He shared his vision with me to such an extent that I too was captured by the opportunities to take the Gospel into prisons. Could this be the continuation of the 'Thin Gold Line?' Oliver Stott firmly believed that, if the Evangelical Alliance made the need known, there would be immediate support for such a project. But first it had to be 'tried out'.

On 6 November 1955, armed with our borrowed copy of *Oil Town USA*, Oliver Stott and I paid our first visit to a prison together. It was a fascinating experience. In those days there was little else on in the prisons other than our film show and the programme was timed to take place during 'association' time when the prisoners were unlocked from their cells.

---

* See Copyright acknowledgements, 'Chapter 8', page 277

All of the 800 or so prisoners in the jail attended (except for about 20). It was an incredible film show. I immediately discovered that a prisoner's reaction to certain scenes in the film was entirely different to the reaction of the everyday audience. After all, I had shown the film in public showings many hundreds of times in preparation for the crusades. I knew *exactly* the points in the film where the audience laughed or caught their breath. It was the same everywhere. But not so in prison! Reaction there was entirely different and in quite different places in the film.

At the end of the film show we were allowed to make a brief 'appeal' and to invite any prisoners who wished to do so, to come and receive a small booklet from us. Person-to-person counselling was not allowed. The most we could do was to share the Gospel through the film and through a small well-written booklet. We distributed almost 100 booklets on that first occasion.

Oliver Stott wrote up the story for the EA's Newsletter which was circulated just before Christmas. He invited support for this ministry. The response was phenomenal and immediate! The ministry had clearly captured the imagination of the EA's constituency and within a few weeks enough gifts had been received to keep the ministry going for at least a couple of years.

Oliver Stott shared his vision with Gilbert Kirby. He accepted Mr Stott's request that the council should appoint me to do this ministry on a full-time basis using the Billy Graham Films. On 15 December 1955 (after an initial hiccough by the council), I was appointed as extension secretary of the Evangelical Alliance with a brief 'to show Billy Graham films' – at first in prisons. But that commitment was soon overruled by Lieutenant General Sir Arthur Smith, as chairman of the EA, who firmly believed that those in the army, navy and air force were just as needy for the Gospel as the men and women in prison. The original 'brief' had already been greatly extended before I had even started to work on it! But it was still with the Billy Graham Films and it was a confirmation to me that the 'Thin Gold Line' was asserting itself yet again! God had brought me back into the periphery of the Billy Graham ministry.

Two things happened at about the same time. First was a temptation to depart from the calling God had now given to me.

There was a danger that the 'Thin Gold Line' could have been terminated there and then. This was a temptation which was to be repeated numerous times – and in different ways – as the years passed by.

Just as soon as my appointment to this film ministry was confirmed I had nine offers of leadership jobs – all within a space of seven days. Stephen Olford, at Duke Street Richmond Baptist Church, invited me to join him as administrator; The Regions Beyond Missionary Society offered me the of job general secretary; Tom Rees put out feelers to see if I would go back to work full time with him – and so on. I had nine openings in all. Some of them were very attractive. Of course, long before that there had been the Kelvin Lodge situation at Frinton. Somehow the Lord steered me through all these distractions, and kept the 'Thin Gold Line' going in the right direction. Once more, God had enabled me to resist this type of temptation.

With the EA's work running on a shoestring (although we had more than adequate finances for the prison and forces film ministry), there was no assured future. I found a note in my father's diary in which he said: 'This has been an eventful year. Maurice and Marilyn went to the USA for four months and on their return Roy Cattell had left the Evangelical Alliance. Also Mildmay (the Movement for World Evangelisation) has separated from the EA. Maurice is doing films in prisons etc., at present, and we await future developments in keen anticipation wondering where it is all leading to!'

The second thing that happened came as the result of looking at the many slides I had taken at the Wembley Crusade in 1955 – both of the preparations and of the event itself. As I went through them a story emerged and I found myself telling it over and over again. Suddenly the thought occurred to me that if I could tell the story on tape it would always be accurate and the same. It would also save me a lot of breath! A development of that followed when I realised I had some 'sound bytes' which could be edited into the tape to make it more informative and attractive. The EA gave me two days off to do the work and to make an interesting sound tape which could be used whenever the slides were shown. The result was *The Wembley Story*. As far as I am aware it was the first-ever sound-strip made and used within the Christian world. Certainly a couple of years later, the Scripture Union had made their first sound-strips in a similar fashion. Soon afterwards it became the 'norm'.

What we didn't realise was that *The Wembley Story* would become a major ministry of the Evangelical Alliance. I myself was invited to take it in person to more than 50 locations. The EA decided that they should make both a film-strip copy and tape available to anyone who would like to buy it. In the end we sold more than 150 copies. It was an unexpected and surprising ministry because, even through that poor vehicle, people were coming to Christ as Billy Graham preached a brief, but significant, message in the story.

In between showings of *The Wembley Story*, I was gradually assembling a schedule of film shows. Strangely enough, Oliver Stott's vision to show Christian films in prisons was slower getting off the ground than was the vision of Sir Arthur Smith. The army, navy and air force soon provided me with many opportunities while I was still waiting for the prison service to get its act together.

Once the prison and forces programme was properly launched I spent two months out of three travelling around the country. During the period up to 1961 I had visited every penal establishment – prison, open prison, borstal, and detention centre – in the country. The chaplains came to know me well and even the prisoners would recognise me as they moved from prison to prison. Often one would greet me like a long lost friend – 'Saw you in Dartmoor, sir,' he would say, and quite often I found another prisoner hugging me because it was through the film that he had found the Lord Jesus Christ as Saviour in a prison elsewhere.

Each prison seemed to have its own characteristics. At the time, Stafford prison was where men went for 'respectable' offences – bigamy, fraud, motoring – etc. The men were so well-dressed there that I facetiously asked the chaplain, 'Do these men dress for dinner?' Conversely, of course, there were those prisons where the 'thugs' ended up. In one prison the chaplain leant down to whisper to me (in the middle of *Souls in Conflict*), 'There are about twenty convicted murderers in the showing today!' It is a little unnerving when you are sitting in a dark room amongst 'who knows whom?'.

But there were the encouragements. One man wrote:

> It is now quite some months since you visited this prison with your film unit and the film which has led to a lot of happenings in my life. I shall never, as long as I live, forget *Souls in Conflict.* It has taken all this time before I could feel justified in writing to you. You see, I wanted to make really sure that I had found God before I started making any commitments. So I purchased Billy Graham's two books *The Secret of Happiness* and *Peace with God.* Since then I have read many books by many authors and as I read so I seemed to come nearer and nearer to God; but it was when I first picked up the greatest Book of all that I started to understand and really started to live. Yes, even here in my present situation, I think I am happier than I have ever been before. My cell no longer seems dull and empty but in my quiet moments I feel that God is with me and, as I read my Bible, I find Him ever near. I would like to take this opportunity to thank you for your visit which was basic to my new-found faith and conversion . . . I am working hard to pass on God's message to other inmates of this institution and in some cases I have met with success. Already I have managed to bring one of my workmates to God. It is often said in here that prison is the breeding ground of crime, but from my own experience I know that it can be also the birthplace of Christians.

One man was in Dartmoor for robbery with violence. He had been so violent to his wife that, when he went to prison, she ultimately divorced him. While in prison he became a Christian through seeing *Souls in Conflict.* His first convert was his mother-in-law, whom he led to Christ through his correspondence from prison. A few years later, after he came out, his mother-in-law found him to be such a changed person that she, eventually, persuaded her daughter to see her ex-husband once again. She too was greatly impressed by the change in him and discovered that it had been through his faith in the Lord Jesus Christ. He led her to the Lord. One of the most fascinating letters I ever received read:

> Since my ex-wife has become a Christian we have discovered how much we really love each other. Now we want to get married again, but because of my parole conditions that cannot happen until six

month's time. Mr Rowlandson, is it alright if I live with my wife until we get remarried?

My reply was, 'That which God has joined together let no man put asunder!' I hope that, if I was wrong, God will forgive me!

Of course, the film ministry with *Oil Town USA* – and later with the Harringay film *Souls in Conflict* – was directly an extension of the ministry of Billy Graham. He could not be there in person, but he was equally powerful as he preached on film.

Apart from the prison and forces film ministry, the Revd A. W. Goodwin Hudson had been appointed by the Billy Graham Team to promote their films in the UK. He organised many dozens of film shows – always launching a new film in a Central London location such as the Coliseum Theatre in the heart of London's theatre-land. Goodwin Hudson and I had the same philosophy about the use of films. We firmly believed that the film should be allowed to do its own job of communicating the Gospel. After all, who better to be the evangelist than Billy Graham himself. Inevitably there were those British evangelists who felt that they were being sidelined because they were not being asked to 'speak at the end of a film show'. We discovered that when they did it was often a disaster. They gave another sermon! But *the sermon had already been given* – either by the evangelist or by the story of the film.

For example, in *Souls in Conflict* the final scenes of this film lent themselves to a very clear presentation of the Gospel. Frank (Frederick Leister), an aircraft designer was sitting at his desk reading the newspaper. As he did so, he quoted a paragraph to Jeff, the test pilot: 'After Mr Graham had finished speaking, he invited people who had lost contact with God to come to the front of the hall and make a decision for Christ.' He put the paper down with a flourish, took off his glasses in astonishment, and remarked, 'Amazing what some people will do!' Jeff quietly replied, 'Amazing? I don't recall anything amazing about it. On the contrary, it seemed the most natural thing I'd ever done.' Frank looked up at Jeff and exclaimed, 'You? Sheer unadulterated nonsense!'

In those two persons are represented everyone present at the film show. There are those who, like Frank, would say 'nonsense' and there are those who, like Jeff, would say that accepting Christ was the most natural thing they had ever done. It all came to a point of decision. I often added that I was almost sorry for them that they had come to see the film. As a result they were confronted with that decision. It was one they had to make. They could go either Frank's way and say that it is all 'nonsense', or they could follow Jeff and make a decision to follow Christ. There was no other way. That was all that needed to be said. As a result, hundreds committed their lives to Christ over the following years.

The long absences from home were hard on the family. For Marilyn these times apart were distressing. I was travelling more often than not. It had not always been easy for her because, as an American, she is a 'displaced person' living in England. (It was an immense step of faith for her when she agreed to leave the land of her birth and at 17 years of age come to live in Britain as my wife.) Marilyn was by now still less than 30 years of age. She was given heavier responsibilities than she should have had in bringing-up four children. Her input in those formative years when the children were small is vividly demonstrated in the blessing we both shared for a long time before two of our family, through accident or illness, were taken from us. As a family they all loved the Lord and His work, and all of them – those that have been taken, as well as the two who are left – were, and are, actively involved and supportive in so many ways. My absences could have been disastrous; 'An excellent wife is the crown of her husband,' said King Solomon (Proverbs 12:4). So if there was any credit due to me for the work I was doing, it can be traced back directly to 'the excellent wife' I had! Marilyn's part in the life of our family is written in the annals of heaven.

To help her during the times of my absences, we regularly had 'au pairs' living with us – ostensibly to learn the language – and they were a great help around the home. We realised that many families and hospitals in our area also had au pairs. With other Christian people in the area we conceived the idea of opening our homes for a monthly 'Overseas Squash'. We passed out invitations and nearly 100 responded. We gave them some good food, good fun and a good 'message' – often in the form of a Billy Graham Evangelistic Film. We had evidence that several of the au pairs eventually returned to their own countries having found the Lord Jesus Christ as their Saviour through the squashes.

Irene Iversen from Norway was prompted to start reading the Bible. Later she told us that through reading Leviticus she had become a Christian. When we expressed surprise that so obscure a book should be meaningful to her, she explained that 'if this God knew all that about hygiene – which I understand as I am a hospital orderly today – then He must be a God worth trusting'. Later she found through reading the Gospel according to St John how she could place her faith and trust in Him.

If prison evangelism kept me busy, the demands from the navy, army and airforce were even greater. In collaboration with the army chaplains, we made three tours of the British Forces in Germany with astonishing results. The chaplains appreciated our efforts and many of them were able to take advantage of doors that had been opened to them as a result of the film show.

I had three helpers who came with me, at different times, on the German visits. We had both a lot of fun and times of great fellowship together. My 'mentor' and close friend, Henry Hole, came with me on one trip. We were accommodated at the headquarters of the British Army of the Rhine. The accommodation was good, but the food was very poor – so poor in fact, that Henry voiced a complaint. A couple of nights later, when we came back after a film show, we went into the mess for dinner. There, on the sideboard, were two magnificent plates of hors d'oevres. Henry's reaction was that they had taken notice of his complaint, so he went and helped himself to the two plates and gave one to me. We had just enjoyed them when the steward came in to the dining room. His face went as white as a sheet. We had, he said, just eaten the hors d'oevres which had been prepared for the brigadier and his guest! Too bad! It was the first good meal we had had there!

On another trip we were on our way home from Germany when we stopped overnight in Amsterdam. Will you forgive me if I say that, in the hotel in Amsterdam I discovered the 'perfect flush'! In the bathroom was a toilet system that just couldn't go wrong – so unlike the cisterns in England! So I determined to bring a set of the equipment back to England with me. The hotel porter told me where I could buy it, but the builder's merchant wouldn't hear of selling me just the 'flush'. I had to have the whole 'package' (pan, pipes and flush) or nothing! However as I had a car full of film equipment and luggage, I said to him, 'There's no way I could get all of that in.' The Dutchman replied in his broken English, 'If I can get it in, will you take it?' I said 'yes' because I knew he couldn't – but he did! So on our return to Harwich we had the experience of going through customs: 'Anything to declare?' they asked. I told them to come around to the other back door of the car. There, in all its glory, sat 'the equipment'. The customs officer scratched his head and said, 'That's the first time I've seen one of those in a car!' What a great joy it is to share true Christian 'fun' with each other.

Another of my companions was my friend Trevor Brient. He was an enormous help throughout the tour. That week we had shown *Souls in Conflict* about ten times. At each showing there were young soldiers and airmen who undoubtedly found the Lord Jesus Christ as their Saviour and Lord. At the end of the film, I made a brief application of the story along the usual lines, and then led the audience in a prayer that, in their own hearts, they could pray along with me – a transaction between themselves and God.

The prayer I used was: 'Lord, I am a sinner. I confess my sin. I turn from my sin and right now I turn to You. Cleanse me from my sin, Lord, and put Your power within and help me to live for You. Amen,' I then asked that any who had prayed that prayer to come and tell me afterwards, so that I could give them a copy of Billy Graham's book *Peace with God*. I also warned them that, on the following morning, the world would not necessarily be 'in technicolor'! They would probably cut themselves shaving; argue with another soldier in the barracks; find a button off their shirt and many other annoying things – to the extent that they would begin to wonder what happened the previous night. That is the way that the devil tries to attack – but they had to *believe* that their prayer of commitment the night before was real.

The army gave us a night off after the series of showings and they had booked rooms for us in the Park Hotel in Dusseldorf.

Trevor's room was about five rooms away from mine on the sixth – top – floor of the lovely hotel. I phoned him on the house phone the next morning to ask if he would join me for breakfast. He said he would be along in a couple of minutes. I waited for the knock on the door. It never came! Instead, there was a knock on my window. Trevor had climbed out of his window, walked along a narrow 4-inch parapet six stories up, and had reached the window of my room. How he didn't fall to his death was a miracle to me! He got the sharp edge of my tongue for this fool-hardy enterprise, because if he had fallen, I might have been delayed in Germany for an inquest! But that apart, he was both good company and a strong spiritual support to me in the ministry.

On one German trip, Marilyn was able to come with me. One of our film shows was at the RAF station on the island of Sylt. It was remote and, in March, a bleak place. There was only one small hotel where the RAF had accommodated us. We reached Sylt by train (taking the car with us on a special truck). We found our way to the hotel and then on to the RAF station. To do a journey like this is a lot of effort but it is so worthwhile when you see the spiritual results of the film show. We spent overnight in the hotel and the next evening we had another film show to do at RAF Jever back on the mainland. Because of that we had to make a very early start. It was essential for us to catch the first car train back to Hamburg.

We got up at about 6am. With our bags we went to the front door only to find it locked. There was no key and no one was about in the hotel. The urgency of that early morning train prompted me to investigate other possible exits. I tried the kitchen doors but they too were locked. In the end, I found a window that did not have any security locks on it. Marilyn and I clambered out of that window with our bags. Anybody watching us would have decided that we were 'doing a runner'! Indeed, as we hadn't paid our hotel bill the night before, Marilyn said it made her feel like a fugitive! All the way back to Hamburg on the train she had expected the police to board at every stop! She was immensely relieved when we arrived at Hamburg and there were no police there to arrest us! Later that day, I sent a cheque to the hotel to pay the bill!

The ministry, the experiences and the fun of the German tours were matched by the knowledge that there were many who would be in heaven as a result of this unusual and effective ministry – using Billy Graham 'by proxy'.

Back in England, the Revd Keith Ensor who was the RAF chaplain at Stafford decided to have a week's mission, with *Souls in Conflict* being used several times in various parts of the base. I didn't know it at the time, but one young airman had come to see *Souls in Conflict* and the film was the catalyst which built on the chaplain's faithful witness. Through that film Billy Strachan came to Christ. At the time he was the bartender in the officers' mess.

A year later, Keith Ensor wanted another week with the same film. There had been a great change-over of personnel and he was sure that many of the new intake had never seen the film. When I arrived at Stafford he told me that he had a young airman who would like to help me and 'carry my bags'. It was the first time I had knowingly met Billy Strachan.

In the officers' mess one officer asked me, 'What have you done to Billy Strachan? He used to be good for a filthy story. Now all he wants to do is to preach at us!'

That week was to be a very significant week for Billy. We spent many hours talking and praying together and he shared with me his desire to enter full-time Christian service. He knew he needed to be trained, but he had no academic qualifications to enable him to enter a college or university in the UK. I suggested to him that he should apply to Northwestern College in Minneapolis. After my time there the college had promised to accept any UK student upon my recommendation on a bursary scheme at no cost to the student. I told Billy I could get him in to Northwestern, and he immediately accepted the invitation.

A whole book could be written about the stories of the way in which the Lord made it possible for him to go to America, and the many remarkable instances of the Lord's leading during his time there. After three years' training he came back to England to work with the Torchbearer Fellowship at Capernwray Hall, under Major Ian Thomas. It was exactly the right place for him and, many years later, he became principal of the Bible College there – and, incidentally, a visiting professor at Northwestern College in Minneapolis. Many years earlier Billy Graham had said, 'If only one person comes to Christ it will have been worthwhile.' Certainly, if through Billy Graham's preaching in *Souls in Conflict* that 'one person' had been Billy Strachan, his would have been an effective ministry for Christ.

It was also the Revd Keith Ensor who 'paved the way' for the ending of my prison and forces ministry. After that second visit to Stafford, Keith took me aside and said, 'Maurice, the spark is going out.' He went on to say that the continuous ministry with the films was becoming 'mechanical' and that he had noticed a change in my presentation between the first and the second visit.

It started a train of thought in my mind and I began to wonder if the Lord was trying to tell me something – or possibly prepare me for something new. I shared my concern with Gilbert Kirby (my 'boss') and he urged me to ease up on the film ministry for the time being, and to get involved in Billy Graham's crusade in Manchester in the summer of 1961.

There were to be relays too from Manchester and I took on a young man, Harvey Thomas, who had been a member of my church youth group. He was 'betwixt and between' having just been rejected by the police force because of colour blindness. To serve in the police force had been his lifelong ambition and the rejection was a bitter blow to him. He was grateful for the opportunity to work in Manchester and promote the relays whilst at the same time he sought out God's perfect will for his life.

Once again Northwestern College came to the fore, and I suggested to Harvey that he should take advantage of the bursary scheme for a three-year study time there. Harvey did so and for him it was the start of a new direction to his life which included time working with the Billy Graham Radio Station in Hawaii, setting up crusades for Mr Graham in Australia, Denmark and Britain. He served the BGEA at Spre-e73 and Eurofest in Belgium before being appointed as a coordinator of meetings for Mrs Margaret Thatcher when she became Prime Minister in England. He served in that capacity throughout her premiership and eventually set up an international ministry on a similar basis. Everything he did was coloured by his strong Christian faith and he became a powerful force in many political situations.

Both Billy Strachan and Harvey Thomas would never have had the significant ministries that both of them had, but for that invitation given to me in 1948 by Billy Graham to go to Northwestern. Mr Graham's influence may have been 'indirect' but it was real and made an enormous contribution to Harvey's effective ministry in many parts of the world.

Although in effect my work in film evangelism in prisons and in the forces ended in the autumn of 1961, there were a few advance engagements which kept me busy through to the end of 1962.

There were also some new films to release. In the summer of 1962 we had the latest Billy Graham film (made by World Wide Pictures), *Touch of Brass*. It was a profoundly 'Northern' story and had been made during the Manchester Crusade the previous year. For several nights, at London's City Temple, we premièred that film. Unfortunately it coincided with a transport strike in London. Our audience had to struggle into the City. Nevertheless we were full each night.

One last word to this chapter! The Revd Keith Ensor was so impressed with the powerful message of *Souls in Conflict* that for the rest of his life he continued to buy copies to distribute far and wide. In all he must have given away more than 100 copies of the film which, although made more than 50 years before, was nevertheless contemporary and effective in conveying the message of Billy Graham.

CHAPTER NINE

A CHANGE IN DIRECTION

GEORGE M. WILSON had been the business manager at Northwestern College when I was a student there. In that position he was the one to whom I had to report. As far as he was concerned I had three strikes against me throughout my time at Northwestern!

First, he was never totally happy that his president (principal) Billy Graham had been so rash as to invite ten young men from Britain to come to Minneapolis and to study 'at the college's expense'. 'There's no taste in nothing,' he used to say and he felt that there should have been some financial contribution by us to the cost of our education. Had that been necessary it would have been impossible for any of us to come for at the time the British Government allowed overseas travellers a mere £25 to take out of the country! So we were grateful to Billy Graham for his abundant generosity.

The second strike against me related to my employment by Mrs Sargent as her 'butler'. George Wilson thought that all of the ten students from Britain should work for the college – free labour as it were – as a way of repaying our debt to the college. But that had not been part of the agreement made with us in London. There was no 'if you will do this, then we will do that' situation. All of us considered that we were free to obtain whatever employment we could. It was necessary anyway because we had to earn enough money to pay our fare home at the end of our course. So two of us were out-of-favour: eight of the ten *did* work for the college, which may explain why only the two of us ever came back to England!

The third strike did not become apparent until nearly five months later. As I have already explained, I went to work for Hospitality House whose director was George England! The two Georges were very much alike. Both were superb managers and both had a very similar outlook. George Wilson was per se also the 'manager' of the Christian radio station KTIS – the station founded by Billy Graham and now owned and operated by Northwestern College.

On the other hand George England was per se also the 'manager' of the Christian radio station KEYD. So, in effect the two Georges were competitors in harsh reality. To some extent George Wilson saw me as consorting with the 'enemy' by working for George England. He felt so strongly about it that, at one stage, he tried to have my visa cancelled.

About this same time I received an independent approach from the USA immigration authorities to say that I had 'overstayed my student's visa'. It turned out to be a technical error. My visa clearly showed that I was admitted to the USA as a student until 1/2/49. I understood that as being 1 February 1949. I had not yet realised that in the USA they put the month first and that, in reality, my visa had expired on 2 January 1949. It was now 28 January. The immigration officer called upon me, ostensibly to put me under arrest for overstaying my time. However, he was a very pleasant and reasonable man and he readily accepted my explanation. He revalidated my visa on the spot and it then allowed me to stay until the end of June. George Wilson's action with my visa had not helped in my problems. I went straight down to the British Consulate in St Paul and had it permanently certified as valid!

With those three factors taken into consideration it is a remarkable fact that, once I had returned to England, George Wilson and I became good friends. Perhaps he enjoyed the fact that I had stood up to him. Maybe that had earned me some respect. At any rate, whenever he visited London thereafter, he always extended an invitation to me to have a meal with him. So it was not an altogether unexpected event when on Wednesday, 12 June 1961, he invited me to have lunch with him at his hotel. I went, altogether unsuspecting. As always we had a pleasant time together talking about many things. And then he dropped his bombshell!

He asked me to tell him about my current responsibilities with the Evangelical Alliance. I told him about the summer programme which included participation in the Keswick Convention. That year Marilyn and I were to run a 'Hotel Party' there for the Evangelical Alliance. This was to enable some of our members and supporters to attend the convention in company with other like-minded people.

Then, during August, we had our family vacation planned at Frinton-on-Sea. There were also one or two prison film shows during August but, by the end of that month, there were no further fixed plans.

'What are you going to do then?' he asked. I had to tell him of my conversation with Gilbert Kirby when we had discussed my future with the EA. There seemed to be no immediate plans for the autumn.

I also told George Wilson there was another project which had taken a great deal of my time for the past four years. In 1958 I had decided to enter politics and to fight a parliamentary election for the City of Bedford. At the time I had been rather radical, and was standing for the Liberal Party (before the days of Liberal Democrats). My four predecessors in Bedford had all lost their deposits (which seemed to be the fate of Liberal candidates in those days)! Although I did not get elected in the 1959 election, I *did* save my deposit which brought an even bigger ovation than the winning candidate received! All in all it was an interesting experience.

'You'll have to give all that up,' he said. 'Then, as soon as your responsibilities with the EA are ended, *that's the date on which you can start with us*'! This unexpected turn in our conversation took me completely by surprise and I did not immediately fully understand what he was saying. He went on to explain that, for a long time he had wanted to invite me to join the work of the BGEA, and now the time seemed just right.

It is to my shame that I did not immediately recognise the prevalence of the 'Thin Gold Line'! It was hard at work again! I told him that I needed to discuss it with Marilyn because it opened up a whole new ball game! However, in my heart of hearts, I knew it was a right move and I was sure that Marilyn would see it that way too. To her credit, she did!

I also needed to talk again with Gilbert Kirby. I explained to him what the invitation from George Wilson would involve. He immediately replied: 'Well! This is truly remarkable. Just yesterday I was talking with Sir Arthur Smith and I had said to him, "I cannot think what in the world we're going to do with Maurice. The EA's ministry is altering so much. We are moving into the world of relationships and Christian diplomacy. That is not really his forte. He's always been a project man."' After I had told him of the invitation from George, Gilbert explained the situation to Sir Arthur. The next day – in his own distinctive handwriting – I had this letter from him:

> If you feel it is 'of the Lord' there is no more to be said. We *all* want God's will to be done. Nevertheless the EA will miss you, though I am sure there will be many opportunities for you in Dr Billy Graham's Organisation in Great Britain. Thank you for all you have done for the EA and may God bless you in your future responsibilities.

Sir Arthur Smith had become part of the 'Thin Gold Line' and two days later I met George once again for dinner and told him that I was sure of God's guidance in this and that I would be pleased and honoured to accept the invitation. He said that he wanted me to arrive in Minneapolis on 18 September 1961 for a period of training before I could be ready to start work in London.

One oft-quoted statement that George Wilson said to me as I accepted the invitation went like this: 'When we (the BGEA) employ you, we do so for 365 days a year and 24 hours a day. Any time left over is your own!' By my calculation I had one, assured, 'day off' every four years – on 29 February! In the event, I learned that what he meant was that whenever the BGEA organisation needed me, I had to be ready to respond. My commitment to them would always take first place after my commitment to the Lord. No excuse would be accepted for non-availability. It turned out to be an exciting way to live and I would not have changed it for any other. Total commitment – a vocation indeed – is a very wonderful thing and is so often missing in today's world.

Just to complete the record, in the 36 years working full-time with the BGEA, only twice was there a serious conflict of responsibilities. Both times were because of my work as secretary of the Keswick Convention. More about that will follow later on. On both occasions, Keswick had to take second place and I found myself making special arrangements to free myself for my responsibilities with Billy Graham.

Because most of my colleagues in the BGEA were American, and lived right across that continent, there were occasions when they forgot about the time difference. It was not unusual to receive a telephone call at 2 or 3am from someone in California. On one significant occasion, Marilyn and I had been on vacation at Frinton. I suddenly got a message to meet one of the Team at London Airport the next day. I planned to go back to our flat in London and spend the night there to be ready for an early morning arrival. At the last minute, Marilyn decided to come back with me. At 2 o'clock in the morning the phone rang. It was my 'boss' Walter Smyth with news of a change of time for his colleague's arrival. Walter started off by asking, 'I hope I didn't wake you up or anything like that?' On those occasions a small white lie is probably allowed as I replied 'No! no! that's alright.' He went on to ask, 'How's Marilyn?' At 2 in the morning I was a bit woozy and replied, 'She's fine thanks. She's down at Frinton!' Marilyn turned over in bed and asked, 'Who do you think you're in bed with?'

George Wilson went on to outline the role he had in mind for me. He said that Jerry Beavan (whom I had come to know during my time at Northwestern and again during the Harringay Crusade) would be moving to London mid-September and that the London Office would become the central office for Mr Graham's International Ministry as from 1 October. He also told me that the first issue of a new magazine, *Decision* – to be published in America and circulated in Britain – would be ready by that date. My task with that would be three-fold. First I would be required to organise the distribution plans to send the magazine freely to some 27,000 people on our mailing list. It was a gigantic task for which I needed to start planning rightaway – even before I came 'on staff' as an associate of the Billy Graham Team.

My second task for *Decision* would be to encourage people to become subscribers and to build up and manage a proper subscribers' list.

Finally, he said that I would eventually become British Editor of the magazine. Each month we would be sent 'silverprints' from which the magazine could later be printed. My task would be to iron out all the Americanisms and spellings, and to make the publication acceptable to a British readership. He said that there would be occasions when an article would need to be replaced. For example, a testimony from a baseball player might need to be replaced with a testimony from a cricket star.

This last responsibility was to go on from 1961 to 1987 and the monthly 're-editing' of *Decision* magazine became a major part of the work of myself and my colleague, Jean Wilson. Sometimes we were up against deadlines. It was not unknown for the British customs at London Airport to hold up the delivery of the 'silverprints' for some technical reason. On many occasions Jean Wilson would travel to London Airport to remonstrate with the Customs people. She often arrived back at our office in the nick of time. We lived dangerously in those days!

Soon after George Wilson had given me the invitation, and I had accepted it, I spoke to Jerry Beavan by telephone. He said how much he was looking forward to working with me once again. I had always found him an inspiring person and one whose positive outlook on life was so uplifting. He went on to say that he could not see the International Office of the Association working out of the present premises at 54a Tottenham Court Road. He gave me the assignment to start immediately to look for more suitable premises; 54a had been found by the Revd A. W. Goodwin Hudson when, in 1955, Billy Graham had asked him to set up enough of an office facility to handle the day-to-day commitments of the BGEA in London. Jerry Beavan thought it was hardly a suitable location for an International Headquarters.

In between my final commitments with the Evangelical Alliance, our family holiday and the few remaining prison visits, I spent a lot of time on the telephone and in the offices of estate agents. There were all kinds of office premises available but, for one reason or another, they were not suitable. Jerry had given me

Thomas B. Rees (Tom Rees) preaching
in the Royal Albert Hall, 7 March 1953.
Photo source: unknown

Earls Court, 29 June 1967.
Cliff Richard with Maurice Rowlandson – making the film *Two a Penny.*
Photo source: World Wide Pictures

The British Board, 29 July 1971, at Shirley House, Camden Town.
(clockwise from left): Maurice Rowlandson, T. W. Wilson, Canon Frank Colquhoun, Cliff Barrows, Canon T. L. Livermore, Sir Cyril Black, Billy Graham, Bishop Goodwin Hudson, George Wilson, Major General D. J. Wilson Haffenden, Bishop Maurice Wood, David Rennie, Jean Wilson, Viscount Brentford.
Photo: Russ Busby

Billy Graham preaching at Spre-e73, 30 August 1973.
Photo: Russ Busby

Marilyn Rowlandson with Ruth Graham
at a London Reception on 25 March 1980.
Photo: Russ Busby

Invitational Group in Manchester, 5 March 1982, Mission England.
Back row: (from left) Victor Jack, Dr Clive Calver, Clarence Jeffries, Val Grieve, Dr Peter English, Alan Boddington, Tony Dann, Raymond Skinner, Brian Mills, Tony Bush, Dr T. W. Wilson, Dr Walter Smyth, Neville Atkinson, Blair Carlson.
Front row: (from left) The Revd Gavin Reid, Maurice Rowlandson, David Rennie, Billy Graham, The Revd Tom Houston, Ian Frith, Bishop Flagg.
Photo source: unknown

Team Members at Mission England, 1984.
From left: Maurice Rowlandson, Dr T. W. Wilson, Dr Walter Smyth, David Rennie.
Photo: Russ Busby

Billy Graham greets Alan Paget – the one-millionth visitor
to Mission England at Ipswich, 27 July 1984.
Photo: Russ Busby

Billy Graham with Maurice Rowlandson and Marilyn Rowlandson at the Team Meeting in San Diego, 19 November 1999.
Photo: Russ Busby

Billy Graham receiving the Templeton Award from HRH The Duke of Edinburgh, 18 May 1982. Ruth Graham alongside Billy Graham.
Photo: Russ Busby

Her Majesty Queen Elizabeth II with Billy Graham
after he had preached at the Royal Chapel of All Saints
in Windsor Great Park, 11 June 1989.
Photo: Russ Busby

Billy Graham at the UK Embassy in Washington, receiving his
Knighthood from Sir Christopher Meyer on behalf of
Her Majesty the Queen, 6 December 2001.
Photo: Maurice Rowlandson

On the platform of the Royal Albert Hall, 29 May 2004,
on the 50th anniversary of the Harringay Crusade
(L to R) Bishop Michael Baughen, Cliff Barrows, Steve Chalke, Franklin Graham, The Revd Preb. Richard Bewes, Maurice Rowlandson, Marilyn Rowlandson, Miss Jean Wilson, and the All Souls Orchestra.
Photo: Walter Dirks

Maurice Rowlandson at the helm of shrimper *Puffin* on Hickling Broad.
Photo: Kenneth Barnes

a list of criteria that he needed the new offices to have – not least was the ability to park his car! Very few offices in those 1961 days had integral car parks. The one place that did was a suite of offices on the second floor of the East Wing of Bush House in the Aldwych. At first they were a little more expensive than my budget allowed, but after extensive negotiations we reached a figure that was acceptable to Jerry Beavan. So I was able to conclude my search by signing a lease for those offices. We remained there until February 1968 during a period of great change and not a few traumatic events.

One final hurdle had to be taken before my appointment could be confirmed. George Wilson had devised a test to be given to all employees of the association. I had to take that test and, subsequently, used it repeatedly with every new employee throughout the next 35 plus years. It was an interesting test. You did not 'pass' or 'fail'. You were either employed or not employed.

Over the years I found the test to be both remarkable and reliable. There were times when, at interview, I thought a candidate for employment was first rate – but their test result was dismal and it was clear they would not meet our criteria. Conversely, I sometimes interviewed a candidate and found them 'rather mousey' or unimpressive. But when they took the test they showed considerable ability. I always lived to rue the day I employed someone who should not be employed after taking the test – whereas all of those who were employed after taking the test were quite exceptional. Many times I had reason to thank George Wilson for his insistence that the test should be the grounds of employment. There were many good results from the test, but only one (in my experience) had a 99 per cent satisfactory response – my colleague Jean Wilson! She even did far better than me!

Tom Rees was the first person to write and congratulate me on my new appointment. His message came on the back of a postcard from New York and he said:

> May God's richest blessing be on you both in your new sphere of service. Yours 'til the devil joins the PBs'.* TOM

* 'PB' – a colloquialism for 'Plymouth Brethren'

Then, early in September, we were packing up to leave for the three-week training period at the Minneapolis office. Suddenly the front doorbell rang and there stood Tom Rees! He had driven all the way up from Hildenborough Hall in Kent, to come to have a prayer with us before we left for this new adventure in our lives. He was such a thoughtful man.

In Minneapolis I spent time in every department of the headquarters. George wanted me to learn the procedures for each one, in order to introduce similar routines into the London office. I was taught everything from card-punching for the computer and handling the finances to mail-opening. I spent time reading some of the thousands of letters which arrived every day. I learned how to identify the main concern in each letter and to translate that into a standard – yet personal – reply prepared by either Billy Graham himself or one of his closest colleagues.

One of the first things I did after I returned to London was to set up the important 'mail reading' part of our work. It was so important and needed careful handling and a sympathetic response. I invited a Baptist minister, the Revd C. Alan Stephens, to undertake this important task. He continued to do so until the office closed in 1987. By then he had written many thousands of counselling letters.

When I got back to London on 9 October I came into the Bush House offices for the first time. Jean Wilson was already there and it says volumes for her grace and stature that she should so willingly accept a newcomer imposed upon her in this way. We were to work together for more than 30 years and, even after the office closed and I had retired, we still kept in close contact and shared information with each other. She is a remarkable lady.

CHAPTER TEN

THE BIRTH OF THE NEXT CRUSADE

BILLY GRAHAM and George Wilson came to London in November of 1961. I had the privilege of attending my first meeting of the British Board in the presence of both of them. Jerry Beavan laid out his plans for the London Office. Amongst them was the take-over bid for *The Christian* newspaper – the subject of the next chapter. He also asked me to plan for a special concert in London's Royal Albert Hall. He wanted to bring Tedd Smith (pianist) and George Beverly Shea (soloist) to London to keep alive the memories of Billy Graham's evangelistic ministry. Having Jerry in the London office meant that he could 'pull strings' for events like that. I loved the opportunity to organise another major event, and entered into the spirit of the occasion with great enthusiasm.

After my 'orientation and training' at the Minneapolis Office, I had returned to London to find Jerry Beavan in situ in the new offices at Bush House in Aldwych. They were, indeed, lovely offices in a good location and Jerry was very happy there.

But, then, on 29 November 1962 the whole of my future changed yet again. Jerry called me into his office to say that there was to be a meeting of the Billy Graham Team at Airlie House in Virginia the following week. He said that he would not be going but he asked me to go in his stead. He only gave me three days notice and I had to change a number of plans in order to accept this invitation.

I was very excited to be asked to represent him at the Team Meeting in Virginia. He had told me a little about it and had said that there would probably be 125-150 members of the team there. I was a little scared to be meeting so many on one occasion, but he assured me that there would be many I had known at the London and Manchester Crusades. The 'Thin Gold Line' was beginning to run through some interesting places. A Team Meeting was one of the most intimate activities of the Billy Graham Evangelistic Association. Jerry Beavan assured me that everybody would give me a very warm welcome.

And so they did! On my arrival at London Airport, on my way to America and Airlie House, I had picked up my airline tickets from Pan American Airlines and was surprised, a few minutes later, to hear my name over the tannoy. I was being asked to return to the Pan American Desk. When I got there, they apologised that they had not given me a letter which had been waiting for me with my tickets. The letter turned out to be from Jerry Beavan. He said:

> Have a good trip. I won't be here when you get back. Doubtless you'll find out why while you are in America.

It was all very mysterious – even the more so because I *didn't* find out what the reason was. It was some weeks later before I discovered that Jerry had resigned from the team 'for family reasons' and I was rarely to see him again thereafter. In fact it was 2001 before we had any real contact again – and then, only by letters and e-mails. The end result was that I found myself isolated in the London Office, and yet required to carry all the responsibilities of Jerry as well as my own.

Then I received a letter from Billy Graham in December 1962, in which he wrote (among other things):

> Just a note to say that I have spoken to a Dr James Jauncey of El Paso, Texas, concerning the possibility of coming over to Britain to replace Jerry Beavan. He would more or less represent us in evangelistic meetings, lectures, debates, etc. The administrative side of things would be more in your hands than it was under Jerry . . . I promise not to make anything definite with him until I have your full views and until you have had an opportunity to get acquainted with him.

In the event Dr Jauncey turned out to be an excellent person – one with whom I could have worked very happily. He came to London and sent a comprehensive report back to Mr Graham – the bones of which implied that he was not really needed – 'Maurice Rowlandson is quite able to do the work you had envisaged for me.' Dr Jauncey decided against coming to England and the future leadership remained in abeyance. In the meantime I carried on as previously.

There was a brief interruption in events when Billy Graham invited the Revd Tom Allen (Minister of St George's Tron in Glasgow) to come and take charge of the London Office and to be the editor of *The Christian*. Tragically Tom Allen had a heart attack and died before he could assume either of those duties. The full story is in Chapter 11.

At the Team Meeting that year Billy Graham made it clear that he would make no more efforts to find someone to replace Jerry Beavan. He gave me the task, amongst my other duties, to promote the ministry of Billy Graham in the UK in every way possible. At the time I was still a member of the Council of the Evangelical Alliance. I had asked Gilbert Kirby to include an item on the next agenda to consider another invitation to London to Billy Graham. In due course the matter was raised and there was, virtually, a unanimous vote against such a proposal. The reason for this was that the members of the EA Council felt that such an event might jeopardise their relationship with the local churches. They had tried to encourage church evangelism and they had felt that there was some 'cooling off' over mass evangelism. They didn't want to take any action which might run against that thinking.

Meanwhile, Marilyn and I received a formal invitation from Billy and Ruth Graham to attend the wedding of his daughter, Gigi Graham, in Montreux, Switzerland. We were deeply touched to have been included in that important event and we had a great time there.

For such a high-profile family the wedding was low-key. There was nothing flamboyant about it, although the bride was, of course, beautiful and in a stunning dress. It was an unusual wedding because her bridegroom was Stephan Tchividjian, the son of an expatriate Armenian financier, who lived in Switzerland. Billy

Graham had received a letter from Stephan in which he had enclosed another letter asking Gigi for her hand. At the time she was only seventeen but declared to her father, 'This is of God, Daddy!' The wedding was conducted by Billy Graham in a picturesque old stone church, Le Temple de Montreux, down by Lake Geneva. A lovely reception was held at a hotel across the road.

Just a few days after the wedding we attended Billy Graham's Crusade in Paris together with most of the staff from our London office. It seemed a good opportunity to allow them to experience a crusade and to learn what their work was about.

As so often happens at a Billy Graham Crusade there was the charge of 'emotionalism' – even in France! One of the staff with me remarked: 'I don't know how you can be emotional, sitting on hard, backless, wooden benches while the rain is pouring through gaps in the marquee making you very wet and when there are rats running in between the rows!' It was a good experience for them all nonetheless.

After the Paris Crusade, Billy and Ruth Graham flew to London to arrive on Thursday, 27 June 1963. As we drove into London, Billy Graham told me of a conversation he had had with David Frost – the famous radio and TV interviewer. David Frost had asked him whether he thought he had done the right thing to follow the advice of the Archbishop of Canterbury after the Harringay Crusade. The Archbishop had said that he thought it would be wise for Mr Graham to leave the British churches to cope with the aftermath of the crusade. He thought it would be best not to attempt any immediate continuation elsewhere in the country. Billy Graham was non-committal in his reply to David Frost who asked Billy Graham when he was coming back to London for a crusade. Billy Graham replied, 'I haven't been invited,' to which David Frost said, 'I want you to come. I am giving you an invitation right now!'

It appeared that the conversation had started a train of thought in Mr Graham's mind. He asked for my opinion about coming back to London for another crusade. I said there were one positive and two negative factors. The first negative problem arose from the Evangelical Alliance. I told Mr Graham that the EA had unanimously rejected the idea of a crusade. The second negative fact was that I knew the clergy, by and large, wouldn't support it. However, on the positive side, I said that I believed that the majority of the laity would back a crusade to the hilt. That prompted Mr Graham to ask, 'Why then, do we not mobilise the laity to produce an invitation?' And so it happened.

In the national news about that time there was much concern about nuclear disarmament promoted by the Campaign for Nuclear Disarmament's so-called 'Committee of 100'. The idea came to us that we should try to find 100 significant names amongst the laity who would be willing to issue an invitation to Mr Graham to come again to London.

Many Christian people were conscious that a whole new generation had grown up since Harringay. There were parents of young people who desperately wanted their children to be involved in a crusade and to hear the message of the Gospel. As a result it was not too hard a job to find 100 leaders who would lend their names to such a project and we assembled our own 'committee of 100'! Having identified them we then invited them to a special luncheon. We prepared a parchment invitation for those present at the luncheon to sign. Those of the 100 names who were unable to accept the invitation to lunch sent us their authority to add their names to the document. We finished with the full number of signatories that we wanted. Deeply moved by the level of support that was forthcoming, Mr Graham accepted the invitation to come back to London in 1966. My hands were full now with planning for this new crusade.

It was therefore something of a shock to be brought up sharply with a severe angina attack early in 1965. My National Health doctor had diagnosed it as 'chronic indigestion' but my osteopath urged me to see a Harley Street doctor privately – and that encouragement virtually saved my life. He made arrangements for me to see a Dr T. R. Williams who promptly marched me up the street to a cardiac specialist. He made the correct diagnosis and recommended a complicated routine of medications. Dr Williams, however, discounted all of that and said that, in his opinion, I should take 400 units of Vitamin E a day, together with a glass of red wine each day. 'Do that,' he said, 'and you'll live to be 100!' Ever since then, that is what I have done and I have had no further heart problem since. As I write this it is 2006 so I have 19 years left to his target!

Once again some members of the Billy Graham Team came from America to help us bear the brunt of the day. They were under the direction of Bill Brown (whose wife, Joan Winmill, had been converted at Harringay). They established temporary offices in Piccadilly Circus. We needed to appoint a staff to assist him and I spent a couple of days interviewing prospective staff. Two of those I almost rejected but, encouraged by my colleague Harvey Thomas (and by the excellent results from their 'tests'), I decided to take them on. One was Stephanie Wills who a few years later became Mr Graham's own private secretary (and still remains so). The other was Judy Butler who, today, is companion and personal assistant to the famous quadriplegic Joni Eareckson. How wrong I nearly was! The story of 1966 and 1967 is in a later chapter.

CHAPTER ELEVEN

THE CHRISTIAN

THE STORY of the Billy Graham Evangelistic Association and *The Christian* is a difficult one. It was probably one of the most traumatic periods of my work with Billy Graham because it brought me into the conflict between the staff in the office, the British Board and the American Board. It was a period when the 'Thin Gold Line' wavered considerably and, but for the goodness of God, might have terminated then.

The story started with news from the publishers, Marshall, Morgan and Scott, that they were preparing to close down the long-established evangelical weekly newspaper *The Christian*. At the time there were three major interdenominational newspapers (apart from *The Christian*): *The Sunday Companion*, *The Christian Herald* and *The Life of Faith*. In addition there were also the weekly denominational papers and a wide variety of monthly magazines. Both *The Christian Herald* and *The Sunday Companion* had a largely elderly and shut-in readership with news that was, usually, several weeks old. They included romantic stories with a Christian emphasis as well as feature articles. *The Life of Faith* had grown out of the world-famous Keswick Convention and concentrated on reports from Keswick, some news of other Christian activities and a Bible Teaching ministry – especially concentrating on the Victorious Life. *The Christian* was first and foremost a Christian newspaper.

Its loss would be severely felt by the evangelical Christian public. The news of its impending demise reached Billy Graham.

He had long wanted a medium for a regular 'voice' to believers in the UK, and he saw that such an opportunity presented itself if he became the proprietor of *The Christian*. Early in 1962 he made an offer to the publishers to buy the newspaper. That offer was accepted, and the Billy Graham Evangelistic Association (BGEA) became the owners and publishers of this old-established newspaper.

With the paper, we 'bought' its editor. She was exceedingly competent at her job and had previously worked with the magazine *Crusade*. She had been editor of *The Christian* since the retirement of Dr Charles T. Cook who had steered it for many years. He was an old friend of ours and I have already recounted how he happened to be in Minneapolis at the time of our wedding back in 1949. He had heard that the wedding was taking place and had surprised us all by turning up. He was, after all, a good old-fashioned journalist!

The current editor was, however, one of the modern breed of journalists who was very conscious of the 'freedom of the press' and of her responsibility to be an unbiased editor. This meant that, from time to time, she had made critical comments both about the Billy Graham Evangelistic Association and upon evangelists in general. Now that the BGEA was her proprietor, to continue in that vein would mean that in effect, she was 'biting the hand that fed her'. Eventually, she was called to task by Mr George M. Wilson, the chief executive officer of the BGEA. He challenged her by giving her the option of being totally loyal to the Lord and loyal to the ministry of Billy Graham as her employer. He said that we needed a more sympathetic approach. She said that she could not work under that restraint and she resigned her post.

Thus the search was on for a new editor who would exercise that sympathetic approach. Amongst those approached for this role were the Revd Gilbert W. Kirby, the Revd John Caiger and the Revd A. Morgan Derham. The first was deeply involved in the work of the Evangelical Alliance and did not feel the call to be an editor. The second was heavily committed to his church where he had been for more than 28 years. He did not feel God's call to this task. Morgan Derham, however, felt very sure that this could be a call of God. Before he accepted the position, however, he expressed ten conditions that he would regard as important.

As most of these conditions were the very causes of the former editor's resignation there seemed to be no point in proceeding any further with this invitation.

Then, a year later, Mr Graham wrote to tell me that he had invited the Revd Tom Allen from Glasgow to fulfil two functions. First he was to become the editor of *The Christian* and second he would be head at the London office. Tom and I knew each other well and got on very well together. I was thrilled to think that he was to become my colleague in these two functions. He wanted to make a success of the newspaper whilst, at the same time, doing all he could to promote the evangelistic ministry of Billy Graham. It immediately became clear that he was the right man for the job. Our search was over! God had led us to the man of His choice.

Tom was to be introduced to the whole Billy Graham Team at the next Team Meeting to be held at Miami Beach in Florida. We were all shattered to hear the news that, on the way over, he had had a heart attack and had passed away. Billy Graham asked to see me at the Team Meeting and he confirmed to me that he would be making no further attempts to find someone to head up the London Office. He now wished to appoint me to that role.

One thing was clear. Billy Graham had the interests of *The Christian* very much in his thoughts. He wrote to me on 26 December 1962:

> It is my thought that *The Christian* could be improved by adding more thoughtful articles. I do not think the tremendous news coverage should be curtailed. In fact, the paper has by far the best news coverage of any of the religious newspapers in Britain. This should be continued and even expanded. I do believe that each issue should carry thoughtful and hard hitting articles on evangelism, the deeper life, the church and its ministry and should be sympathetic to what we are trying to do, etc.

He went on:

> In addition I am most anxious that a couple of pages in *The Christian* should be devoted to carrying reprints of editorials in other religious periodicals throughout the world. Something like the *Reader's Digest* is now doing.

The main problem still was to find the right person to be the editor. Through the good offices of the American publication *Christianity Today* the name of Jim Douglas was presented to us. He was a person of high integrity and with exceptional academic qualifications. He was also an established and acceptable writer. With all of those attributes, Billy Graham had no hesitation in inviting him to take on the mantle of the editorship of *The Christian*. He was appointed on 8 January 1964. In accordance with Mr Graham's letter the previous December, it was agreed that *The Christian* would draw heavily upon *Christianity Today*. In order to reflect this association, the name of the paper in the UK was changed to *The Christian and Christianity Today*.

Meanwhile, in a telephone call to me, Billy Graham had confirmed his wish that I should assume full responsibility for the office in London. This would include the supervision of the editorial department.

Once the appointment of Jim Douglas was confirmed he lost no time in setting up a strong editorial team. The team included journalists, writers, artists, photographers and administrators. Altogether there were about 25 or so on the staff. The finances of the London Office, as they stood, could never absorb the cost of such an operation and from the beginning it was agreed that the American Office would give a substantial subsidy to support the newspaper. Some £20,000 a month would be needed and the Americans agreed to contribute that amount to establish the newspaper as a major force in the UK. It was clear however, that it would be a long time before the circulation would be anywhere near a figure large enough to sustain that sort of subsidy.

Without a doubt the newspaper flourished. The watchword from Jim, reflected by all of his staff was that 'people are interested in people' and the newspaper sought to honour that code.

Unfortunately the spectre of the 'freedom of the press' reared its head repeatedly, and articles started to appear which were both critical of other evangelists and – occasionally – even of Billy Graham himself. At the time Bishop A. W. Goodwin Hudson was the Chairman of the British Board of the BGEA and the American board put increasing pressure on him to both instruct the editor and his staff and to encourage more positive articles. The bishop passed that responsibility on to me. Between April 1965 and April 1969 I had repeated confrontations with the editorial team, to try and persuade them to fulfil more completely Billy Graham's vision for the newspaper.

Franklin Graham wrote:

> It saddens me to see *The Christian* jump on the bandwagon of the secular media. I question the motives of writers who sling mud by reporting scandals within the body of Christ. They defend it, saying it is their obligation. The Scripture carefully warns: 'If you keep on biting and devouring each other, watch out or you will be destroyed by each other (Galatians 5:15 NIV)'.

On 24 August 1968, Mr Graham wrote to me:

> I am terribly sorry about the problems in relation to *The Christian* . . . I think this is going to have to be handled with a great deal of discretion, love and understanding. I share some of the reservations that the Bishop has. This does not come through personal knowledge but through general impressions given me by members of the team and by friends in Britain. I think you should call the entire British Board together and have an all-day discussion – making your own decisions. Be assured that I will be in much prayer concerning these problems.

The Americans saw some comments in the paper about *other* evangelists as implicit attacks on Billy Graham's own ministry. For example, the report of a crusade held by one British evangelist declared that 'when he gave his invitation to come forward, *predictably* most of those who came forward were children'. Because the Bishop was at the meeting reported, he knew that this was just not true. He saw it as being 'slanted' in a way that seemed to denigrate the work of that evangelist. It was this and other similar negative reports which, bit by bit, made the American board members unhappy. They looked at the £20,000 a month subsidy and asked, 'Why are we subsidising a paper which attacks mass evangelism?' There were, of course, many good and helpful articles also in the paper but the American Board were concerned about these critical reports.

I received a letter from Mr Graham early in 1967 in which he said:

> We have been going through a rather agonising time with our budget for 1967. Therefore I am having to cut in every field of our work. Please write to me as quickly as possible where and how you think you can cut the work in the British office by at least a quarter.

This concern about money was to be a recurring theme in many of the letters I received from Billy Graham in the following years. On this occasion, it led Bishop Goodwin Hudson to have a long talk on the telephone with both George Wilson and Billy Graham himself. He expressed to them his view that the biggest cut could be made if the large monthly subsidy for *The Christian* was reduced or discontinued. This provoked some strong comments from George Wilson about the content of the paper. To him it seemed that the paper had become more and more opposed to evangelism, and he said that the American Board was very concerned.

An ultimatum, directly from the American Board, was given to the bishop. Either the content and emphasis of the paper should change, or the subsidy would be discontinued. The American Board gave three months grace to allow this to happen. Unhappily there was no change and on 20 May 1969 the American Board requested that there should be an emergency meeting of the British Board to determine what action should be taken. At that meeting they took the decision that there was no option left open to them but to close the paper.

It fell to me to convey that decision to the editor. Inevitably, as I was the one who conveyed that unpalatable message I became the bête noir. It appeared to them that I was the blockage in the pipeline because I was the one who had always been suggesting ways in which their approach might change. Now, in the eleventh hour, I had to wield the final axe. I met with Jim Douglas on 22 May 1969 and told him of the American Board's decision, and of the acquiescence of the British Board.

The news leaked out, and on 23 May 1969 I told the staff. There was an immediate adverse reaction. On 27 May, Philip Crowe, then the editor of the *Church of England Newspaper*, hurried around to meet the bishop and me to see if he could rescue the paper. On 28 May I had to go to Richmond to tell the printers that our contract would be terminated. It was a very hard day – a 'jet black day' I recorded in my diary.

On 30 May 1969 it all happened. There were several conferences in the office – not least with John Capon who was managing editor of the Church of England newspaper. Later that week the entire staff of the newspaper left the office for the last time. George Wilson flew in from America to support the bishop and me. John Pollock, Billy Graham's official biographer, had an idea to rescue the paper. But the American Board was adamant, and we were left to pick up the pieces.

It was not easy for the large *Christian* staff to assimilate all that had happened. Quite naturally very few of them had any good words to say about the Bishop and me. Indeed I got some quite abusive letters from one or two of them. Also some friends of mine in other ministries did not understand the reasoning behind our actions and the constraints under which we had been operating. How could you explain the complex background behind all that had happened? Some of my best friends gave me 'the cold shoulder' for quite some time. However, looking back from the perspective of more than 35 years later, I am glad to say that most of those staff members who felt so strongly about it at the time are now my very good friends. Some years later one of them apologised to me for some of the things that had happened. With another I was reconciled a year or two later when we met and prayed through the hurt in his heart. I am sad that all this happened. It was, as I have said, a horrendous period of my life. But I knew the Lord was by my side, and 'if the Lord is with us, who can be against us?'.

* * * *

This distressing time leads me to write about the second of four digressions. The story of the first – the Venturers Cruise – has already been told. The remaining three all involved me in some participation in a secular activity to 'keep my feet on the ground'. It was at a time like this that my spirit could have been broken but for the fact that there were these other interests in life which occupied my mind. In Chapter Four I referred to my service with the Royal Naval Reserve and the difficulty I expected to have because of medical problems. However, I got through those.

When I was interviewed by Captain MacGregor of HMS *Northwood*, he explained to me that we were 'simply another pair of hands' to help in the NATO responsibility for the Naval Control of Shipping. In the event of war we would be in charge of any convoy arrangements. He emphasised that there was no opportunity, within the service, for promotion.

I always enjoyed anything to do with the sea and was glad to learn all about plotting techniques and all the intricacies of convoy management. All of that was a great diversion to my mind. During the difficult times in the office, I returned after an RNR training night, refreshed in body, mind and spirit. I am sure that the Lord provided this diversion for me and it was a lifesaver to me. To be forced to think of other things than the problems of the office for two hours each week (and, once a year, during a two-week 'exercise') enabled me to expand my mind and renew my energy.

It was an enormous surprise, two years after joining, to be told that I had been selected for a commission in the Royal Naval Reserve. A problem arose however. Apparently to gain a commission I needed to have had at least 40 days of sea time on my record. For the whole summer of 1960 I was sent off to sea at every available opportunity. I sailed – a day at a time – aboard the *Thames* (three times); *Salisbury*, *Hermes*, *Kent*, *Bossington*, *Grafton*, *Pellew*, *Danae*, *Stubbington*, *Ashanti*, *Leopard* (twice), *Falmouth*, *Brighton* (twice) and *Gurka*. I probably sailed on more ships than many a regular naval officer during that period! This programme enabled me to amass the forty days I required for qualification!

Now, as an officer, I qualified to serve aboard the Sail Training Association topsail schooners – the *Sir Winston Churchill* and the *Malcolm Miller*. These duties as purser aboard were allowed to me in place of the annual exercise and, although terribly hard work, were immensely pleasurable. Each of the nine two-week voyages I completed involved visits to numerous European ports. We were fêted at each port of call – none less than the Festival of Sail in Bremenhaven. While I was there I met a group who had been involved in Billy Graham's Crusade in Essen the year before. I remarked to my fellow-afterguard officers that 'when you are a Christian it is like being a member of a club with branches everywhere!'

There were eight officers – two full-time (the captain and the first mate). The other six were volunteers who shared the confined area of the afterguard accommodation. I learned very soon that to say I worked for the American Evangelist Billy Graham, destroyed any possibility of a relationship with my fellows. When the captain performed his introductory duties the first night aboard, I always said that I worked for 'World Wide Films' (which was a department of the BGEA). Over the next few days there was time to establish a relationship with the other officers before the inevitable question came, 'What sort of films does World Wide Films' produce?' My explanation always started by saying that, in America, World Wide Films was called World Wide Pictures. We had to change the name in the UK, because World Wide Pictures in Britain were distributors of pornographic films! Then I could tell them of the different nature of our films. By then, they had discovered that I was a normal person. I was not some eccentric, raving religious weirdo! So, not only did they accept what I told them, but they always wanted to know more! It was a wonderful open door of opportunity.

In October 1962 the international Cuban crisis arose. NATO was put on 'red alert' – the closest we ever came to nuclear warfare – and my participation in the Royal Naval Reserve meant that I was 'on call' for several days. This was the only occasion when something else took precedence over my work for Billy Graham. It was a national crisis that lasted for four days. It also involved a number of extra duties at the Northwood Headquarters. Jerry Beavan realised that I had no alternative but to obey orders and he supported me in the extra commitment which I had to make.

Becoming a Royal Naval Reserve Officer was a whole new aspect of life. I had to learn, for example, that in the mess (dining hall) there were three topics of conversation that were not allowed – religion, sex and politics. This raised a problem because, when I sat next to a regular RN officer at table, I often got the question: 'What do you do in Civilian life?' To that I replied: 'I work with Dr Billy Graham, the American Evangelist.' Sometimes that was the end of conversation! More often there followed a further question: 'That's interesting. Is he genuine?' Or, sometimes, 'What does he really believe?' Now you have to understand that, in answering any of those questions I was talking about Dr Billy Graham – not about religion! This too gave many opportunities for witness.

When the admiral commanding reserves would come for his annual inspection, he would pause and talk to most officers. Some conversations were quite lengthy – especially when the admiral recognised some Service medal. However, when he reached me I had no medals to 'read'. So he too would ask the question, 'What do you do in civilian life?' Upon receiving my reply the usual reaction was to say, 'That's nice,' and move on to the next in line. Until, that is, Admiral Sir Peter Hill Norton was the inspecting officer. He was a great Christian and a supporter of Billy Graham. When he asked the question and received my answer I had an extended conversation with him which prompted many of my fellow-officers to ask what in the world he had been talking to me about – the conversation had gone on for so long. By this, and other means, there was a silent witness to my fellow-officers in the unit. From time to time this was compounded as I received a telephone call from one or another: 'Maurice! May I come and have a chat with you?' So often it was some personal problem that was troubling them. They all seemed to know where I stood, and it was yet another diversion from my daily work.

Eventually there came a time when I had to retire, through age, from the Reserve. I missed it enormously and was profoundly thankful that there were other diversions which occupied my mind – but the stories of those must wait for a later digression!

* * * *

In spite of the closure of *The Christian* the thought of a regular publication was never far from Mr Graham's mind. He wrote to me on 26 July 1976 as follows:

> I just returned from the Continent of Europe last night and have read your recent letter. I was most encouraged by the groundwork you have already done about the possibility of reviving *The Christian* in England. I think you are on exactly the right road and I shall await further developments with great anticipation.

Bishop Goodwin Hudson and I ran into considerable difficulties as we continued in an exploratory mode. There seemed to be insurmountable problems – not least in finding the right editor for such a project. On visits to London Mr Graham often spoke to me about it and continued to wonder if there was any future for such a project.

I had a letter from him in November 1979 when, once again, he returned to this burden on his heart. He said:

> I have been giving a great deal of thought to the discussions we have had over many years concerning *The Christian*. I remember that we had several approaches to either sell, give or cooperate with others in bringing *The Christian* out again. As I have prayed, thought and discussed it with several others since I have been home, I would like to share my thoughts with you.

It was interesting that, in spite of the fact that Jim Douglas had been the editor when the paper was closed in 1969, Billy Graham still held him in high regard and suggested that he might be re-appointed. He went on to say:

> We should think in terms of bringing *The Christian* out again, very much as it was when it was closed down, under an entirely new Board *fully responsible for the business administration*. This would have all the possibilities of becoming by far the most significant evangelical religious publication in Britain. It should possibly be published under the name of BGEA in order for people to know where it stands. We should send it to all evangelical clergy in the country as well as all the bishops, chaplains, divinity professors, etc.

In a later letter Mr Graham named seven key people whom he felt could be involved. Finally he said:

> I think that any plans should be done in connection with any crusade plans in the early 1980s. I think we should have several months of build-up with ads, letters, promotion, etc., with the possibility of it coming out about November 1981 on either a weekly or a bi-weekly basis.

All of this prompted long discussions in the British Board but, sadly, nothing ever came of it. Whether this was due to reluctance by the American Board to get involved in subsidising another periodical, or whether the British Board advised against it, I know not. All I do know is that for one reason or another it fell by the wayside. It did, nonetheless, demonstrate Mr Graham's concern for Britain and his desire to keep the Gospel message to the forefront.

A few years later the name of *The Christian* was revived. *The Christian Herald* decided that it was too good a title to be lost. They made enquiries of us and learned that there was no legal bar which might have prevented them from adopting, and using, the name for their publication. At first it was a tiny 'by-line' which appeared below their major title of *The Christian Herald* – with *The Christian* appearing in small type below it. However, as the years passed, the title was reversed and the main and major title in big letters became *The Christian*, with *The Christian Herald* appearing in small type below. Sadly in 2006 that periodical too ceased publication bringing to an end the era of independent Christian newspapers.

CHAPTER TWELVE

THE SECOND LONDON CRUSADE

FROM THE time in 1963 when Mr Graham arrived from Paris, until the end of the Earl's Court Greater London Crusade in 1967, our feet barely touched the ground. At first I found it frustrating that my angina attack had slowed me down. I wanted to play my full part and I had to find out how best to contribute to the overall planning. Then my doctor gave me a clue: 'Carry on as usual,' he said, 'but when you get tired, don't push yourself. Just pack up and go home.' It was a formula that worked well, and I was able to be involved, as much as my strength would allow, in all the planning for the Greater London Crusade.

Earls Court was selected as the venue and was available for the five weeks of the crusade. Major General D. J. Wilson Haffenden became the chairman of the committee once more. He and I went to discuss the arrangements at Earls Court with Major General Ritchie (the general manager). It turned out that the two of them had served together in the Western Desert under Field Marshall Montgomery so they quickly had a good rapport. Major Ritchie introduced us to his clerk of works, Mr Matthews. He was a tower of strength to us throughout the time we were at Earls Court. Nothing was too much trouble for him and he fulfilled every need we had with speed and efficiency.

Having said that, the management still needed us to agree to a contract of some 250 pages long! We remembered the three-page letter of intent which was all we had at Harringay! Naturally, 250 pages opened the door to endless negotiations on all sorts of points – and usually carried an extra charge for whatever happened outside the agreement!

Two rather amusing factors arose from our time at Earls Court. When we finally reached the end of our five weeks, Major General Ritchie presented Henry Hole and me with Earls Court ties. He told us that those ties would get us in to any event at the arena without paying! And they did – until General Ritchie retired and 'there arose another manager who knew not the Greater London Crusade'! The other thing was that Mr Matthews showed us a back – and secret – door which, he said, would always be open to allow us in so long as he was still clerk of works. That too worked well for many years. Using Earls Court had its perks.

I had a telephone call from the Rev. Gilbert W. Kirby early in 1964. He was concerned that the Evangelical Alliance was not involved in the plans for the Greater London Crusade. He wanted to know why I had not approached him for the EA's support. I explained to him that I had remembered the virtually unanimous vote against a crusade by the EA Council when I had raised the question of extending an invitation to Mr Graham. Mr Kirby recognised that I had been justified in my view, but he said that now the crusade was a foregone conclusion, the EA wanted to be involved.

The matter was taken back to the Crusade Committee who had been concerned that the EA had not been involved. They remembered that Harringay may never have happened but for the EA's support. It seemed inappropriate to them for any crusade to go ahead without the EA's involvement. A complicated procedure was devised by the committee who 'backdated' several of the initial decisions to allow the full participation of the EA. From that day onwards, the crusade was officially sponsored by the Evangelical Alliance.

Naturally there were many organisational details to be completed. Bill Brown, with his competent staff (assisted by Harvey Thomas) and many members of the Billy Graham Team from America coped magnificently in bringing it all together.

As at the time of Harringay, a gigantic publicity campaign was launched. The American Team carried a large proportion of the cost of that and the British committee was exceedingly grateful.

A year later the controversial poster campaign declaring 'Billy's Back' (with a photograph depicting a back view of Mr Graham preaching) was also supported heavily by the American Team.

For us there were counsellor training classes to be organised; choir and stewards' teams to be recruited, and the physical arrangements within the building of Earls Court to be planned. It was a busy period.

One member of the Billy Graham Team to arrive in London was Dr Robert Ferm. I went to London Airport to meet him on 18 January 1965. While I was waiting in the Arrivals Lounge a message came over the loudspeakers: 'Would Maurice Rowlandson please proceed through the doors to immigration where his presence is required.'

When I got there I found a distressed Robert Ferm because he was having difficulties with the Muslim Immigration Officer. The officer seriously doubted Dr Ferm's intentions and needed my authority that he was coming to London at our invitation. As he stamped Dr Ferm's passport the immigration officer said: 'If I had my way, I wouldn't let you into the country. You Billy Graham people are an anathema to me!' I could scarcely believe my ears and wanted to make a complaint to the Home Office. However, Robert Ferm restrained me and, instead, gave the immigration officer a warm invitation to come to Earls Court – which he subsequently did and, later, he was converted!

* * * *

Coping with this very busy time, and my own health problems, leads me to discuss the third digression which helped me through this difficult period. The period of the crusade preparation ran from early 1963 to the start of the meetings on 31 May 1966. The busyness of this period could have been a disaster for me as I learned to live with the aftermath of my angina attack.

I therefore needed some activity to 'keep my feet on the ground'. It was my membership of the Magic Circle that provided that catalyst. My activities there diverted my mind away from the day-to-day pressures. Helping at the Magic Circle during this time was a lifesaver to me.

Ever since my father had shown me his 'party trick' with a short length of string, I had been fascinated by magical tricks. Of course there was the great danger that some people would see it as 'black magic' – and for me as a Christian that was totally 'out' (even if it ever existed)! I always said, 'I do illusions: you see magic.' Actually every magical trick usually followed one, or a combination of, seven magic principles (such as production; disappearance; multiplication; levitation, etc.). 'The quickness of the hand deceives the eye' – and distracting the viewer's attention had a lot to do with the way that many magical tricks mystified.

In 1983 I became more deeply involved when a magician friend, Michael Candy, invited me to join the team who provided all the back-up for the monthly 'Magic Circle at Home' days. These were two or more evenings each month when the Magic Circle was 'at home' to the public. They were interesting evenings comprising a visit to the Magical Museum; almost an hour of close-up magic around a group of tables; a short lecture on the history of magic and then, after a break for refreshments, a three-act magical show in our own theatre. They were good evenings which took – and still take – a great deal of team work by back-room behind-the-scenes helpers. It was quite an organisation and I became part of that team for 18 years. In 2001 I ended up as the leader of the team helping to provide training in lights, sound, and stage management. I also compiled the working rota. It didn't take long for both the members of the team, as well as members of the Magic Circle itself, to discover that I worked for Billy Graham – and that nailed my colours to the mast! I had some great times of discussion at the Circle.

To those who question how, as a Christian, I can be an Associate of the Inner Magic Circle, I give the answer expressed so clearly about the late Pete McCahon by his friend Toby Travis, the American magician. Pete was the president of the Fellowship of Christian Magicians. He was the son of a Baptist Minister and was an active magician until his untimely death just before Christmas in 2004. Toby wrote:

> Pete McCahon would have said that there are at least two meanings to the word 'magic' in the dictionary. First is 'the art of producing effects by what are claimed to be SUPERHUMAN means via

occult powers'. The second definition is 'the art of applying NATURAL causes, whose operation is secret to produce a surprising effect'. That is what magicians (or illusionists) do today.

Psalm 72:18 and Psalm 136:3, 4 clearly say that God alone can perform the miraculous. Even Satan is unable to perform the genuine miraculous. In passages like 2 Thessalonians 2:9, Satan's powers are described as 'lying wonders'. But in Exodus 7:10-12 Pharaoh's magicians attempted to duplicate the genuine miraculous performed by God through Moses and Aaron. It appeared to indicate that their illusionary wonders were accomplished by their 'secret arts'. In the original Hebrew the word here is 'lahat' which, literally translated, means 'to perform covertly'. This does not mean an indication of genuine miraculous ability, but rather that it was a trick or a sleight of hand.

In his tribute, Toby Travis goes on to give his own view:

I have been questioned as to how I can justify using that form of deception. I can't! I don't. Like any magician, I am an honest man because I *tell* you I am going to fool you and then proceed to do it! Secrecy is part of our hobby but that does not equal an evil deception. Secrecy is an integral part of my work just as a certain recipe is a secret for Kentucky Fried Chicken. It is simply a matter of good business!

Everything I do, I do for the glory of our Lord Jesus Christ and for the purpose of spreading the Gospel. My presentation of illusions and magic tricks has provided me with the opportunity to share Christ with millions of people. As a result I have witnessed thousands' trust in Jesus Christ as Lord.

This has been the reasoning behind my own involvement with the technical team at the Magic Circle headquarters. It was a great thrill when one of my technical team stopped me in our wonderful new headquarters near Euston Station. He told me that he had recently become a Christian and he wanted me to be amongst the first to know. He wrote to me shortly afterwards and said:

I know now that God managed to get through to me and I bought a small travel Bible thinking that no one will see it. When the coast is clear I could read a few bits . . . being a bit of a 'techie' I sat down at my computer and searched for local churches and found out about a local church – the Dartford Christian Fellowship. I wanted to know what happened at the service and a cup of tea at the end sounded great. I went to the church and as the service progressed I knew then that something had happened to me. The pastor was great and he made the Bible come alive for me. God has given him an incredible gift. That is where and when I became a Christian and I know God is always around us. We only have to listen. I have discovered that you can't get a better manual to life than the Bible.

Without a doubt, serving with the Magic Circle is an exceptional opportunity for covert evangelism. You never know what influence a life led for God will have on others.

* * * *

Early in May 1965, with Mr Graham's approval, another diversion came about. I was invited to become the chairman in Britain of the Christian Missionary Radio Station, Trans World Radio. I asked Mr Graham if he would wish me to do this and he concurred – even encouraged me to do so. He said that I should pay an early visit to the European Studios situated in Monte Carlo, Monaco. That August, Marilyn and I flew out for five days to the Principality – our first ever visit there, and our first sight of the Apostle Paul's Mediterranean Sea! We were warmly welcomed and it was to be followed by many more visits there over the following years.

The full story of the two Greater London Crusades in 1966 and 1967 has been written elsewhere and this is not the place to tell it all over again. There are, however, a few stories which directly involved my participation with Billy Graham and the Team. They may not have been recorded elsewhere.

The crusade meetings closely followed the former Harringay pattern and continued to draw capacity crowds night after night. There was a little more flexibility at Earls Court because there were two adjacent massive exhibition halls into which we could expand the meetings by using Closed Circuit Television (CCTV). It made no difference whether the meeting was live or televised. When Billy Graham gave his appeal, people streamed to the front to stand by the platform or, in the CCTV areas, in front of the screens. There were adequate counsellors in both places. Countless thousands date the crusade at Earls Court as the time that they found the Lord Jesus Christ as their Saviour.

We had our problems. The whole culture of the day meant that we received several warnings of 'a bomb in the building'. They all turned out to be hoaxes – one a carefully prepared hoax when the police found a heavy cardboard box with wires coming out of it. When they took it away they found it contained only bricks. In the end, after the first two or three hoaxes, the police took a calculated risk and decided not to vacate the building.

I had the same team of stewards, with Henry Hole now fulfilling the role of chief steward. His back-up team were all Venturers Cruise officers, and they worked well together. By now the entire leadership team was equipped with two-way radios. The flexibility they allowed contributed largely to the excellence of the work that the stewards did. We also had a large contingent of policemen (out-of-uniform), all volunteers from the Christian Police Association (CPA). They came into their own one night when we had anti-Vietnam war protestors who dropped leaflets from the roof and, simultaneously, ran into the building to try and disrupt the meeting. The CPA boys moved into action and, in no time at all, they had rounded up the protestors and had escorted them out of the building. It was a highly professional job which brought a commendation to me from the Inspector of Police who said: 'Mr Rowlandson. Your stewards did a magnificent job in handling that problem!' He had no idea that the CPA men there were, in fact, his own men!

One story certainly wouldn't be recounted in any other history of the Earls Court Crusade. It was too personal! Two Elim pastors had volunteered to be drivers for Mr Graham and Cliff Barrows during the entire period of the crusade. One of them cultivated strawberries at home. One night he brought a wooden box of some of the largest and most juicy variety to Mr Graham's room. There were twenty-four strawberries in the box, each one about the size of a small peach and in its own little paper cup. I happened to be in Mr Graham's room when the box arrived and he handed them around to the four of us who were there. Our initial impressions were confirmed: the strawberries were perfectly ripe, sweet and tasty.

Mr Graham looked around at the four of us and held up the remaining strawberries in their box. He said, 'What in the world am I going to do with these?' Then, in what seemed to be a moment of inspiration, he looked directly at me and said: 'Maurice, take them home to Marilyn and the family.' I thanked him profusely! We left his room and made our way to the platform.

Because there were many administrative jobs to be done throughout the meeting, it was not unusual for some of us to leave the platform after the first hymn or two. We usually returned in time for Mr Graham's evening message. On this occasion, a little earlier than usual, I suddenly thought of those strawberries. Oh the temptations of the devil!

I left the platform and made my way back to Mr Graham's room. There I collected the box of strawberries and took them out to the car park and put them in my car. As I came back into the hall I spotted Dr Walter Smyth and Dr T. W. Wilson striding purposefully towards Mr Graham's room. They emerged a few minutes later looking puzzled. We all went back to the platform and soon afterwards Dr Smyth scribbled a little note that he passed along the row to me. It read: 'Maurice! Do you know what happened to those strawberries?' I realised that I had beaten them to it by just a few seconds! When he heard what I had done, he forgave me and said that he hoped Marilyn would enjoy the strawberries!

There were two 'big nights' during the weeks at Earls Court. One was the night when the Revd Maurice A. P. Wood (later Bishop of Norwich but at the time of the crusade, principal of the Oak Hill Theological College) brought some 23 of his ordinands, all of whom traced their conversion to the Harringay Crusade of 1954. It was a moving experience to see them there.

The other big night followed a little hand-written postcard which I received in the mail. It came from Mr David Winter who, at the time, was the editor of the magazine *Crusade*. It simply read:

> Dear Maurice, Cliff Richard spent yesterday evening at our home and we satisfied ourselves that he really *is* a Christian now! We (his closest counsellor and I) both feel a wise letter from Billy G,

> perhaps specifically inviting him to Earls Court – but *not*, we suggest, asking him to make any public pronouncements for the present – could do a lot of good. Yours sincerely, as ever, David.

The letter of invitation was duly sent and, to Mr Graham's surprise, back came a message from Cliff Richard to say that he would like to sing at the meeting. Mr Graham happily accommodated him in the programme and Cliff not only sang 'It is no secret what God can do', but unashamedly gave his testimony. He really 'nailed *his* colours to the mast' on that occasion and he has never looked back. Since then he has taken part in many Billy Graham Crusades across the world, singing and giving his testimony.

It was following that occasion that I had an unusual experience. World Wide Pictures – the American film 'arm' of the BGEA – decided that they would like to make a feature film of the Earls Court meetings and, if he was willing, to use Cliff Richard as the 'star'. He *was* willing and the filming of *Two a Penny* was started during the last two weeks of Earls Court. By then, the announcement had been made that Mr Graham would be returning for a further week in June 1967. It was decided to complete the filming the following year.

One scene included Cliff Richard as he attempted to bluff his way on to the platform. He pretended he was a VIP guest and was to be stopped by a steward at the foot of the platform. To my immense surprise the film team asked me to act the part of that steward. All I had to do was to say 'I'm sorry you can't go up there' (on to the platform), and appear to restrain him – but without success. Only half of that scene was finished in 1966. The director of the film then told me that I needed to put away the suit I was wearing, together with the shirt and tie, in case I wore it and it was damaged. I would need to wear exactly the same outfit for the completion of the scene in 1967. So, for a whole year I was deprived of some of my clothes! It was all a matter of 'continuity'.

The sequel to that event came later when the director told me he had a problem. He said that everyone with a speaking part would normally be included in the 'credits' for the film. But, as I had no equity card (from the actor's union), he could not legally do that for me. 'But,' he said 'I've taken care of it another way.' He wouldn't tell me what he had done, and I had to wait for the première on 29 June 1968. I then discovered how he had solved his problem.

One scene in the film was of the young actress selling hats in a millinery department. She was doing a poor job of it. Cliff Richard (Jamie in the film) was her boyfriend and turned up in the middle of this difficult sale. He took over the sale, full of charm, and did a marvellous job and ended up by selling a hat! Then the lady customer looked at the female assistant and said, 'I shall certainly complain to the director of this store – Mr Rowlandson. The Rowlandsons are personal friends of mine!' Many of the audience at the première were personal friends of *mine* and that line 'brought the house down'! Unfortunately the film did not do very well on general release because it portrayed Cliff Richard as a thug – and to everyone who knew him (and his fans) it was totally out of character.

Shortly after the 1967 crusade was over, the Scipture Union, on behalf of the Evangelical Alliance, published a book entitled *On the Other Side*. Gavin Reid says: 'It proved to be a very low-key and realistic assessment of the situation. It recognised that it would probably prove a disappointment to many of its readers hoping to find some master plan for the conversion of England. It was critical of crusade evangelism, without discounting it entirely.'

I was undoubtedly one of its critics. For one reason I felt that the report had made some unfair and erroneous comments. For example, on page 93 there was mention of the apparent signs of increasing disillusionment in the churches. It then went on to cite the fact that one church had run five trains to the crusade in 1966 'but in 1967 they ran one train only'. The report did not go on to say that there were five weeks to the crusade in 1966, but only one week in 1967. There was also a rather snide comment on page 89 where it referred to evangelism being 'a group sitting around a polished desk in the wall-to-wall carpeted offices of an evangelistic association discussing a West End première for a film'. In the BGEA offices we found it rather hard to take this thinly disguised criticism of what we were doing. Bearing in mind 1 Corinthians 14:40 we were only trying to make sure that things were done 'decently and in order' – sadly not always the way that things were done in some other Christian organisations.

In my opinion the report put evangelism back 16 years. I had a hard time trying to keep the 'Thin Gold Line' from becoming fractured! Things did not really recover until the very successful Mission England in 1984. More about that later on . . .

CHAPTER THIRTEEN

1970–1972 AND SPRE-E73

I HAD a long letter from Mr Graham, dated 8 January 1971. In it he gave me some specific instructions relating to the British Board. He said:

> I would like to suggest that the entire British Board become more involved in the decision-making as it affects Britain. I was somewhat embarrassed to sit at the recent board meeting and practically no one made a statement except one or two. I also do not feel that it is within the best interest of the ministry for the board to be simply a 'rubber stamp'. Second I believe that the board chairman should be rotated about every two or three years. Third I suggest bringing two or three younger men on to the board to help us apply our ministry of evangelism to a contemporary society. Fourthly I suggest that the Board take up the matter of salaries of our staff. I feel that some of them are underpaid – even by British standards!

He continued:

> I feel that our financial commitment to Britain is still larger than our board in America is going to accept in the present economic situation. We can carry our present budget for the coming year, but I am thinking in the long term.
>
> Ruth and I just got back from our experience in California as marshalls of the Tournament of Roses. It was a fantastic opportunity to witness to the entire nation. I was able to speak twelve times.
>
> Finally you will be interested to know that I have accepted an invitation to come to Britain in early November to address the Institute of Directors at the Royal Albert Hall.

> Maurice! I have the greatest confidence in the leadership of yourself and of Jean Wilson. I also have the highest esteem for the vision of Bishop Goodwin Hudson as the chairman of the board.

Marilyn and I had been present in Pasadena, California for the Tournament of Roses. We sat in the public stands which were fairly close to the road. As the marshall's car passed us, we stood up and waved. Billy Graham spotted us immediately and called out 'Maurice!' and he gave us a warm wave.

Just a few months earlier Dr Sherwood Eliot Wirt (founder-editor of *Decision* magazine) had come to London. We took advantage of the occasion to hold a public welcome to him in Church House, Westminster. We called the occasion 'Meet the Editor'. It took the form of a dramatic presentation of how the magazine was produced and gave the editor a chance to meet and address his readership.

We also took advantage of the 350th anniversary of the sailing to America of the Pilgrim Fathers. I had asked Mr Graham if he would help us to commemorate the occasion and he readily agreed.

On 23 November 1970 we had produced a remarkable programme, in a somewhat unusual style for Mr Graham, at the Royal Albert Hall. The band of the Grenadier Guards provided the music and, after the singing of the National Anthems of America and Britain, Henry Hole (my colleague of many years' standing) produced a four-act pageant, specially written by C. Alan Stephens. It depicted the Plea for Freedom which led the Pilgrim Fathers, through many traumatic times, to sail for America and seek the disciplined freedom that they intended to set up there.

The chairman for the commemoration was Admiral Sir Horace Law, a fine Christian gentleman serving with the Royal Navy. He introduced the American Ambassador who made a speech and handed a message from the President of the United States to Mr Graham.

The augmented London Emmanuel Choir sang the Battle Hymn of the Republic before the chairman introduced Billy Graham as speaker. It was impossible for Mr Graham to address any meeting without making it a Gospel message which, on this occasion, led to an Act of Re-dedication by all those present. To close the programme Bishop A. W. Goodwin Hudson pronounced the Benediction. Then the band of the Grenadier Guards played us out with a musical finale.

Two publications enhanced the occasion. The first, on simulated parchment, was the programme which sketched the historical background of the occasion. The other was a mock-up of *The Pilgrim Times* dated September 1620 with the headline 'Mayflower sails for New World'. This 12-page newspaper contained many historical stories and the full text of Mr Graham's message at the Royal Albert Hall. The Revd Eddie Stride told about the spiritual history of the Pilgrim Fathers. The cost of the publication was covered by the sale of advertisements and it was a little incongruous to have a full-page advertisement, on page 2, by the Automobile Association inviting membership of the AA and saying 'You may need us today!'

Before the next major event in London in which Mr Graham was involved, there was one final opportunity to remind the public of his ministry. In May 1972 Ruth Graham came to London for a parental visit to her son Ned at Felsted School in Essex. During his stay there, and throughout his time in Britain, my wife and I were Ned's guardians. As we knew that Mrs Graham would be here at that time we decided that it would be a good idea to use the occasion to commemorate the great Harringay Crusade in 1954. Without any other specific reason, we booked the main ballroom of the Grosvenor Hotel in London and invited the Christian public to come and share the occasion with us. Hundreds accepted the invitation.

The programme started with a Salvation Army band playing melodies from the Harringay hymns. After a suitable introduction during which Ruth Graham spoke, we showed the Harringay film story *Souls in Conflict* and had a slide interview with the star of the film, Joan Winmill. We then produced a 'chain' of testimonies. Five people each told how they had come to Christ. The first was converted at the Harringay Arena. She had led a friend to Christ and so on through all five – one linking with the other – bringing us right up to date. It showed how the witness of Harringay had spread through the generations.

Following the Harringay reunion, and during these preparation days for Spre-e73, Ruth and Billy Graham came again to London for another parental visit to Ned. I met them at London Airport and took them straight on to Felsted School. On the way there I had an intimate insight into the amazing 'public relations' that Mr Graham has always had. In the car, en route to Felsted, Ruth Graham briefed him extensively about all that he needed to know concerning Ned's school. She reminded him of the name of the headmaster; the names of Ned's friends; of his teachers; his House; his sporting interests, etc. And in typical fashion, Mr Graham remembered all he had been told. When he arrived at Felsted, it was as though he had been a regular visitor. Ruth and Billy Graham made a great team!

I had a telephone call from Mr Graham on 23 March 1972. He told me that he had a burden on his heart for Ireland. He asked me to assemble a group of influential leaders and to take them to Belfast and Dublin. Our brief would be to find out if it would be feasible for a crusade to be held in either place.

With Sir Eric Richardson, Viscount Brentford, Mr Neville Knox (the town clerk of Harrogate and a big supporter of Billy Graham) and – at Mr Graham's request – an American, Mr David Enghauser, we flew to Belfast. We met government and church leaders there. The day after we left there was a bomb in the hotel in which we had stayed. From there we went to Dublin and met with Miss Margaret Hamilton-Reid, a significant protestant leader, and a large group of inter-denominational church leaders. After we had had discussions with as many Irish representatives as we could, our report back to Mr Graham was negative. We came to the conclusion that, for Mr Graham to visit either Northern or Southern Ireland could add confusion to a situation already very confused. He accepted our judgement as he, and we, realised that there was already a strong Christian witness – especially in Ulster.

* * * *

The fourth digression from the stories is about my appointment in 1971 as a magistrate (Justice of the Peace). My appointment was due to Major General D. J. Wilson Haffenden, and Bishop A. W. Goodwin Hudson nominating me. Both of them felt that I should receive this honour and be allowed to contribute to public service in this way. They had sought the approval of Billy Graham, and he had graciously agreed.

Any appointment as a Justice of the Peace (JP) is voluntary – unpaid – and for life. I was appointed and sworn in by a judge of the High Court on 22 March 1971 and I sat in court for the first time seven days later at the Harrow Court House in the Gore Division of Middlesex. At the time I had practically no experience and very little training.

No legal qualification is required to be a JP. You simply sit in judgement on your peers, using fact and evidence as the essential means of determining guilt and sentence. If a 'point of law' is applicable, there is the clerk of the court sitting just in front of you, and he will explain that to the Bench. The Justices must then accord to it.

A bench consists, normally, of three Justices and they – in effect – act as judge and jury. They try cases from parking fines to murder (the latter to see if 'there is a case to answer'). Some 92 per cent of all criminal cases begin and end in a magistrate's court and it is speedy justice. If you offend on Monday, it is probable that you will be tried and sentenced by the following Monday.

Once I had sat I attended court most weeks – either for a day or a half day. Attendance at court became a way of life and yet another 'life-saver' to me in the high-pressure life in which I lived and moved. There were occasions, of course, when court duties clashed with my responsibilities at the BGEA. On those occasions I had to find a substitute magistrate to sit for me.

In 1983 we moved to Frinton-on-Sea, and I applied to be transferred to the Tendring District Court at Clacton-on-Sea. They were so short of magistrates that I sat for the last time at Harrow on 24 December 1983 and sat for the first time at Clacton on 19 January 1984. Normally a Bench transfer can take up to two years to complete so I was particularly fortunate in these circumstances. Ten years later I was elected as chairman of the Bench of Magistrates at Tendring and found myself sitting almost daily either in court or upon some committee.

Because of my appointment as chairman, Marilyn and I received an invitation to the Royal Garden Party at Buckingham Palace on 13 July 1993. It was a terribly wet day, but a great experience nonetheless. Unfortunately we were not amongst those selected to talk to Her Majesty. Had we been, I am sure a conversation about Billy Graham would have developed!

A similar situation had arisen a short time before when, as a serving magistrate, I had been invited to St James's Palace for a reception to meet the Queen. As she walked along the lines of magistrates she spoke at length to every third or fourth one. I calculated that I would not be the one for a long conversation with the Queen. In the event our conversation was very short. All she asked me was, 'Which Bench do you serve?' to which I replied 'Gore, Ma'am'. That is all I said to the Queen on that occasion!

The day coincided with the BAFTA film awards at the Wembley Conference Centre. The 'star' (Jeannette Clift) of our film *The Hiding Place* had been nominated for the 'Best Actress' award. The commercial distributors of the film insisted that I should be there. The Queen's meeting with magistrates ended at 6pm. The awards ceremony started at 7.30pm. In between I had to change into evening dress, and drive (in the rush-hour traffic) to Wembley to arrive on time. In fact, I was a few minutes late. Having nowhere else to change, I found a convenient bush in St James's Park and hoped that I would not fall foul of some observant policeman. In the event, I got safely changed from my lounge suit to evening dress. It was quite an experience. I am sure that not many people will have used St James's Park as a changing room.

My 24 years as a magistrate were fascinating and vital to my health and sanity! Although I didn't *enjoy* sending people to prison, I did find a real sense of satisfaction in the work of a magistrate and felt privileged to be able to do it. It did not take long for my fellow-magistrates, either in Harrow or Clacton, to learn that I was a committed Christian. That gave numerous opportunities for witness and it was also a useful service to the community. It helped me enormously in coping with the pressures of my daily work with and for Billy Graham.

* * * *

Which brings us to the next major event with Billy Graham in the UK. I think that during the planning for Spre-e73 I came closer to the heart of Billy Graham than at any other time.

It all started in 1972 when Billy Graham asked George Wilson to invite me to Dallas Texas to share in the great Explo72 event to be organised by Campus Crusade for Christ. It was an unexpected invitation and one that I greatly appreciated. I had seen an announcement about this seven-day event in the magazine *Christianity Today*. Billy Graham was advertised as the keynote speaker. I had looked at those advertisements with some degree of envy because I could not be there. So my joy in receiving the invitation knew no bounds.

When my son Gary heard that I was going to Dallas he said that he wanted to be there too. He had saved up enough money for his fare and, as there would be an extra bed in my hotel room, accommodation would not be a problem. He followed me five days after I had left. We were both involved in the daily training programmes and as stewards at the evening events in the stadium.

Day by day the morning was given over to intensive training in personal evangelism. We were encouraged to share the Gospel by using the *Four Spiritual Laws*. 'Witness to others in the power of the Holy Spirit and leave the results to God' we were told. Then, in the afternoon, two by two we went out on to the streets of Dallas to witness to whosoever would listen to us. It was exciting and spiritually productive work.

Afterwards I said that, in an evangelistic crusade, the counsellors were taught how to lead someone to Christ *after* the evangelist had done his job. Here at Explo72 we were taught how to do the job of an evangelist. It was a whole new ball game.

At the packed stadium each evening there was lively singing, bands, testimonies of what had gone on through the day, and a closing message (with an appeal) from Billy Graham. On the last night the stadium was plunged into total darkness as Billy Graham lit a candle whose flame he passed on to others on the platform. They dispersed in different directions and passed on the flame to candle-holders in the audience. With each passing of the flame to another it was not long before the vast and entire stadium was ablaze with the light of candles – 25,000 'candle power' – as we sang 'It only takes a spark to get a fire burning . . . pass it on'. It was an emotive evening.

Earlier that same evening Gary, who was stewarding on the opposite side of the stadium to me, walked over to see and greet me. It was, virtually, the only time we met at Explo72 (except in our bedroom at night) and he was only with me for five minutes. Later, when Campus Crusade released the filmed story of Explo72, Gary and I were astounded to see that the cameras had caught that special moment, in the stadium, of the two of us together!

I came back to Britain 'on fire' with Explo72 and deeply convicted that something of a similar nature should be made possible to young people in my own country. From the pictures I had taken at Explo, I assembled another sound strip *The Story of Explo72* and I showed it around wherever I could (including to audiences at the Keswick Convention). I wanted to encourage British people to be inspired with the same vision as I had had. It was at Keswick that I first met Charitie and Victor Pippett from Australia. They too had been at Explo72 and, when they heard of my dream and vision, they encouraged me to keep going.

It did not take long. I soon began to get telephone calls: 'Can't we have something like that over here?' On Monday, 15 July 1972, I telephoned Billy Graham to share my vision with him and – specifically – to ask him, 'If we have an event like that in Britain, would you be willing to come?' I followed it up with a letter, extending a firm invitation to him. I had no authority to do this from my board, nor from any other individual or group. The Lord had just laid this heavy burden on my heart and I felt led to take executive action. I hoped that others would back me up when the time came.

On 8 August, 1972 I had a reply from Mr Graham. He said:

> Yes, I think there ought to be an 'Explo-style' gathering in Britain. I think it could possibly be sponsored jointly by BGEA and about a dozen other youth organisations such as Campus Crusade, Inter-Varsity, etc., if they are willing. Also the Evangelical Alliance could be brought in. It might be a series of events. Perhaps we could have Earls Court for a weekend – with Trafalgar Square, a torchlight parade, singing some of the new and more popular songs like 'Pass it on', with all kinds of signs, placards, etc. It would be great if we could mobilise all the Christian forces of Britain for one great

> outpouring and set a goal of 200,000 young people in the march. Naturally no expense should be spared.
>
> Unless the Christian forces of Britain rise up to do something dramatic like this I am informed on the highest levels that Britain is in deep and dire and desperate difficulty. It seems to me that this ought to be organised and planned for late next August or early September. These are just top of the head thoughts. Naturally I would be delighted to participate as one of the speakers – one of the leaders – honorary chairman, or anything you like. I am certain that I could get my board to help finance it. You might want to get a different name from 'Explo'.

Before the next letter arrived, a great tragedy was to hit my family and cause the 'Thin Gold Line' to waver considerably. Following Mr Graham's letter in August, I set about making known his acceptance of my invitation. In accordance with his wishes I first contacted the Evangelical Alliance who, true to form at that time, really didn't want to know. Inter-Varsity Fellowship said that they had their own programmes and couldn't officially back it. The only organisation who responded enthusiastically was Campus Crusade for Christ. But then, Explo72 had been their dream child like this event was mine. Many felt that the event had been imposed upon them and there was great criticism from those who misunderstood the project. I told those antagonists that it's only because I have lived so close to the event, that I have not been disillusioned by all the criticism.

It seemed to me that the only way forward was to form an ad hoc committee who would catch the ball and run with it. Youth was the keyword, and I considered it important to have a young chairman and members who represented that constituency. David Pickford was selected as the chairman with about 26 others – mostly young – to help him. We met on Monday 4 September in our offices in Camden Road. Only Dr Walter Smyth from the Billy Graham Team met with us and he brought us Mr Graham's greetings.

The Board of the BGEA decided that they needed to take control of the project and formed a separate, older, committee under the chairmanship of Mr Philip Henman – a man with great business experience and a capable man. They felt that he would be the right person to see it through. Someone facetiously remarked that they saw this special 'senior' committee as the 'House of Lords' while the younger working committee they saw as the 'House of Commons' and the BGEA's own board a 'Privy Council'!

One problem was to find a name for the event. Mr Graham himself had urged that we move away from 'Explo'. Names such as 'Bang on'; 'Hit it'; 'Outspell 73' and even 'ReachOut' were bandied about and, one by one were rejected. Then Bishop Goodwin Hudson turned to me and, in his characteristic and bluff way said: 'Jamboree! That's what we want, or something like it. Get out your Roget's *Thesaurus* and see what it can offer.'

I got the book and turned up 'jamboree'. About eight alternatives were offered like 'knees up', 'shindig' and 'carnival'. Last in the list as I read down was 'spree'. 'Spree73' I said 'had a ring about it' but, when I looked it up in the dictionary, 'spree' meant 'a drunken orgy; bacchanalia'.

'What a pity we can't use that,' I said. It had such a flowing 'sound' to it. As I spoke, Jean Wilson was standing in the doorway and she asked, 'Why not? S-P-R is Spiritual, and R-E means re-emphasis. Spiritual Re-emphasis! Isn't that what it's all about?' We instantly agreed – provided that whenever it was used, the hyphen was always inserted between the first and second 'e'. So *Spre-e73* it became! The ad hoc committee could now begin to talk about an event with a name!

As we got to that point in the committee, the door opened and my secretary, Dawn Chandler, appeared and asked me to come out. I replied, 'Later, Dawn. I'm in the middle of the committee right now.' She insisted, 'I think you had better come now,' and I got up from the committee and went out with her.

As I came out, my wife Marilyn was waiting for me in my office. Gently, she told me that the police had been on the telephone earlier that morning to say that our dear daughter Cherylyn had met with a car accident, just outside Colchester. She had been returning from a Christian conference in Swanwick, and was coming back to Frinton to work in a hotel for the summer. She had died instantly from her injuries. It was terrible news. I went straight back into the committee and told them. I asked them for their prayers. The devil was launching an attack upon our onslaught on his kingdom.

Dr Walter Smyth came out of the committee to comfort us and I told him that, for me, Spre-e73 would become a memorial event for my daughter.

What a mixture of emotions and feelings followed! At first there was the inevitable reaction: 'It can't be true. They must have made a mistake – maybe it's mistaken identity.' But gradually, the recognition that it is true sinks home, and you realise the delicate thread upon which all of us live and move and have our being. The one true comfort we had was that Cherylyn had a deep and real faith in the Lord Jesus Christ as her Saviour and Lord. So for us, we knew that she was now in His presence and more alive than she had ever been on earth. Human sorrow is real, but spiritual joy can enable us to cope at a time of loss. How the event affected our younger son, Julian, is described in Chapter 21. It is then that you realise that all you have said you believed over many years is true. God *is* the God of all comfort, and He does sustain in time of need. It was the reality of that experience which enabled us to live through those early days.

The next few days were some of the saddest and hardest to live through. But the Lord gave strength to us at the funeral. We were encouraged by Ruth Graham's presence with us. Later there was a memorial service at Cherylyn's college in Cheltenham which also brought encouragement to us. Later Dr Sherwood Wirt, editor of *Decision* magazine, asked Cherylyn's mother to write a piece about the way she coped with the loss. It was published in the magazine and afterwards there were a great many requests for a reprint of it.*

Meanwhile the ad hoc committee had decided that a general director should be appointed to run Spre-e73. We interviewed 19 possible candidates but only one was suitable. We invited him to take the post and he accepted. Then, in the eleventh hour, a death in his company gave him the chance of the top position. It was offered to him and he realised that he might not have another

---

* Copies can be obtained from the BGEA (UK). See page 273 for the address

opportunity if he didn't accept it there and then. Because of that he had to pull out. With absolute unanimity the committee agreed to invite me to be the general director of the event. I accepted the committee's wishes and said: 'I want to see Christians as more useful to their ministers and congregations. I want to see them excited about their faith and able to articulate what they believe and why.'

I was asked why I had not consulted others before launching the plans for Spre-e73. 'Whom do you consult at such times?' I asked. 'When the Lord gives a vision does He not give the drive to carry it out? Did Wilberforce consult anybody before he set out to free the slaves? Did Florence Nightingale consult anybody before she went out to serve the soldiers in the Crimea? In short, how many events that have shaped history have been the result of consultation?' Also it was probable that nobody else but the BGEA would have been prepared to put up the finances.

From that point onwards it was 'full steam ahead'. The complete story of Spre-e73 has been written by David Coomes in his book *Spre-e73* so, apart from one story about chairs which has not been told elsewhere there is no need to repeat the full story here.

We discovered that we would need some 30,000 chairs to be put on the arena floor at Earls Court. The cost of hiring these would be considerable. John Dillon hit upon the idea of buying a 'job lot' of chairs, and then selling them to churches afterwards.

In order to select the best chair for the job, John had about 12/15 sample chairs, from different manufacturers, delivered to the office. Then, one night, after everybody had gone home and there was no one about below, he dropped the chairs one by one out of our second-floor window on to the concrete pavement below. Every chair, except one, shattered under this treatment! The one that survived this ordeal was manufactured by Remploy. John concluded a deal with them for chairs at £1.46 each. After Spre-e73 was over, they were offered to churches at £2.50 each (as against a normal price of some £10 each). They were snapped up, and Spre-e chairs are to be found in churches, and church halls, all over the country.

On the last day of Spre-e, we needed to stack the chairs ready for collection. Earls Court quoted £3000 for this job. Henry Hole, as chief steward, had an inspiration. As the meeting finished he came to the microphone and instructed everyone to turn around, pick up their chair and walk to the left or right, where stewards would supervise the stacking. It was all completed in 10 minutes – and, at no cost! It was a brilliant manoeuvre!

I considered it to be of major importance that all the ad hoc committee should acknowledge the graciousness shown by Mr Graham as they took decisions that were hurtful to him. For example, they wanted neither Cliff Barrows nor Bev Shea, two of the stalwarts who always gave their entire support to Mr Graham in everything he did. The committee too, wanted to give Mr Graham the subjects on which he should speak. They did not want any American influence to dominate the planning – although that was exactly what I *had* wanted.

Early in 1973 (before Spre-e73) Mr Graham wrote to me again:

> I just talked with the American Chief of Chaplains in Washington and the Chief of the European Operations happened to be in his office. We had a chat (about Spre-e73) – he is very enthusiastic. He said they will definitely cooperate. It might be preferable to have Bishop Goodwin Hudson go and see him in Germany. He should go in his bishop's stock and dog-collar. If they were so disposed they could probably bring hundreds (of servicemen from Germany) over – and I think they are so disposed at the moment. If the Bishop, as a rather high-level churchman from England, contacted them it would give them a great impetus. They are often afraid of anything non-denominational – though they know that this programme is similar to Explo.
>
> I will be most delighted to speak each night at the Earls Court – but would not want to be limited to the subjects assigned me. I will certainly bring those thoughts into my address each evening but may not feel that I can make that my entire address. I have learned long ago that I just am not capable of being put in a strait-jacket on subjects. This is one of my weaknesses and I hope they will accept it.

It was the fresh and innovative approach of our American brethren that had so 'set me on fire' at Explo72. I had wanted the entire team to be imported to London – and they would have been willing to come. As it was the programme was taken over by British young leaders. As far as the training programme was concerned, we reached a compromise and I was allowed to bring in half of the training team from the USA. The other half would be British. Strangely enough, when Spre-e73 was all over and we organised a survey to be answered by all the participants, the American training team received high assessment, while the British training team just 'scraped by'.

I quickly realised that being general director was no sinecure. 'The buck stops here' as the Americans would say. One day I telephoned Mr Graham to ask if there was an American member of the team who could come and help me. He immediately assigned John Dillon to that task. He could not have sent a better lieutenant. John and I hit it off from the very beginning and he was a tower of strength to me in the many decisions – and quick responses – which had to be made. After all, we only had until August 1973 and it was already February! At the time I did not fully realise the significance of his arrival. There were light-hearted moments too as we worked together. Some of them are recalled in *Life with Billy*.

Three times between February and July 1973 Mr Graham asked that we cancel the event. Each time John Dillon took the phone from me and explained in no uncertain terms that we had already gone too far to cancel. Each time, Mr Graham accepted John's judgement. It might have been different had I been left on my own. I could not have spoken with the same authority as John Dillon.

When Spre-e73 actually started it was clear to me that Mr Graham really felt the absence of Cliff Barrows and Bev Shea. The British committee had tried to pour him into their mould, and it simply did not work. In my opinion, that, coupled with the refusal to use all American seminar leaders, were two of the failure points of the event – although in many other ways it was highly successful. There are countless people in Britain and across the continent of Europe – who were young people in 1972 – who look back upon the event as the catalyst that changed their lives. So, whatever the failings that I felt personally, God used the event in a remarkable way both to bring people to the Lord and to teach young people how to witness.

In my book *I'm Going to Ask You . . .* is a testimony of one man whose life was dramatically changed. He was the treasurer of the

Mafia and his lifestyle changed from a life of depravity to a life of full-time service for the Lord.

As Spre-e73 came to an end, it was clear that we had been seriously over budget. Although we had kept a careful check on a day-by-day basis, and it appeared that all was well, during the event itself there were many unknown and last minute extra costs. For example there was a 5-figure bill from Earls Court which was considerably more than we had anticipated – chiefly because of the items we *had* to have but which were outside the terms of our 250-page agreement with them. Every additional item was charged. The final accounting disclosed that we were almost £100,000 'in the red'.

Mr Graham wrote to me on 3 October 1973:

> I am going to have to have a great deal more information from you to present to our American Board which meets on 20 October. There is quite a division of thought about this deficit on Spre-e73. Neither George Wilson nor I have the authority to do anything about it.
>
> Please, therefore, give me a complete breakdown of the bills that you owe. It is terribly embarrassing for all of us that the budget got so completely out of hand. Perhaps, unfairly, we gave Jean Wilson far too much responsibility. We needed a full-time accountant, using modern methods and technology in keeping the accounts.

He concluded his letter on a positive note:

> We just concluded in Raleigh, North Carolina, and had a glorious time, especially with the university students. More than 10,000 people responded to the appeal in the eight days.

To end Spre-e73 in that sad way was a great sorrow to me. After I had sent Mr Graham the information he had asked for, he wrote again:

> I have studied the financial statement concerning Spre-e73. Frankly, I do not understand it. Perhaps at the Team meeting you can give a small group of us a confidential explanation. In the meantime I have instructed George to settle these bills.
>
> I am most hopeful that you will give very careful attention to the planning of the budget of BGEA for the next twelve months. I

> can assure you that the executive committee of BGEA is very unhappy. It was only after careful explanation and a defense of you and the Spre-e committee that they have agreed to continue our British work for another year.
>
> I am looking forward to meeting with the British Board when I come to London on 10 December.

It was a gentle censure which I took to heart and John Dillon and I set about assembling a file of positive reactions to the event, which we could present to the Team Meeting when we met in December. Two days later another letter came from Mr Graham in which he said that he would be unable to come to the board meeting on 10 December. In the meantime, the Spre-e73 committee had planned and held their 'wrap-up' meeting in early November. They expressed their deep gratitude to Mr Graham for settling the outstanding bills.

The reason why Mr Graham could not be with us on 10 December was that he now needed to be in Geneva for meetings on that day. This coincided with the period when Marilyn and I were taking all our family to America – amongst other things – to attend a Team meeting and then to spend Christmas with her parents in Phoenix, Arizona. Marilyn and I left London on 22 November 1973 (the family followed later). We went first to that year's Team meeting at Porte St Lucie in Florida. The only mention of Spre-e73 at the Team meeting came through a report of the event that Billy Graham had invited me to give. He said nothing more to me about the financial problem. From Porte St Lucie Marilyn went to Minneapolis to spend time with her brother's family there. Meanwhile I flew to Switzerland. Billy Graham had written to me on 31 October to say:

> I have just heard that you may not be able to be at the board meeting in London on 10 December. I think it is rather important for you to be at both the Spre-e committee in November and at the 10 December meeting – even if you have to fly back from America for them.

In the event the London Board meeting never happened. Instead, the board was invited by Mr Graham to meet him in Geneva. On my arrival in Geneva there were some preliminary meetings with Billy Graham. Bishop A. W. Goodwin Hudson, (chairman of the British Board) together with Dr Walter Smyth, Grady Wilson and Cliff Barrows and I were there. It was a very positive meeting when, once again, the financial problems of Spre-e73 were put behind us and we looked forward to an active and productive period ahead of us.

I had an earlier letter from Mr Graham (in October 1973) in which he had urged that there should be some new, and younger, board members appointed to the British Board. He said:

> I am convinced that if David Pickford, Sir Kirby Laing, Douglas Malton, Charles Green, Richard Bewes and Michael Baughen were brought on to the board, they would not only strengthen it, but bring new ideas and new life to our ministry in Britain. Maurice! Just as George Wilson has had to adapt himself to a very strong American Board I think you will have to learn to adapt to a strong British Board. This is not so easy for any of us, yet I feel it is God's way as we get older and as the organisation grows and becomes institutionalised.

Then, in his own distinctive handwriting he added this note:

> Perhaps we ought to plan a full-scale board meeting in December and a day of planning with Dave Foster and others on a future Spre-e.

That last sentence was the formulative birth of two similar youth-oriented events – the great Eurofest in Brussels in 1975 and Christoval in Essen, Germany in 1976. In both of those events, those of us from London were deeply involved. The suggestion that there should be a board meeting in December came to fruition with the meeting in Geneva.

As a result of Mr Graham's letter in October 1973, we extended invitations to most of the men on his list but had passed over a few who did not really come within the range of 'youth'. Now in Geneva these new board members were invited to join with us and Richard Bewes (who ultimately was the only one who survived as a board member), David Bubbers, Robin Oake, and Gilbert Kirby met with the established board members and Mr Graham and some of his colleagues. David Pickford and Jack Stordy had been invited, but were unable to join us. The day after the board meeting I flew back to America to join the family for our Christmas plans.

One of the outcomes of the meeting in Geneva was that all the American Team members (including Mr Graham) were now to be considered as ex officio board members whenever they were in London. Mr Graham said that they would have the privilege of attending the meeting and speaking but without a vote. In his letter of 3 October he ended: 'I continue to get good reactions from Spre-e73.'

One of my more treasured letters from Mr Graham is one that came immediately after Spre-e73, and before the events described above. It was dated 3 September 1973. In it he said:

> I've never seen anyone with a greater dedication to a Christian project than you gave to Spre-e. It was certainly largely your vision and labor that brought it about. I would deeply appreciate you thanking Jean Wilson for the many extra hours she spent – to John Dillon for his willingness to carry the load with you, and the many others that participated. I hope you will especially greet the office staff and apologise to them for me, that I was unable to stay and come and greet them personally.
>
> I think the overall impact of Spre-e will be positive. It is extremely difficult to evaluate such a conference immediately afterwards. It will take several months to see it in its true perspective.
>
> However, I think it is very important public relations wise that you frankly admit that some things could have been done better, and that we will learn from the mistakes of Spre-e.

He then went on to evaluate some of the lessons learned from the event. Most of his observations arose from the 'control' exercised by the young organising committee. Had we followed more closely the ambience of Explo72, I feel sure that it would have been a different story. For example, a leaflet had been designed to publicise the event. That leaflet had been based entirely upon the striking publicity for Explo. The British committee would not allow us to use that leaflet but, instead insisted upon rather third-rate and unexciting 'newspaper-style' publicity. To me it was neither attractive nor appealing. Had the more colourful leaflet been used, I believe that our 15,000 numbers would have been boosted to well over 25,000. However, by now it was academic and we would never know.

I agreed with all of Mr Graham's conclusions and, with John Dillon, felt that we both knew the reasons why Spre-e73 had been less successful than we had hoped. But there was nothing we could do about it.

Finally, in his letter, he went on to lead us into the next phase of our ministry. In this the 'Thin Gold Line' would clearly be continuing in the foreseeable future and I still would have a part to play. He said:

> Now I write concerning the future of the BGEA in Britain. I think I am in favour of continuing the ministry. I would like to see at least ten new men added to the board. In my judgment, board meetings should be held at a more comfortable hotel and all the expenses of the board members should be met. I was terribly impressed by the new leadership that emerged in SPRE-E. This may be one of the more lasting results.

He concluded on a personal note:

> You and Marilyn certainly deserve a holiday. I hope you will take a couple of weeks rest, perhaps in the South of France – at our expense!
>
> With warmest personal affection and admiration, I am your co-labourer in witnessing to the saving grace and power of our Lord Jesus Christ.

The 'paid for' holiday was a nice thought but, for one reason or another, we did not take advantage of it.

CHAPTER FOURTEEN

AFTERMATH, FINANCES AND MISSION ENGLAND PREPARATIONS

SPRE-E73 SPAWNED Eurofest75 in Brussels and, in turn, that inspired Christoval in Essen, Germany in 1976. In a sense all of these had been the result of Explo72. One cannot help but wonder if Bill Bright, the founder of Campus Crusade for Christ, ever imagined what a gigantic impact his vision would have both in America and across Europe.

The stories of Eurofest and Christoval have already been told in separate picture books published in the USA by the BGEA – now out of print. Two stories, however, may not have been related before. One concerns the public address system used at Eurofest and the other is about Bishop Festo Kivengere.

With nine different languages to contend with, the cost of separate translation systems was prohibitive. David Rennie (from the UK), technical advisor to the Billy Graham team, came up with a unique solution.

He suggested that, in the main hall, each different language should be fed to a separate and directional loudspeaker pointing directly downwards. His theory was that delegates would walk around the hall until they heard a language that they recognised. Then they would sit down on the floor, right there, for the duration of the session. I tried it out with the English language and found that it worked perfectly. It was a low-cost but exceedingly practical and efficient method of dealing with all the languages.

The story about Festo Kivengere is very 'cloak and dagger'! We were in the City of Bath visiting our son Julian (who was at Monkton Combe School) when I got an emergency telephone call! The call was from Dr T. W. Wilson and he gave me some very disturbing news. In 1972 Idi Amin, the evil dictator of Uganda, had started a programme of violence which was to continue for several years. In 1977 Archbishop Janani Luwum was detained and murdered, and a rapidly escalating series of events threatened many other church leaders.

Just about the same time as Christoval a rumour was circulated that Bishop Festo Kivengere had also been murdered. T. W. Wilson was deeply concerned and telephoned the bishop in Uganda from his home in America. Relieved that the rumour was untrue, they had a guarded talk for no one knew who else might be listening. Fifteen minutes later Dr Wilson telephoned back again but there was no answer. Immediately his concern was rekindled and he wondered if, in the interim, Festo had been taken by Amin's people.

For the next 48 hours it was as though the Kivengeres had dropped off the face of the earth. In reality, Festo and Mera had left their home between the first and second call and had been taken by car 'going like the clappers' he said, through the streets of Kampala, heading for their home in Kabale. When they got there however, their house had been watched and already searched three times that day. If he and Mera went there he could have been immediately under house arrest – which in Ugandan terms almost assured execution.

Things had happened so fast that events caught up with Festo and Mera. Their friends urged them to flee, and after praying together, they decided to take their chance and get out. They did not unpack the suitcases with which they had returned home. They didn't stop to collect anything, but of course, they left everything behind – personal papers, sermon notes, books, and all their possessions and furniture.

Eventually they crossed the border between Rwanda and Uganda and they were safe . . . for the time being. Later when they tried to fly out to Europe, the immigration officer at Kingali Airport demanded to know why their passports did not have a proper stamp. He declared them 'illegal immigrants'. For that the punishment could have been deportation back to Uganda. But God was in it, for the young pastor who had brought them to the airport told the immigration officer that Festo's exit from Uganda 'had been on a Sunday' – implying that there had been lax control at immigration on that day.

Surprisingly the explanation was accepted and Festo and his wife were able to fly out to Nairobi where they found several more Ugandan bishops who had fled there.

At that point I had that first telephone call in Bath. T. W. Wilson brought me up to speed on the current situation and the ongoing implications. No one knew at that time whether Festo would come to London or wherever. All T. W. Wilson wanted me to know was that, at any moment, I might need to go to the airport at short notice to meet him and ensure his safety during his time in Britain. It was a wonderful example of the way in which the Billy Graham Team looked after their friends. Festo and his family were eventually brought to safety and it was a privilege to have been involved in the situation. It was particularly encouraging to find Festo as one of the speakers at Christoval. He gave a masterly address which, if he had finished at its climax, would have been one of the best addresses given. Unfortunately he launched enthusiastically into one passage and then got carried away completely. The red warning light on the platform (telling him his time was up) flashed urgently to stop him but to no avail. In his enthusiasm he had placed his Bible over the light and did not see it. The ensuing story is best told in Anne Coomes' words in *Festo Kivengere*.

> Richard Bewes, platform chairman, could see the Americans on the platform beginning to twitch. The minutes ticked by. They stared at Festo's back in anguish, trying to make him *feel* their urgency. One finally leaned over and pleaded with Richard to 'have a word with Festo'. Bewes gaped helplessly: Bishop Festo was in full flow before 8000 people. 'I can't!' he hissed. More minutes went by. The Americans were by now in torment. 'The programme! We've got to get on with the programme!'
>
> Desperately, Richard Bewes devised a plan. After all, the platform was very high off the ground, and edged with huge floral displays

> . . . these would provide some cover, at least. So he slipped off his chair and, on his stomach, wriggled slowly across to the pulpit. If the congregation didn't see him, neither did Festo – not until Bewes reached out a hand, grabbed his ankle and squeaked 'STOP!' Bishop Festo froze in astonishment.
>
> Then he rallied: 'The Lord bless you!' and left the pulpit, leaving Bewes supine on the platform in relief. He stood up without thinking a moment later and many in the audience blinked in astonishment: where had he come from?

But to return to the financial concerns of the BGEA, in 1972 Bishop Goodwin Hudson and I had flown to New York at Mr Graham's request when Mr Graham first put forward his idea that the overseas offices should become 'agencies' of the BGEA rather than 'branches' of the Minneapolis office. He reinforced this two years later in a letter:

> I would like to see a cutback made in all the offices around the world. Why cannot they all be made 'agencies' of the BGEA? London could be the first experiment. We just cannot continue to pour out all this money.

Our immediate need now was to demonstrate that we could save money. To do that would mean cutting the present staff from 28 to 5! At first that seemed an impossible task but, by October 1974 we had achieved our target. We did this in three ways. First, we discontinued the practice of keeping statistics. That had been a major part of our work hitherto – regarded by George Wilson as giving essential information to the BGEA. But to keep the type of statistics that Minneapolis required needed about four staff members.

Second, we changed the philosophy of keeping a mailing list. George Wilson's thinking was that every name and address – however it may have come to us – should be added to our ever-growing mailing list. He once remarked, 'Take away all my offices, all my equipment and all my staff but leave me my mailing list and I'll have it all back in twelve months.' That may have been true in America but it was a doubtful philosophy for the UK. So we sent a 'trial' mailing to some 14,000 people to see what sort of response we got. We had had no identifiable response from this

14,000 over the past three years. Ironically – and to confuse the issue – only *one* letter came back from that trial mailing, and with it a cheque for £1000 was enclosed 'for Spre-e73'! In spite of that we agreed to reduce the numbers on the mailing list from around 27,000 to about 13,000!

Postage alone was an enormous saving. We could save too on printing costs because 27,000 was an uneconomic number to print. So, from 1975 we decided that there should not be a separate British edition of *Decision* magazine. From that year we used the American edition which was printed and mailed in the USA. Our colleagues in America were careful to introduce some articles of British interest into the international edition.

Third, we invited International Films to become an 'agency' of World Wide Films in the UK. This meant we could pass to them all the storage, maintenance, booking, distribution and finances of the film ministry from which we simply received a royalty.

The changes within the routine of the office enabled us to cut back to just 8 staff with an enormous saving on our monthly subsidy from Minneapolis. All of this coincided with a change of management from the head office. George Wilson, who had been in charge of the London office since its inception, was now taken off overseas responsibilities to concentrate on the continued expansion of the Minneapolis Office. Dr Walter Smyth was to be our new supervisor.

This made a change in the style of management. When George Wilson was in charge he came to London about twice a year. Whenever he came I had never done anything right! However hard I tried, he could always find areas in which I could improve. It meant a constant 'honing up' of all our operations so that we could continue to claim 1 Corinthians 14:40.

Once Walter Smyth took over I never did anything wrong! He was always a great encourager and he gave me constant support during his many visits (far more than George's) to the London office. Of the two, I think I learned most from George Wilson.

A big change took place as the result of another letter I received from Mr Graham on 18 June 1975. In it he said:

> I would deeply appreciate it if for future appeals/prayer letters – from this point on – you would draft a suggested letter for me.

> I am so far removed from the British scene that it is extremely difficult for me to write such a letter. I can put in small personal items but when it comes to the major content and the appeal itself, I think you or some other person there should draw it up for my approval.

The routine as far as compiling the prayer letters was concerned was a simple one. Every month I received the monthly prayer/appeal letter sent out by the American office (in the UK we only circulated three letters a year). From those letters I would compile a composite letter, omitting those paragraphs which did not apply to the UK. Then I wrote and inserted a few extra paragraphs with UK news. To that compilation I added any paragraphs that Mr Graham had sent me. The finished letter was then sent to him for his approval and signature. Rarely did he change anything that I had written. After all, the bulk of the letter was taken from what he had already written before for the USA.

Then, one day, I had a telephone call from Billy Graham who was in Paris. He told me that he had been talking with George Wilson about the future of the office in Minneapolis. George had told Mr Graham that he needed an understudy who could be his right-hand man. He wanted someone to fulfil two functions. First, to relieve the heavy and constant pressure under which he worked. Second, he was anxious that there should be a plan of 'succession' in place should anything happen to him.

Billy Graham came straight to the point with me – and virtually took my breath away! 'Would you,' he asked, 'consider coming to Minneapolis to understudy George Wilson with the ultimate thought that you should succeed him in due course?' It was probably the least likely proposal that I had ever expected to hear, and I was deeply moved that both George and Mr Graham should feel I would be capable for the task. He said he would get back to me later on.

I came to think that it was one of those many 'ideas' that Billy Graham had from time to time. I am sure he had shared this one with me on the impulse of the moment. Later, as he listened to the advice and guidance given to him by other Team members he probably realised then that I was hardly suited for the job. Certainly

I never heard it mentioned again! I don't think I had either the experience or the wisdom. I looked upon George Wilson as someone quite exceptional. I feel sure it would never have worked out, and in many ways I was greatly relieved that it went no further.

Out of the blue an invitation came from the BBC to plan a *Songs of Praise* programme using the Billy Graham musicians – Cliff Barrows and George Beverly Shea. The idea had come from a Scottish Minister, the Revd David McLagan. David was one of four men who had been part of a panel that had interviewed Mr Graham on television a few years earlier. Unknown to Mr Graham, the four men on the panel were all completely opposed to his ministry. However, the graciousness of Mr Graham in the face of harsh criticism caused David to radically rethink his position. Within a very short space of time he had done a complete U-turn and was now a different man.

As part of his new 'image' he had conceived this idea of bringing Cliff and Bev to Britain and for the programme to originate in his church in East Kilbride. The idea concurred exactly with my own desire to keep Mr Graham's name and ministry before the public. In the event, Cliff and Bev flew to Scotland from the USA. David McLagan invited Marilyn and me to attend the recording on 12 December 1974 in his church and the BBC was delighted with the programme that resulted.

Wednesday, 1 October 1975, was to become a significant date in the history of evangelism in the UK. On the morning of that day, accompanied by my personal assistant Rosemary Wheeler, we went to see Lord Luke in his offices at the Bovril headquarters in London. Over the years he had been a stalwart supporter of Billy Graham and he had also backed up all the plans for Spre-e73. If there was any one person whom I felt would capture the vision of another crusade in Britain, I knew that Lord Luke would be that man.

My confidence was rewarded when he gave me every encouragement to take matters a stage further. 'Consultation,' he said, 'is vital. Call together a representative group to whom we can put your thoughts and plans.' We left his office in high spirits, firmly believing that God had led us there and that He would guide our steps as He had promised. In the event, and as the years unfolded, it became quite clear that 1975/6 was not God's best plan for us but, when 1984 eventually emerged as Mission England, the timing was exactly right. But, meanwhile, there were to be eight and a half years of frustration and heartbreaking activity. There were countless hours of seemingly unfruitful meetings before the hour of God's timing came.

Following Lord Luke's request, we set about assembling a group of Christian leaders who we knew would be sympathetic and supportive. Bearing in mind our 'committee of 100' in 1963, we set our target once more on 100 names. It was not a hard job to find them. Everyone we asked said 'yes' to a meeting in Church House, Westminster, on 6 November 1975. A few days before I had a telephone call from Gordon Landreth who, at the time, was the general secretary of the Evangelical Alliance. He said that, in his estimation, the 100 people we had invited would all be 100 per cent for a crusade. He knew of others who felt differently and he felt that some of them should be invited also. We agreed between us that about 20 of his nominees would be right.

At the meeting I introduced Lord Luke and described the purpose of the meeting. Lord Luke then spoke in support of a crusade and his hope that some positive result would come from the meeting. He then introduced the Revd David Bubbers who spoke on behalf of the clergy. He said that many of those he knew would add their support to the idea of Mr Graham returning for a crusade. There followed a time of question and answer.

It was significant that, during that time, about 20 people raised questions. Every one of those who spoke came from the twenty names that Gordon Landreth had suggested. Not a single person from the original 100 spoke at all!

As a result of the questions raised, the consensus of the meeting was that we should go for a series of consultations before proceeding. It was clear that there was no immediate and positive support to the idea of a crusade. Afterwards many people came and said to me, 'I don't agree with what was said!' I had to point out to them that no one from the original 100 had spoken up. There seemed to be no opposition to the strong criticism of 'the 20'.

So to consultation we went – from November 1975 to July 1981 – eleven different committees in all (including a 'select committee', a working group, consultation with the Archbishop of Canterbury, a meeting with Mr Graham in Copenhagen; a 'steering' committee – and six other committees! Altogether 236 individuals were involved). Along the way came an Anglican programme called 'The Decade of Evangelism'. The Evangelical Alliance announced a programme they called simply 'Power'. Two other programmes devised at that time were called 'Let My People Grow' and the 'Nationwide Initiative in Evangelism.' Not one of these programmes captured the imagination and one by one they fell by the wayside. Just after one of these projects had been rejected, the Revd Tom Houston sidled up to me. He said, 'Maurice! You've done all the right things. I would say that the door is now open for you to invite Billy Graham.' As he had been chairman of the original 'Working Group' to consider an invitation, his words carried some weight. But it was not quite as simple as that! I could not work unilaterally: I needed very wide support for Mr Graham even to consider an invitation.

Eventually, the Revd Gavin Reid (later Bishop of Maidstone) could stand it no more. He wrote an article in the *Church of England Newspaper* in which he said: 'Two and a half years of consultation have got us nowhere. We haven't got Billy and those who originally felt strongly about inviting him are becoming dismayed with three years of ecclesiastical chatter.'

A writer for *The Guardian*, the Revd Peter Mullen, didn't like the import of that article and he wrote a very critical piece in the paper. The headline declared: 'Stay away Billy Graham; for God's sake stay away!' This *Guardian* article provoked the Revd Ian Barclay to write a positive response the following week. Both he and Peter Mullen were then invited to confront each other on BBC radio and debate the issue. It was an emotive debate which prompted the producer of the programme, on the spur of the moment, to announce his own national poll. He asked for a simple response from listeners. 'Send me a postcard,' he said. 'If you want Billy Graham to come just write "YES". If not, then write "NO"'. A week later he gave the result: 14,990 plus cards had come in. Of them 13,825 said YES and 1165 said NO. It was the biggest response thus far to any single announcement on the radio.

Moved by the result of that poll the Evangelical Alliance sent a telegram to Billy Graham giving him a warm invitation to come to Britain. That was on 15 March 1979. Twelve months later on 24 March 1980 Mr Graham came to London and met with around 65 Christian leaders in the Waldegrave Hall at All Souls' Church, Langham Place. They put heavy pressure upon him to come to London, but he made it clear that God had not yet laid that burden on his heart. He asked if his response could be postponed for some while.

'Testing the water' had been a strong element in all the consultations. To do this, Mr Graham agreed to conduct university missions at Oxford and Cambridge in February 1980. I believed it to be important to get my family as much involved in evangelism as possible. Julian, my younger son, volunteered to help with the sound at the Cambridge University Mission. At Oxford we had a couple of bomb scares and on one evening, the police insisted on checking my car before Mr Graham got into it. But to all intents and purposes, it didn't faze him. He still preached a powerful message at both Oxford and Cambridge – and the students in both places responded well. It was in Cambridge that one of the 'gems' of conversation took place with Dr T. W. Wilson. I tell the story in *Life with Billy:*

> Because of the pressure of students wanting to see him, Mr Graham took to having his meals in his room. Dr T. W. Wilson (whom we called simply T or TW) would keep him company there. One day, after lunch, I had occasion to explain to TW the difference in meaning and idiom between Cambridge English and American English. As I came up from the restaurant, T. W. Wilson was coming out of Mr Graham's room. He looked a little crestfallen, and I asked him: 'T! What's the matter?'
>
> 'Maureece,' he said, 'I think I've upset the chambermaid.' I asked him: 'What happened?' He replied: 'Well, Maureece, I was having lunch with Billy when I upset the to-may-to soup all down the front of my pants [American for trousers], so I went along to the chambermaid's room and I said, "Ma'am, can you help me? I've soiled my pants!" '

I had to explain the English meaning of what he had said and he was devastated!

Mr Graham also accepted an invitation to conduct a mini-crusade in Blackpool in 1982, described later on in this chapter. Both of these events showed that his message and methods were still relevant 15 years after his last crusade. But still the consultative committees had failed to come up with an answer.

On 4 March 1981 there followed one of the most important meetings in the whole of the consultation process. It involved the members of the so-called 'steering committee'. David Rennie was in the chair, and we were discussing the interminable 'consultations' that had been going on and the apparent failure to get a significant reply from Mr Graham.

Suddenly, Gavin Reid spoke up. He referred to the success of Terry Waite (the Archbishop of Canterbury's special envoy to the Ayatollah Khomeini). Terry, through face-to-face negotiation had succeeded in getting a group of hostages in Iran released. Others had failed in their attempts. Gavin said, 'If face-to-face contact is the way to get things done then let us have a face-to-face meeting with Billy Graham.'

The idea immediately caught on and efforts were made right away to find a time when this might happen. We discovered that, in a couple of months, Mr Graham would be in Nice in the South of France. Both practically, and economically, it seemed a good idea to arrange our meeting while he was there. He expressed a willingness to see us.

On 6 July 1981 five members of the steering committee (David Rennie, together with Eddie Gibbs, Clive Calver, Gavin Reid and I) flew out to Nice. For Gavin it was to be the first time he had ever seen the Mediterranean Sea – and that alone was an excitement for him! As it happened, Mr Graham's associate, Blair Carlson, met us at the airport. He took us to the basement car park from where we drove through a tunnel, right into the basement car park of Mr Graham's hotel. There we met with Dr Walter Smyth, Mr Fred Dienert, Blair Carlson and Mr Graham in a nice basement room. After our meeting we returned by the same route and all that Gavin Reid saw of the Mediterranean that day was from the aircraft window!

I had first met Blair Carlson two or three years earlier on his first visit to England. He came with Dr Walter Smyth who told me, 'I want you to spend some time with Blair and teach him all you can about the Billy Graham Team.' We were in Cambridge at the time, and Blair and I went for a long walk up The Backs and talked at great length on the many aspects of working with the team. Blair was a very suave young man. He was of striking appearance, with pleasant wavy hair. He always dressed impeccably. A few years later, when the Mission England team had a conference at Cumberland Lodge in Windsor Great Park, he and I went for another long walk through the woods and out, to our surprise, onto the polo field. A match was in progress, and it didn't take us long to discover that Prince Charles was mounted on one of the ponies.

There was a public stand of seats alongside the field and we were told that they were available and free. So we sat up there and watched the match. In the interval, Blair 'went walkabout' while I stayed in our seats. Half an hour later he was back, looking very sheepish and with a big smile on his face. It was clear he had a story to tell! Apparently he had come across an enclosure. Looking very smart and acceptable, he had no difficulty in entering the enclosure – which turned out to be the royal enclosure. He saw a young lady struggling with her car keys and he went over to see if he could help. That was the way in which the incorrigible Blair Carlson spent nearly twenty minutes chatting with Princess Diana! It could only have happened to him!

At the meeting in Nice, Eddie Gibbs presented his vision of a crusade to be held in several centres. The idea had resonance with Mr Graham and he quickly warmed to it. There was some discussion about the name 'Crusade'. In order to avoid offence we agreed to call any event a 'Mission'. The whole meeting was entirely positive and we came away with the assurance that Mr Graham would give us a firm answer in the very near future. The whole group felt encouraged as they flew home.

We saw the urgent need to consult church leaders in each of the potential mission centres. Seven of us, in two cars, spent two weeks mid-October visiting Newcastle-upon-Tyne (Sunderland was the location selected), Coventry (where we chose Birmingham as the best centre), Bristol (the location for the launching of Mission

England) and Norwich (later Ipswich was also included). At this stage, Liverpool had not yet been considered, but it was added later. Sheffield was another city that was added a year later. We had with us John Mallison from Australia who spoke enthusiastically from his recent experiences of Mr Graham's ministry there. Also in the group was Brian Mills who, on a journey between centres, gave birth to the idea of the Prayer Triplets scheme. This prayer-based activity was so successful that the Billy Graham Team adopted its use for their future Crusades in the USA.

At each place we went to there was a contingent of protestors from Northern Ireland. They saw Mr Graham as compromising with Roman Catholics and made vociferous protests outside each of our meetings. Dr Smyth's reaction was quite positive. He asked, 'Is Billy Graham allowed to preach the Gospel to anyone except to Roman Catholics?'

Just about that time Mr Graham had received an invitation to be the 'Banquet' speaker at the annual Christian Booksellers' Convention. It was to be held in Blackpool. When some of the Christian leaders there heard about it they put forward a proposal that Mr Graham should conduct a mini-crusade in the town. The steering committee saw this as an ideal opportunity to prove that Mr Graham's ministry was still effective, and we encouraged him to accept the invitation. In the event, three other interesting things happened at the same time as the Blackpool visit.

The event itself was completely successful and justified the time and effort put into it. From the steering committee's point of view, it was just what they needed for reassurance.

In *Life with Billy* I have described one of the three things that took place in Blackpool:

> The visit to Blackpool took place at the precise time when Billy Graham had received an invitation to speak at a peace conference in Russia. He was in two minds whether or not to accept. Throughout the Blackpool crusade he privately struggled to reach his decision.
>
> He was staying in a hotel seven miles south of Blackpool, and it was my privilege to travel there and collect him for his engagements. On the journey in, with T. W. Wilson in the front seat of my car, Billy Graham rehearsed with us all of the pros and cons of the

invitation from Russia. If he went, there would be some politicians in the United States who would criticise him. If he didn't go, he would miss an opportunity – one which, incidentally, might open other doors for ministry in the Soviet Union. Throughout the journey into Blackpool we went over and over the arguments on both sides.

We arrived at the Winter Gardens and I was inevitably thinking to myself: 'How in the world can this man be effective in his preaching when he has so much on his mind?' But when he arrived on the platform he was a different man. All of the uncertainties of the Russian invitation were put behind him for the certainties of the message of the Gospel. He preached with power and authority, and he gave a strong appeal to accept Christ at the end. Many responded. As always, after preaching, he returned to the car doubtful that he had been faithful to his calling. We encouraged him and told him how effective his preaching had been.

No sooner were we back in the car, than we returned to the old arguments about the Russian invitation. All the way back to his hotel we rehearsed again new and different angles. Some of these had come to him during the meeting. There is a feeling of utter helplessness as you seek to advise and counsel him in these matters. It must be between him and God – and that is what we told him. In the end, a few days later, he decided to accept the invitation and I was commissioned to write the letter of acceptance.

The negotiations with leaders in Eastern Europe and in Russia had been conducted by Dr Alexander Haraszti. He was a Christian Hungarian-American doctor who had translated *Peace with God* into Hungarian. He worked closely with Dr Walter Smyth and Dr John Akers – a recently appointed young adviser to Mr Graham.

When the negotiations first started Dr Haraszti was still living in Hungary. He came to the West in 1956 during a time when the borders were opened for a brief time during the revolution.

It should be remembered that, at the time in question, the Soviet Union was still a communist state and the countries of Eastern Europe were dominated by the communist philosophy. Anything religious was not received with enthusiasm. Dr Haraszti spent many hours over several years visiting government leaders in Poland, Hungary, Bulgaria and Romania. He also visited Moscow on many occasions. His exploits there entered the public domain when he told his life story which was released in his memoirs and on video and cassettes.

In 1959 Billy Graham had visited Moscow for the first time. As he sat, with Grady Wilson, in the empty Lenin Stadium he prayed that, one day, he would be able to come and preach the Gospel there. Through the efforts of Josip Horak, Mr Graham's first visit to preach in Eastern Europe had been to Zagreb in 1967, but this was not too helpful in breaking into other Eastern European countries, because Yugoslavia (as it was then) was not considered a truly communist state by other communist countries.

When Dr Haraszti asked Billy Graham why he wanted to go to the Soviet Union the evangelist gave his reasons. He said, 'I am an evangelist. It is my task to preach the Gospel to as many people as I can, all over the world. The communist states are part of that world. Therefore I must endeavour to preach the Gospel also to them.'

One of the most interesting exchanges during the negotiations was one of the conversations between Dr Haraszti and the Soviet Ambassador in the presence of Billy Graham. The ambassador asked the question, 'Why does Dr Graham want to come to the Soviet Union?' In his reply Haraszti first said, 'Why does he want to come? Well simply because he wants to preach the Gospel in Moscow.'

After listening intently the Soviet Ambassador said, 'When does he want to come?' Dr Haraszti said that it would probably be in the Fall (Autumn). The Ambassador immediately reacted, 'Why does he want to come in the Fall rather than in the Winter?' Dr Haraszti replied that Billy Graham thought that the Fall – or even the Spring – was a better season in the Soviet Union, but the Soviet Ambassador reiterated, 'I think it would be better for him to come in the winter.'

Dr Haraszti said: 'Mr Ambassador. Winter is too cold. People in overflow meetings could not stand outside. Nor could Mr Graham take that cold!' The ambassador replied, 'If he loves the Soviet Union, he can come in the winter!' Dr Haraszti was faced with a dilemma because he knew winter was not a good time. On an inspiration he said: 'Mr Ambassador. To be very straight with you, two people tried to come in the winter – and both people regretted it very very much. One happened in 1812 and the other one in 1941. Both Napoleon and Hitler regretted it very much.' This reply brought laughter to the lips of the ambassador and he capitulated. 'Alright,' he said, 'let him come in the Fall.' Then the ambassador asked, 'To what places would Mr Graham like to come? What about Siberia?' When Billy Graham heard that he laughed and said, 'Alright, if you will let me out!'

It was clear that if Mr Graham accepted an invitation to go to Russia, he would be faced with the agonising task of explaining his reasons to his supporters in America. He finally gave six reasons for his acceptance: First, that the Lord had opened the door. Dr Haraszti added, 'You are clearly pledged to go, because you have been praying for a door to be opened.' Second, it was clear that, by accepting this invitation, all types of Christians from the most Orthodox to the Free Church leaders would be involved. Third, the Soviet Union would learn that there are honest church leaders in the West. Fourth, it would help the Baptists, because they had been successful in securing Billy Graham as a speaker. Fifth, Dr Haraszti said that if Mr Graham went to Moscow, every Eastern European country would fall into line and would be willing to allow him to preach there also. Finally, Mr Graham knew he would be allowed to preach the unabridged and unaltered Gospel without restriction.

In the face of many major criticisms Mr Graham went ahead with his acceptance. That courageous decision ultimately led to the widespread proclamation of the Gospel in the Soviet Union, culminating in a major stadium in Moscow.

In his memoirs, whilst recognising the Hand of God in all the negotiations, Dr Haraszti attributes the collapse of communism and the freedom which came to Eastern European states to the work and influence of four men – Ronald Reagan, Mikhail Gorbachev, the Pope, Billy Graham; and finally to his own influence as an intermediary between all of the other four.

On the Saturday afternoon, after we got back to London from Blackpool, Dr Walter Smyth and Dr Haraszti came into my office. Dr Haraszti dictated the letter of acceptance and I sat at the word processor and typed it out. The draft, when printed out, was altered again and again until it was exactly right. That signalled the start of Mr Graham's ministry in Russia including, eventually, the crusade in Moscow.

The second thing that happened during the visit to Blackpool was an amusing incident involving both Dr Walter Smyth and me. After extensive investigations he had *just* confirmed the Rai Centre in Amsterdam. It would be the location of the great International Conference of Itinerant Evangelists (ICIE). It was a dream of Mr Graham's, and Dr Smyth had been working on finding a suitable venue for months. As I drove Mr Graham to his hotel one morning, he remarked on the rows and rows of hotels in Blackpool. 'You know,' he said, 'this would be an ideal place for the ICIE. I like it for three reasons. First, there are plenty of inexpensive hotels. Second, Blackpool would have a much lower profile than Amsterdam, and third, we would not expose these overseas evangelists to the temptations of Amsterdam.'

At that moment we were passing the Imperial hotel. 'Let's stop there for lunch,' he said. Then he added, 'Call Walter and ask him to join us.'

Minutes later Walter Smyth arrived. Billy Graham went up to him and said, 'You know, Walter, Maurice has been saying what a good place this would be for the ICIE!' I looked rapidly at Walter and he gave me a cut-throat sign. As he did so I exclaimed, 'Walter! Please! It was not me. It was Billy's idea!'

The third and most important thing that happened just after Blackpool was the occasion of Mr Graham's acceptance of our invitation. On our way to Manchester airport Mr Graham wanted to meet with some 20 representatives from the six areas to which we expected any mission to go. We selected a hotel in Manchester for the meeting. It was there that Mr Graham first gave us his firm answer to our firm invitation. He *would* come for a six-centre mission that we would call Mission England. It was a moving moment and as we heard Mr Graham commit himself to coming, Gavin Reid spontaneously led everyone in singing 'Praise God from whom all blessings flow'.

Over lunch a young, somewhat tongue-tied clergyman sat next to Mr Graham. At a loss to make conversation he turned to Mr

Graham and asked him, 'Which day do you take for your statutory day off?' Mr Graham replied: 'I beg your pardon? I'm not quite sure I understand you.' The young man replied, 'Well, I mean what day do you take to "do your own thing"? I usually take Friday off, but some ministers take Monday.' 'Oh my!' exclaimed Mr Graham. 'I don't think I've have a day like that since 1949!'

Another event during this period was the news that Mr Graham had been awarded the Templeton Prize. This international award was held in such high esteem that it was to be presented by the Duke of Edinburgh at Buckingham Palace. The Templeton people sent cars to collect Mr Graham's party and I was both amazed and thrilled when he included me amongst those he wished to be with him. It was a wonderful occasion.

Just around the corner was another major shock for my family. We were just going to bed one night, after a Bank Holiday weekend, when the telephone rang. It was a lady's voice. 'Are you the father of Jacqueline Rowlandson?' she asked. When she found out that she was speaking to the right person she told me that our lovely daughter had been involved in a car accident. She was in Bishop's Stortford hospital and the nurse advised us to come straightaway. I turned to Marilyn and said, 'I can't go through all that again!' She replied, 'You'll just have to – but the Lord will see us through.' And He did!

CHAPTER FIFTEEN

MISSION ENGLAND

THE JOURNEY to Bishop's Stortford was a problem. To start with I had less than a gallon of petrol and, so close to midnight, very few petrol stations were open. It so happened that a police car was sitting at the end of our road and I stopped to ask him where I would find the nearest fuel supply. But for his help, we might have wasted the precious last drops of petrol.

On arrival at the hospital we found that Julian our son, with his wife Fiona, had just reached there too. Julian had his Bible open and was keen to read some supportive texts to us! It was a comfort to have their presence with us at this stressful time.

The Asian doctor who met us told us that our daughter was in a critical condition with serious head injuries. 'We have a good hospital here,' he said. 'But not good enough for your daughter's injuries.' He asked our permission to transfer her to St Barts Hospital in London where they had a special unit for head injuries. He had an ambulance and a police escort all ready for us and, at breakneck speed we went to the City of London. 'Just follow us. Go through red lights if we do!' the policeman told us. As we reached the border for the Essex and Metropolitan police, the Essex car pulled into the slip-road off the M11, and the Met. police car came out the other side. It was a smooth and well-organised transfer.

At Barts they were ready and waiting for us. We didn't know then, but it would be 50 long and anxious days before Jacky awoke from that coma. The doctors and nurses were wonderful throughout those dreadful days.

A whole book could be written of the day-to-day experiences of those 50 coma days, but four stories will suffice in this writing.

The second day a senior member of the nursing staff, Sarah Whitfield came to see us. She said that she would be looking after our welfare for as long as it took. It was a tremendous joy to find that she was a committed Christian, so we had much in common. She was a tower of strength to us throughout the long recovery period. On the third day she handed me a 'sick note' to say that Jacky would be unable to return to her nursing career 'for four weeks'. I looked at the note and saw it said 'four weeks'. Strangely that was a great comfort to me, because my reaction was 'they must think she will live'!

About 20 days into the coma, one of the young nurses came in to see Jacky. True to all that they had taught us, she talked to Jacky as though she were quite normal. It is a strange feeling when someone is in a coma. She told Jacky's inert form, 'It's my 21st birthday tomorrow, and I'm taking my friends to the Royal Ballet.' On the Monday following, she brought in a tape of the Royal Ballet music, and lent it to us to be put on Jacky's pillow speaker. About thirty days later, after Jacky 'woke up', I was trying to find out what she could remember from before the accident. She told me that it had been her 21st birthday just before (and it had)! She then went on to say that she had taken her friends to the Royal Ballet. When I remonstrated with her and said that that was nonsense, she replied, 'I know I did Dad, because I can still hear the music!'

On the morning of the 50th day, Marilyn my wife had gone into the office on her way to the hospital. One of the ladies reminded her that 50 days was the day of Jubilee. Marilyn said she didn't feel much like celebrating today. Then she went into the hospital and, with the nurse, wheeled Jacky in her wheelchair to the physiotherapy ward. Marilyn was helping the physiotherapist and learning from her, because she might have had to care for Jacky for a long period.

While undressing her, Marilyn ran her finger up the ball of Jacky's foot. As she did so she said to Jacky, 'One of these days you'll tell me to stop doing that!' She had hardly got the words out of her mouth when Jacky replied, 'Stop it mum!' And that was the moment she woke up!

I was sitting as Chairman of the Bench in court at that moment. My mobile phone vibrated indicating that a call was coming in. As I knew it must be from the hospital, I asked my two colleagues if we might retire for a few moments. When we entered the retiring room, I accepted the call on my phone. It was the nurse's voice: 'I have someone here to talk to you,' she said. Immediately, Jacky's voice came over the phone, 'Hi Dad!' she said. My two colleagues in the retiring room joined in the emotion of the moment and we all had tears in our eyes.

After that she was in recovery mode for many months, and there were many experiences to go through. Suffice it to say that, long before this story was written and since the accident, she has married and has three lovely daughters (two now in their teens). She has been to college and has gained a BA Honours degree. So we have much to be thankful for.

So much so, in fact, that on 19 March 1983 we decided to hold a service of thanksgiving for her recovery. We held it at St Paul's Church, Robert Adam Street, and the church was packed with our relatives, our friends and many of the nurses and doctors from the hospital. Shortly before the service I had been listening to a tape of the broadcaster David Kossoff. He was reading a soliloquy in memory of his son. What he read was exactly our experiences of Jacky's recovery – apart from the fact that David's son had died. I felt led to telephone and ask David Kossoff if I might read the piece at the service. I explained to him the alterations I would need to make. He was so touched that he said that he would like to come and read the piece himself – which he did. We later discovered that our thanksgiving service commemorated also the day on which his son had died. It was a moving experience.

All of that took place in the early days of preparation for Mission England. It was, naturally, a struggle to keep up with the office work whilst spending most of our days with Jacky at the hospital. But God gave us the strength and we emerged, at the end, not only up to date on the work, but conscious of God's hand upon us through those days. It was wonderful to have so many of my colleagues on the Billy Graham Team in London, and Jacky had many visitors from amongst them. We were also conscious that our needs were on the Billy Graham Team prayer list. Mr Graham himself was constantly on the telephone asking for a progress report.

Jacky was first able to come home from hospital for just the three days of Christmas. On Christmas day, the telephone rang. I answered it and, at the other end of the line, was Mr Graham. 'I don't want to talk to you,' he said. 'I want to talk to that wonderful daughter of yours.' I put Jacky on the line and for twenty minutes he simply encouraged her and congratulated her on her recovery. That is the sort of man he is!

During the days of Jacky's hospitalisation, many of my colleagues from America had arrived. A large contingent was necessary because a mini-team presence was needed in each of the six locations. We were, virtually, setting up six crusades at the same time. Our resources were stretched to the limit. We maintained a central planning office in Harrow through the kindness of David Rennie (the BGEA chairman) who made space available at the factory and warehouse of his company Microlease Ltd. In addition we had regional offices in each of the cities where the mission would be held.

Most of the Team members had never been to Britain before and they all needed some considerable training. To do this, Bob Williams, the (American) director of the mission, took us all away for a weekend to the Shillingworth Bridge Hotel, near Princes Risborough, where we had a high-powered two days' training. Amongst other things, Eddie Gibbs gave a potted history of the church in Great Britain. It was a masterly presentation which took us right back to the early church fathers, and gave an understanding to the American Team about the Anglican and nonconformist traditions. He quoted Tom Rees's description of the three types of Anglican churches – 'The High and hazy; the Broad and crazy, and the Low and lazy!' He described the wide variety of worship styles within all the churches. Marilyn gave a talk to the Team wives, orientating them as far as possible about British culinary matters – an American explaining to American wives the differences in weights and measures; ingredients and language problems. For example, she explained that the simple sentence 'I was mad about my flat', in England meant 'I was thrilled with my apartment', whereas (as all the Americans knew) in America it meant 'I was furious about my punctured tyre!'

Once the conference dispersed to the extremities of England, it was hard work for everybody. The usual crusade training applied equally to this mission, and there were counselling classes as well as orientation for the stewards and rehearsals for the choirs.

Mr Graham arrived at London airport for Mission England on Thursday, 3 May. As I met him, I discovered that he had a serious throat infection and could hardly talk. The infection had developed during his Alaskan Crusade a few days before and was so bad that one of the Associate Evangelists had to take over and complete the evening's message.

His first engagement the next morning was to visit his doctor, Dr T. R. Williams. He marched him straight up the road to see an Ear, Nose and Throat specialist – Mr Ian Fraser. It was the May bank holiday weekend, and Dr Williams had tried between 11 and 12 other specialists, but they were all away. So, in desperation he tried 'the top man' and he was there. 'That's why he's the top man,' remarked Dr Williams.

At twelve noon precisely, Mr Graham came downstairs from his consultation with Mr Fraser. 'He wants to put me in hospital and operate tomorrow,' he said. My mind did a quick double-take and rehearsed all the engagements that Mr Graham had during the next few days – starting with a preaching engagement for Dr R. T. Kendall at Westminster Chapel.

Mr Fraser followed Mr Graham downstairs. 'Bring him to the Royal Masonic Hospital tomorrow morning at 7am, and I will operate.' When I heard that I said, 'Anywhere but the Royal Masonic Hospital,' but Mr Fraser explained that was his operating base and it was there, and there only, that he had his operating team. Off the cuff I remarked, 'That will be good for 300 or more letters!' And it was! They started as soon as the story appeared in the newspapers – 'Billy Graham enters Royal Masonic Hospital for operation' said the headline. The first letter came two days later; 'Is Mr Graham a Freemason?' There were so many letters, that I had to compile a standard reply which the staff could send out in reply to all:

> Mr Graham arrived in England with a throat infection. An operation was required to overcome the problem. During the Bank Holiday weekend, the only Ear, Nose and Throat surgeon on duty was Mr Ian Fraser who operates only at the Royal Masonic Hospital. It was there that Mr Graham was successfully operated upon. He is not a Freemason but was treated at the only available hospital that weekend. He will fulfil all his engagements for Mission England.

It didn't stop the flow of letters – and I still received assertions that Billy Graham was a Freemason more than 20 years later!

I asked Mr Fraser if I should cancel his immediate engagements, but he assured me that Mr Graham would be recovered enough to complete them all. The operation was first thing on Saturday morning. T. W. Wilson and I visited him an hour later and found him a little woozy from the anaesthetic, but alert enough to give both of us our marching orders for the day!

On Sunday afternoon I collected him from the hospital – still wearing his hospital identification wristband – and took him to Westminster Chapel. He preached as powerfully as ever, although his voice was somewhat subdued. After the service I returned him to the hospital where he remained for another 36 hours. He was discharged in time for his next major engagement which was to meet the editors of all the national daily newspapers at the offices of *The Times* and a luncheon hosted by Rupert Murdoch. From there he went to the BBC Television studios at Lime Grove where he completed five 10-minute interviews.

Shortly afterwards Mr Graham went to the ABC Studios to be interviewed by Michael Parkinson. It was an early morning show and the interview before Mr Graham's was with a London 'stripper'. She emerged just before Mr Graham went in and, as she did so, she was wearing very little. T. W. Wilson was standing by me and was astounded by what he saw. The team photographer, Russ Busby, was standing by his side and said: 'T. You can't help the first look – but the second look is sinful!' TW replied, 'Man alive! I haven't finished the first look yet!'

After that traumatic weekend and major meetings before he left London, the pressure in Bristol did not lessen to any extent. There was an immediate press conference and numerous receptions and consultations with the Bristol committee. The day after he arrived in Bristol he had 14 press interviews and a 30-minute radio programme to cope with. His programme would have floored many a patient who was just recovering from surgery. However, he survived it all and was ready for the dedication meeting on the Friday evening.

A week after his operation the first meeting of Mission Bristol attracted more than 31,000 in attendance. No one had known how it would go. Would people even turn up? Would they sing the old songs? Would they respond to Mr Graham's invitation to 'get up out of your seat and come and stand at the front'?

There were tears in the eyes of most of the organising team as the Ashton Gate Stadium, home of the Bristol City Football Club, opened its doors to the crowds outside. We stood there watching in amazement as the crowds poured in and the stadium rapidly filled up. And they sang! It was no problem! And when it came to the 'invitation' there was the moment of complete silence when nobody moved. We all held our breath until, all of a sudden, the flow started and it seemed as if nothing would stop it. On that first night in Bristol there were over 2239 enquirers who responded at the end.

I had been assigned a new job for Mission England. For the first time in my experience I was invited to be in charge of the media – radio, television and press interviews. It was a major job for which I felt ill-equipped. Indeed, I would not have been able to do it at all save for the magnificent support I had from (almost) 7-foot tall Larry Ross who was Mr Graham's personal press representative. Larry took me under his wing and taught me all that he could of what he knew. Thanks to his tuition, I was told that I did a creditable job in keeping the media happy – and in their place!

In a recent interview with Dan Wooding of Assist Ministries, Larry Ross told how he had become associated with Billy Graham.

> The first Billy Graham crusade that I ever attended was in 1962 at Soldier's Field in Chicago when I was 11. I remember that the

> temperature was over 100 degrees and all I wanted was something to drink. We sat way up in the corner and Dr Graham was a little speck on the stage with everyone else. Years later, my first crusade as a media man for Billy Graham was in Baltimore in 1981 when I had the opportunity to provide a professional public relations dimension for Dr Graham because they were getting so many requests for interviews. Then I went full time with the crusades in 1984, beginning with Mission England. Mr Graham's last crusade in New York was my seventieth crusade. It's just been a tremendous privilege to have a small part in the ministry of this great man of God.

Larry Ross 'held my hand' throughout all of Mission England. Like most of the other major Billy Graham activities the story has been told in *One in a Million* by Derek Williams and it will not be repeated here – except, as usual, for three stories which can bear repeating!

The first refers to the meetings at the Roker Park Football Stadium in Sunderland. This large complex is right on the edge of the sea and the cold north-east wind blows right across it. During the days of our mission meetings, the weather was exceptionally cold. Mr Graham took to preaching in his overcoat with a 'Geordie' cap on his head and – as the tabloids loved to announce – 'two sets of thermal underwear'! In spite of that, it was so cold that the Sunderland committee had to erect a perspex screen in front of him, to prevent the cold taking his breath away.

In spite of those inhospitable features, more than 19,000 came on the last night, filling the stadium to capacity, and there were 1849 enquirers. It was an exceptional meeting in the coldest setting we had ever known. We came away from the fourteen days in Sunderland with a miner's lamp given to each of us as a token of the appreciation of the Sunderland committee.

The second story had rather humorous connotations involving, as it did, my tall colleague Larry Ross. We were in Liverpool for the mission when it happened. One morning, Larry announced that in Texas he had that day rented a massive road-side advertising board (bill board in America) and had had the message 'Autumn, will you marry me?' painted upon it. The board was on the route that he knew his girlfriend would take to work.

The next morning, at the crack of dawn, Cliff Barrows (having received a telegram overnight from Autumn in Texas) and Bev Shea with Johnny Lenning each bore a breakfast tray to Larry's bedroom. On Cliff's tray was a large 'Y'; on Bev's tray was a large 'E', and on Johnny's tray was a large 'S'. Thus Larry got his answer.

The Holiday Inn, in which all the Team were staying, was so intrigued by the story that, on the big Holiday Inn signboard outside the hotel, they put the message; 'Autumn says "yes" to Larry!' There was great rejoicing in the Team hotel that day!

Finally we got to Ipswich. As press representative for the Mission, it was made known to me that on one special day at Ipswich, the one-millionth visitor would be coming to the mission. The question was, how to select the person who would be the millionth visitor! In the end, we decided that Liz Fane (my PA) and I would take up a position at the main entrance to the stadium. There, with our backs to the entrance turnstiles, we would count 150 people through. We would then accost the 151st person whom we would determine as the one-millionth visitor. Derek Williams takes up the story:

> The fact was probably irrelevant so far as God's economy goes, but to the media it was a little milestone they did not want to ignore. Maurice Rowlandson, with his colleague Liz Fane, went into action. Standing at the main entrance, they turned their backs on the streaming crowd so that they would not be influenced by a face, and began the countdown as people passed them. Nervous Team members prayed that the person upon whose shoulder Maurice Rowlandson's hand fell would be young and *male!* (Young and female on a newspaper front page might look embarrassingly similar to sales hype which spread girls across car bonnets!) Old of either sex would be untypical of the high percentage of young people who came to hear Billy Graham.
>
> At 7.20pm Maurice Rowlandson sprang and some prayers were answered! Alan Paget, looking a little older than his 15 years, was escorted on to the turf to meet Billy Graham who presented him with a Bible and a Mission England sweatshirt. The electronic scoreboard announced the magic number to the crowd.

It could, however, have been a disaster. For, as I stopped Alan Paget, No. 151, the very next person turned to me and said, 'You're Maurice Rowlandson aren't you? I've been in your house, and I'm a friend of your son.' Had it been him I had chosen, I could have been charged with some kind of nepotism!

If all had gone according to plan, the mission at Ipswich would have been the final event of Mission England. But it didn't happen like that. A group of leaders from Sheffield came to one of the Mission England centres. There they accosted Mr Graham and, figuratively speaking, held his arm behind his back until he agreed to a final mission meeting being held in their city. It was impossible to accept the invitation in 1984. In any case, Mr Graham was very tired by the time Mission England was over. But he did agree to return in 1985 and thus the final meetings of Mission England were a very successful eight days in Sheffield – making it the longest of any of the Mission England locations. Attendance was in excess of 160,000 with more than 14,000 enquirers. One of those who responded to Mr Graham's invitation was a macho motorcyclist enthusiast named Jean Lupton. She had her own paint-spraying and customising motorcycle factory near Derby and it was from there that her mother persuaded a rather reluctant Jean to travel by coach to Sheffield. She takes up the story:

> My mum asked me to go with her to hear Billy Graham. For some reason I could not determine at the time I accepted my mum's invitation and found myself on the bus. When I looked at it, it was a most decrepit bus. By today's standards it would not have been allowed on the road. I found myself in this rickety old bus shaking, rattling and rolling all the way – with a load of religious weirdos! I felt aggravated and wondered what insanity had prompted me to come!
>
> When we arrived there was a crowd of around 45,000 in the packed stadium. Every seat seemed to be filled. I thought to myself, 'There must be something about it, to have all this lot here.'
>
> 'Billy Graham said his bit,' she recalls, 'and I can't really remember very much except when he got to the bit where he said, "If you want to commit yourself to Christ; if you want to join yourself to Jesus; if you want to be reconciled to God – then come forward and stand at the front of the platform." '
>
> I said to my mum, 'If I go forward, will you come with me?' And there I was, the managing director of this macho company, walking to the front with my mum. I felt like a little child.

> All of a sudden I was confronted by a teenager – with a clip-board – who asked me to tell her what I knew about Jesus. So I told her what I knew. She said, 'You know more about Him than I do. Let's say this prayer,' she said, and repeated a prayer that sounded a lot to me like a wedding vow – 'I'll be yours and you'll be mine . . .'
>
> Anyway, I said the prayer and nothing happened; nothing was changed: there were no angels flying; no bells ringing; my face was the same, and no hairs were growing on the backs of my hands! 'That's it then,' I thought. 'It hasn't taken!'
>
> I walked out of the stadium and back into that old rickety bus – but suddenly it had turned into Starship Enterprise! Smooth and fast down the motorway it ran as we drove home. The people all around me were still the same people – but now they all seemed nicer and lovely!

The persistence of the Sheffield group had paid off and there were countless numbers, like Jean, who would look back to Sheffield as the time when they first found the Lord Jesus Christ as their Saviour.

CHAPTER SIXTEEN

A POT-POURRI OF STORIES: 1974–1984

AFTER SPRE-E73 ended, in September 1973 I joined the *Sir Winston Churchill* – a topsail schooner owned and operated by the Sail Training Association. I knew it would be hard work but it provided total relaxation of mind. This was one of the many voyages that I did on the schooner (and her sister ship the *Malcolm Miller*) serving as purser aboard.

This trip was notorious because we had so many horrendous storms. The worst one was on passage between Southampton and Amsterdam. Just off the Galloper Sands in the North Sea, a 'Force 10' gale hit us. Three of our sails blew out and were in shreds. The wiskeard (stay), holding the bowsprit at the front of the vessel, parted. The mizzen-mast crosstrees (which stabilised the stays that held the mast up) shattered and we had water in the port engine. Most of the teenage crew were seasick below and the captain – Barry Swindell, baldheaded, and looking as tranquil as if there was no storm – was alone on deck and on the wheel. The enormous ship was tossed about like a small dinghy. Eventually the captain decided we had had enough. He turned the ship around and 'ran before the wind' with the gale behind us. With no sails up at all, we were still travelling at 13 knots under bare poles! It was quite an experience. But we survived and went into Deal Bay to lick our wounds and regroup before resuming our journey to Amsterdam.

On the Billy Graham front there was the Team Meeting at Porte St Lucie. Back in London we worked on the release of several new films. These various duties kept us busy – along with planning committees for the Eurofest75 conference. All in all it was a quieter period – until I had a telephone call from Mr Graham one evening.

He told me that he had been invited to be the centenary speaker at the Keswick Convention in July. He went on to say that the council of the convention wanted him to conduct a public open air crusade-type meeting as part of the celebrations. He was very nervous about accepting this and said he would only do so if I was prepared to do a 'mini-crusade set-up' along the lines that he wanted.

It was a challenge that was very close to my heart. Ever since I had received my first 'call to Christian service' at the convention I had always tried to attend whenever I could. The idea of working with their council in preparation for Mr Graham's meeting had a great attraction for me. I told him I would do my very best to set everything up in the way he would wish.

I went to Keswick and the full story of those days is told in my book *Life at the Keswick Convention*. From February to July I worked closely with the Keswick Convention Council in making all the plans. For the open air meeting we used an old farm wagon, suitably enhanced, as the platform. I persuaded Henry Hole to come and organise the stewarding. Musical instruments were found, and Wanda Adams, a young American working with Trans World Radio was enlisted as soloist.

On the day that Billy Graham arrived with T. W. Wilson, I went to Penrith to meet him off the train. He had had a good journey, including luncheon in the dining car which really impressed him. Someone, somewhere, had told him that cider was a drink that Christians accepted, so on the journey he ordered a glass. Later the stewardess passed by his table and said, 'You know, you look just like Billy Graham. But you can't be, because you're drinking cider!' To that, Mr Graham made his usual response when he was flummoxed – 'Oh! My!' He enjoyed telling us the story as he got into the car.

I had no responsibility for the actual Keswick Centenary meeting in the main tent apart from ensuring that Mr Graham arrived there on time. On another day he also spoke at the young people's meeting.

The open-air meeting attracted an enormous crowd to the hillside park by the lake. The approach road was so narrow that the police feared it would be impossible to bring Mr Graham by car to the park. So they suggested bringing him in by boat – which we did. It was reminiscent of Christ speaking from the shoreline of the Sea of Galilee.

Immediately after the meeting was over we went back by boat to Portinscale where I had left the car. From there we set off for Manchester airport as he was flying out the same night. Earlier in the afternoon, my secretary/PA, Rosemary Wheeler, had collected the luggage from the hotel at which Mr Graham and T. W. Wilson were staying, and she was waiting for us in her car, with my wife and daughter Jacky, in a layby on the Penrith road. As we arrived, they fell in behind us in convoy all the way to Manchester airport. We had a walkie-talkie radio to keep in touch with them. 'Who is on the other end of that radio?' asked Mr Graham. I told him it was my daughter. He immediately grabbed the radio, asked how it worked, and then spent some time in conversation with Jacky in the other car.

A month or two later the devil saw his opportunity to make another attempt to divert me from the 'Thin Gold Line' which had guided me thus far. My wife and I were living at Frinton-on-Sea at the time and there was, on the sea front, a lovely Christian-owned hotel. The owner, Frank Houlding was a good friend of ours.

He came to see me when we were in Frinton for the weekend. He said that he and his wife wanted to retire from the Cedars, and he wondered if we would be willing to buy it and take it over. In the past I had often considered running a hotel, but other ministries had intervened. This offer from Mr Houlding seemed attractive to us. However, the price that he was asking was far more than we could afford. After extensive negotiations he came down to a more reasonable price but it was still £50,000 more than we could afford.

In the meantime I spoke to Billy Graham about the Cedars, and he asked Walter Smyth to come and check it out. Walter was in Europe at the time so he and his wife went home to America via Frinton and stayed for a couple of nights at the hotel. His assessment was that if I felt that to be the way that God was guiding me, then I should go ahead. I told Mr Houlding that I could not afford the extra £50,000 he wanted, but that if he would reduce the price by that amount, we would give it serious consideration. In my mind I decided that I would wait until the end of the month. If he hadn't accepted it by then we would take it as guidance that we should not go ahead.

The last day of the month came, and Mr Houlding said that he could not accede to my request. Accordingly I telephoned Billy Graham and told him that I would remain fully committed to the BGEA. He was delighted and told me that he felt that I had made the right decision.

Three days later, Frank Houlding telephoned to say that he had changed his mind and that he *would* reduce the price by the £50,000 I had asked for! I was not in a dilemma because I had committed the matter to the Lord and my 'fleece' had been that the offer should be accepted by the end of the month. That had not happened and Mr Houlding was disappointed but he respected my decision and the grounds upon which I had based it.

Another 'first' followed in December when Mr Graham came to London to accept an invitation to have lunch with Her Majesty the Queen at Buckingham Palace. It was his wish that I should drive him there. Remembering the advice of Major General Wilson Haffenden that 'time spent in reconnaissance is rarely wasted' I did a 'dry run' to Buckingham Palace in the morning. To my surprise the policeman on the gate already knew about my car and, when I stopped to ask him for instructions about what to do later on (when I brought Mr Graham) he told me to drive into the Palace and around the courtyard. He was very helpful, and I felt quite confident by the time I left the palace. On the way back to the office I was stopped by a traffic survey. The young WPC asked, 'Where have you just come from?' I replied, 'Buckingham Palace!' She remonstrated with me, considering that I was a time-waster and said, 'Please, sir, will you give me a sensible answer.'

I explained that my answer had been entirely correct – and told her why! She was very apologetic and waved me on.

In the afternoon with my new-found confidence I drove up to the palace gates with Mr Graham in the car. The same policeman waved me through and I took Mr Graham to the entrance lobby in the courtyard. There he was met by Sir Martin Charteris, the Queen's secretary, while a footman held open my car door.

Dr Smyth had urged me to stay in the palace courtyard, and sit in the car to wait. He said that Mr Graham would feel far more comfortable if he knew I was outside. So I swung around in an arc and parked in full view of the entrance. While I waited, I consumed my lunch of (slimmers') Bisks and a glass of water! I am sure that the food inside the palace was far more salubrious! An hour and forty-five minutes later, the door opened and out came Sir Martin and Mr Graham. The footman on duty turned to look at me and, with a flick of the wrist and with a beckoning finger, he waved me into position. He seemed a little flummoxed when he discovered that I was not a chauffeur, but a friend of Mr Graham's!

It was the first of several occasions when the same routine was repeated as Mr Graham received a number of invitations to similar lunches. On one occasion a few years later I was parked outside the private entrance to the royal apartments when an aerial photograph was taken of the palace and published in the *London Illustrated News*. To my surprise, there was my car parked by the private entrance (and once again I was consuming my Bisks)!

Mr Graham paid other visits to the UK between 1975 and 1978, including preaching engagements and a ministers' meeting in Glasgow. There were more Team meetings in Buena Vista in Orlando one year and in Montego Bay in Jamaica two years later. Coming into the airport at Tampa at night, the man next to me made a remark which has been oft-repeated ever since. As we looked out over the multitudinous lights of the city he said: 'Just think of it! Every one of those lights has been put in by human hand!' It was quite a thought! But an even greater thought would be to look up to the stars and say, 'Every one of those stars has been placed there by the hand of God. What a creator!'

Our new film, *The Hiding Place*, telling the story of the Dutch Patriot Corrie Ten Boom, was completed. I was heavily involved in the film's release all around the country. My American colleague, Ken Bliss, arrived to help me to make the most of the film's distribution. I went to the airport to meet him and took him to the office. There, a message awaited him to say that, through a firearms accident, his son had been killed that morning. I took him straight back to the airport and he got the next flight home. We shared his sorrow at the news, and committed both him and his family to the Lord. As a result I was left to carry the full burden of the film's release.

A formal (commercial) première of *The Hiding Place* was held at the Prince Charles cinema in central London. It was organised by a company called GTO (a company experienced in commercial film releases) – and they were planning the general release of the film. It was nearly a disaster!

About a quarter of the cinema was reserved for the stars in the film and their friends and family. About half of the seats were reserved for the BGEA friends and supporters. The remaining seats were for those from the big cinema chains. GTO had handled the whole pre-release programme so they offered to undertake the organisation of the première.

They did it in grand style! It was a full dress occasion. The Prince Charles Cinema was decorated and special souvenir 'packs' were prepared for everybody. They also booked the Roman Catholic Church hall which was adjacent to the cinema. There they had organised a reception for all of our guests. We made the mistake – rather *I* made the mistake – of leaving everything in their hands. I never thought about double-checking.

Fortunately, about two-thirds of the way through the film I thought I had better go and see that everything was ready for the reception. When I entered the hall, I could scarcely believe my eyes! Table upon table was laden with bottles of hard liquor. Cigars and cigarettes were liberally scattered around for our guests, and I was introduced to 'the entertainment'. She turned out to be a (so-called) exotic dancer!

I immediately sought out the head of GTO and said that, before the film ended and our guests arrived, *everything* would have to be changed! He expressed considerable surprise at my determination and said that all this 'was what normally happens at a film première'. I said, 'Not at ours! I'm sorry but if any of that stuff remains to be seen when our guests arrive they would never understand.' I explained that it could lose us a whole army of supporters.

The next twenty minutes were full of the most hectic activity you can imagine. The refreshment area now displayed some wine (which I felt acceptable) and soft drinks. Everything else was put out of sight. The exotic dancer was despatched with her fee paid without performing. By the time the film finished our guests were welcomed as they should be and I had a clear conscience. How nearly we had courted disaster! But the Lord put into my heart that need to 'double check' – and was I glad I did. The name of the BGEA was safe. Thank you Lord!

I was away a lot from the office, and Rosemary Wheeler valiantly kept things going, but when I got back she had a complaint: 'I am just a machine,' she said. 'Your dictated words come in through my ears and pass out through my fingers. I am not involved!' She started a whole new philosophy of secretarial work. From then on she sat with me as I opened the mail in the morning, and she sat with me again as I signed, and she stuffed the mail into envelopes. As we worked, we talked about all that the correspondence referred to. It made life more interesting to her and for me. She also initiated a new system of printing one extra copy of every letter which she kept in date order. That system has often 'saved the day' ever since when an elusively filed letter could always be found in the 'date' file. I still use the system today.

When Mr Graham had his crusade in Gothenberg it provided us with another opportunity to take a tour group. As always, we took with us a group from our London office staff together with some 50 other people. Amongst our group was a young woman whose mother paid for her to come as a 21st birthday present. We never knew who would be amongst those who came on our tour groups. At first sight, we thought we had been joined by a young woman unlike any that we would normally expect to see in a group of this kind. Her dress was designed to shock with a maxi-mini skirt, low-cut top and with her face more heavily made up than normal. Her application form described her as a 'go-go dancer'. And to every appearance she 'fitted the bill'! It was something of a surprise, therefore, to find her sitting on the plane, reading her Bible.

It was even more of a surprise when we had our devotional times with the party, to listen to her pray in the time of open prayer. It was then, in conversation with her, that we discovered that she was a deeply committed Christian.

We had some great times at the crusade meetings and, each night as we got back to the hotel, we met our group to hear about their experiences during the day. One evening, this young lady was not with the group – nor did she appear when, at midnight, Marilyn and I decided to go to bed. We were not, after all, responsible for her. She was now 21 and carried her own responsibilities. However, we decided to take one last look around the hotel lounge and coffee-bar. It was in the latter that we found our quarry, sitting at a table with a group of eight or ten English-speaking Swedish young men. She had her Bible open in front of her, and she was in full flight of witnessing to them! We quietly slipped away, amazed how God can use anyone who is dedicated to Him, whatever their appearance, to do His work. We quickly recognised that the Lord doesn't see as humans see. They look on the outward appearance, but the Lord looks on the heart (1 Samuel 16:7). A young person, dressed like other young people, is more likely to be able to get alongside them than those of us who wear conventional suits and ties. We must not forget that Jesus Himself did not hesitate to mix with, and make disciples of, all and sundry.

During these 'quiet' years I also organised several tour groups to visit Israel. I did these in conjunction with *Decision* magazine, encouraged to do so by Roy Gustafson, my colleague on the Billy Graham Team. He ran several tours a year, and we found them to be very good public relations for the BGEA.

At Mr Graham's invitation we also attended the National Religious Broadcasters' Conference (NRB) in Washington each year. He felt that it was good for the American broadcasters to know about the situation in the UK. In America they were so used to Christian broadcasting in the USA that they found it hard to understand the restrictions under which we operated in the UK. In fact the only way for Mr Graham's radio programme *The Hour of Decision* to be heard in the UK was on one of the overseas (or 'pirate' stations). Bishop Goodwin Hudson and I talked about the possibilities on many occasions.

Eventually he decided to propose to Billy Graham that, for an experimental period, we should broadcast the programme on Radio Luxembourg. We would include several advertisements for the programme as well as the *Hour of Decision* itself. To our delight, Mr Graham agreed and said he would underwrite the cost.

On 28 November 1980 I had a letter from Mr Graham in which he said:

> I hope we haven't made a very costly mistake in this Luxembourg contract. It was certainly presented to me in a different way. As a matter of fact, in the back of my mind I thought that you were the one who had instigated the 'thrilling opportunity'. I try to deal with so many matters that unfortunately I do not get to think them all through and thereby make a number of mistakes. If this is not a profitable investment I am wondering if there is any way out of the contract?

Actually it had been the bishop who had described the broadcast on Radio Luxembourg as 'a thrilling opportunity'. In the event the programme was not a success, producing negligible response. Fortunately there *had* been a clause in the contract which allowed us to make a break after six months. In the light of our experience, we took advantage of that break – much to Mr Graham's relief!

In the same letter Mr Graham spoke about another meeting for which he would be coming to London. The occasion was to celebrate twenty-five years of the publication *Crusade*. The magazine had been started as a direct result of the Harringay Crusade, and it seemed appropriate to John Capon (currently responsible to the Evangelical Alliance for the publication), to invite Mr Graham to the celebration at the Royal Albert Hall. Mr Graham wrote:

> In any event, I am looking forward to seeing you in January and would appreciate all the help you can give me in preparing my address at Westminster for John Capon. I have no idea what would be the right approach, and unfortunately I have practically no time to prepare it since I am preparing other major addresses that must be given in January both in America, Poland and Hungary.

This letter demonstrated in a graphic way the enormous pressures under which Billy Graham suffered. On an occasion like this, several of us would get together and put down some ideas for him. He had a remarkable ability to take our poor efforts, and to turn them into a masterly address – which is what he did on this occasion.

Because so many Team members attended the NRB each year, it was always like a mini-team meeting. Then, one year, I received an unexpected invitation. Ben Armstrong, who was the executive head of NRB, invited me to come and address one of the sessions the next year. He told me to get my airline ticket and emphasised that I should get a first class ticket (in the days before club or business class). A day or two later the cheque came from him to pay for it. He told me that he had reserved accommodation for me at the hotel. When I bought the ticket, I discovered that, by paying just a little more, I could fly on to Minneapolis, and spend a few days with Marilyn's parents, before going to the NRB convention.

I travelled by TWA in great comfort! The only trouble was that one of the main dishes at lunchtime was lobster. Now I am very fond of lobster, so that is what I ordered. Unbeknown to me, it must have been 'off' because, on arrival in Chicago (where I had to change planes), I was suddenly aware that the airport was going around in giddy circles! Somehow or other I managed to struggle on to the Minneapolis plane but that night, in my parents-in-law's home, I was desperately ill. It lasted all night and through the next day. In fact the salmonella poisoning was so bad, it lasted – on or off – for some eight days!

Rather unsure of myself, I flew down from Minneapolis to Washington to attend the convention. On arrival I registered and looked through the programme to find out when I would be speaking. But there was no mention of my visit, or of the session at which I was to be the speaker.

I sought out, and found, Ben Armstrong. He took one look at me and hit his forehead. 'Oh my goodness,' he said. 'Maurice, I had clear forgotten about my invitation to you to speak!' He went on to say that I would be put on the supplementary schedule to speak on the last afternoon of the convention. But that didn't happen either! In the event the only time I spoke at the convention that year was to ask a question in one of the workshops! I didn't mind, but it had seemed a rather expensive exercise for the NRB – and I had been so ill to boot!! In the end they redeemed themselves, by publishing the address I *should* have given, in full, in the next issue of the NRB Journal – headlined as the 'Address given by Maurice Rowlandson of the UK, at the NRB Convention in February'. It really was a remarkable situation.

There is a sequel however. On my return to England I wrote a strong letter of complaint to TWA. I told them of the illness I had suffered as a result of eating the lobster served in first class on their Chicago flight. Apparently I was not the only one to suffer and complain. They were well aware of the problem and they refunded my fare in full without question. This enabled me to return the cost of the fare to Ben Armstrong. The Lord knows and provides!

Back at the office I had a caller – a young aircraft pilot with British Airways. He told me that he had been 'called to work with Billy Graham' and wanted to discover how that might come about. His calling seemed real enough until I explained the difference between a 'job' and a 'vocation'. I then quoted George Wilson's phrase (365 days a year and 24 hours a day. Any time left over is your own) and his immediate reaction was, 'Oh dear! I couldn't work like that. I like set hours!' He was one of many who came with the same 'calling'.

Another regular question was 'Who will succeed Billy Graham?' Sometimes the question was asked by an active evangelist. I always replied, using the words in their actual meaning (rather than the colloquial idiom) 'God only knows!' I explained that God alone would make that appointment as He prepared His man for the task. Billy Graham never set out to be the evangelist he became. It was God who called him and set him aside.

My duties at the Royal Naval Reserve came to an end in 1977 when the Lords of the Admiralty decided that I was now too old to serve. At the Admiral Commanding Reserves annual inspection that year I was called forward to receive the Reserve Decoration from the Admiral. It was a fitting climax to 20 years of service.

It wasn't always possible to escape from embarrassment when you worked for Billy Graham. One day in the summer I had taken seven friends sailing off Dovercourt Bay. We eventually reached Pin Mill where we anchored for lunch in a sheltered bay. Little did we realise that while we were anchored a storm was brewing. As we left the shelter in which we had been anchored, we felt the full force of the wind. All but one of the sails came down and we had a wild voyage down the River Orwell. As we reached Harwich Harbour it was so rough that my guests were beginning to feel seasick. I decided to use the motor and to take in the last sail. Unfortunately it was a petrol engine and the rough sea allowed the condensation in the carburettor to get into the petrol. As we came out of the harbour, the engine died and I could not get it restarted. We dropped an anchor, but it didn't hold and we were drifting very fast on to the Dovercourt concrete breakwater. Prudence demanded immediate action and I instructed Julian, my son, to fire the Very pistol to summon the lifeboat. They were with us in 13 minutes and towed us safely into the harbour. As we moored and I came up the ladder of the harbour wall, there at the top was a squashy-hat journalist – ready with notebook and pencil for a first-hand account of all that had happened. Before he could start, he took one look at me and said 'Why! You're Maurice Rowlandson aren't you? You work with Billy Graham, don't you?' Sure enough the local paper the next day had the major headline 'Billy Graham man rescued by lifeboat'!

May 1978 saw us travelling to Norwich for the installation of Peter English as Lord Mayor of Norwich. Not only was he an ex Venturer, but he was also the father-in-law of our eldest son. It was an impressive ceremony and, for the next year Peter English kept us up to date with his mayoral programme and activities. He was still Lord Mayor at the time of the 1979 Venturers Cruise, and he invited the entire cruise, boys, girls and skippers to come to Norwich for a reception in the mayor's parlour. He gave them a good 'nosh up' after which – to our immense surprise – he took us into the Council Chamber where we held our fun sing-song and evening prayers. I can scarcely imagine that the serious Council Chamber had ever heard such rumbustious singing before – nor would indeed, ever again. Many a staid former councillor must have stirred in his grave as the strains of 'My bonnie lies over the ocean' and 'What shall we do with the drunken sailor?' echoed around the walls of the chamber. It is probable too that, during the devotional time afterwards, no such clear presentation of the Gospel had been heard in those austere surroundings!

The next two years were the years of my secretary Wendy Mitchell. Many attempts to find a good secretary in England had failed. In the end I asked George Wilson if he had anyone in Minneapolis who would like a two-year experience in the UK. As Wendy had a 'certificate of patriality' (due to her grandfather being British), she was able to come and work for two years without any special permit. From the moment she arrived, she 'took over'. In fact, on the day of her arrival it was Trooping the Colour. She insisted that we stopped in The Mall before going to her hotel. She was so small she couldn't see over the crowd. Then she spotted a milk crate nearby. She commandeered it, turned it over and stood on it with a look of triumph on her face.

We worked well together, but she had a strong mind, and a firm resolve. What Wendy wanted, Wendy got! She kept me in line, and on occasions, refused to type letters I had dictated because she thought they were not good – or right – for the BGEA. She was probably correct in that!

For many years on my birthday (in August) it had been my custom to include my secretary with any other friends going sailing. We often sailed with my friend Norman Farrar who had a lovely Royal Harwich One Design and could take four or five passengers with him. It naturally fell to Wendy's lot to be included in the August she was with me. We had an interesting day which resulted in the following story which she presented to me a week later.

> I remember Norman Farrar. He was a photographer, but, in real life, he was a sailor. He came from a fine sailing family. His brother was a sail-maker. Norman Farrar was a proper old man with not much white hair. When I sailed with him, I remember that he arrived at the marina in a dark suit, white shirt, tie – and right there he changed into rubber-soled shoes and snapped a huge plastic raincoat over himself.
>
> Tradition has it that on Maurice's birthday, he takes his secretary sailing. Maurice would take his wife, but Marilyn quite happily remains home annually for the occasion: she doesn't like the water! Maurice is another sailor. Since I was his secretary that year it was my duty to sail so I went along to sail in Norman's boat.
>
> The day was a fine one and Maurice and Norman thought that we might sail to Harwich Harbour: what did I think? Of course, I had no preference. That was fine with me. I was along for the lunch – a fine selection of apple and marmalade sandwiches; cheese and date; peanut butter and bacon (Maurice always likes two fillings in his sandwiches)! There was cake too. So we set off and eventually I could see the Harbour off in the distance.
>
> And then the wind came up. I mean the wind came up! Maurice says it increased from a 'force 3' to a 'force 5'. And there were waves! Maurice and Norman quickly decided that a trip into the harbour was not such a good idea after all – and this time they didn't ask my opinion.
>
> The sailing was rough. The wind blew and the sea was wild. The water came sloshing over the sides of the boat – which rocked a lot too. It was kind of scary I guess. But I watched Norman. He sat in the back of the boat, his hand on the tiller and he directed Maurice. Maurice was tacking. 'Come about,' Norman would say, and Maurice would scramble, making the sail do what it was supposed to do. I was sitting near the front, getting wet, hanging on, and watching Norman. He sat on his throne in that raincoat. He would turn his head slowly as though he were beholding all creation – and he did seem to be taking it all in. At the right moment he would call out a command in his old-man voice, 'come about', and Maurice would fly from his rest position and wrestle with the ropes and canvas. I remember his skinny white legs! I still

don't think I was afraid. I knew that Norman, in all his years, had never gone down, never! And I was perfectly confident that Norman, with Maurice, would get me back to land. I was kind of cold and wet, but still I had no fear.

Sometimes I think I'm still in that boat, only it isn't Norman sitting back there. It's God. Life is fine and we sail along. Sometimes there isn't much wind and living's a little dull, and then of course there are the good, enjoyable, happy times in the boat. And exciting adventurous sails too, and then sometimes storms blow up and life is so crazy and all I can do is hang on.

Oh for sure I get wet, maybe cold, pretty uncomfortable, but Maurice followed Norman's directions. He never paused or argued, he never even offered alternatives (which is pretty unusual for Maurice!) and we came through.

Unfortunately, I have a tendency to jump out of the boat. I've told God, time and time again, it seems that my destination would be so much better than His, or that I know the best way to get there; and silly old God doesn't even seem to listen! So I plunge out – and talk about wet and cold and uncomfortable! Sometimes it takes a while, but it's always awful in the end. I shamefacedly swim back to the boat; or, to be more honest I'm usually rescued at sea. Thank God! And oh, the Lord Jesus always welcomes me back and it's so wonderful to be on board again.

You see, I'm learning what I already know. I know that God will not fail me. I have His Word. 'I have been young, and now am old; yet I have not seen the righteous forsaken, his seed begging bread. (Psalm 37:25). Two sailors took me for a sail I shall not forget: and I can only hope I remember the lesson they provided. Read Psalm 107:23-30.

During these years we took every advantage of Mr Graham's visits to Europe for crusades. We organised tour groups to Dortmund, Stockholm, Copenhagen and, of course, Paris. On each of these trips we included those members of staff who wanted to come. I firmly believed that it was good for them to see Mr Graham in action and to experience the ambience of a crusade.

In late 1978, Dr Walter Smyth came to London again. This time he brought a message from Mr Graham. It was, once again, the question of saving money and reducing the subsidy from

Minneapolis. We had already reduced the staff. Now all we could do was to reduce our office space – so we set about doing that. We had a grand move around and this enabled us to dispose of about half our floor space. In addition, we hived off Miss Jean Wilson's work and made it a separate operation. She now rented office space from us. So, all in all, we were able to make the savings that Dr Smyth looked for – whilst still maintaining our level of ministry.

At this point we were on the threshold of a major change in my own ministry and yet another means to save the association some money. Ever since I had worked with the Keswick Convention Council at the time of the centenary meetings, I had looked back on that time with immense happiness. They were a good crowd to work with. Then, in the Keswick News Letter in October 1978 there was the announcement that the present secretary would be retiring and an invitation was extended to any who might wish to apply for the position.

I was in a quandary. Things were moving ahead towards a return to Britain by Mr Graham, and I didn't want to be left out of that. At the same time, planning was going ahead for the great International Congress of Itinerant Evangelists to be held in Amsterdam in 1983. For that I had already been asked to hold myself ready to be chief steward. At the same time the position at Keswick was one which attracted me enormously. I needed to see if the 'Thin Gold Line' included that direction! I decided to telephone Mr Graham and to talk it over with him. I pointed out to him that, if I worked for Keswick, the BGEA work would still have priority, and I felt I had time enough and strength enough to cope with both jobs. Mr Graham agreed. In fact, he seemed relieved because, as he said to me, he felt that there were elements in my present 'holding' work which did not use my talents to their full advantage. Furthermore, Mr Graham said that he saw the Keswick Convention as complementary to his ministry, and he did not believe it to be incompatible for me to be involved in both.

Thus encouraged, I sent off my application to become the secretary of the convention. There followed a series of interviews, first with the entire council and subsequently with the chairman, and then the treasurer. At that point I decided to share the situation with the British board of the BGEA. Dr Walter Smyth was present, and Mr Graham had already told him of his support for me to take on this new work. Dr Smyth also pointed out that the Keswick Convention would share in the cost of the offices and in my salary. Both of these factors would enable us to make further cuts in our BGEA budget. So I felt that it was 'all systems go'. I now just awaited the word from Keswick.

That word came on 27 January 1979 that my appointment as secretary had been confirmed and on 30 April the same year I started work with them. There followed 14 years of very happy association during which the new Keswick building was envisaged and completed and the convention went on from strength to strength. The full story of those 14 years is told in my book *Life with the Keswick Convention*.

The first ICIE congress was in 1983 and my involvement there produced the first clash of loyalties. The first week of the convention overlapped with the ICIE dates. In accordance with my promise to Mr Graham, I put the ICIE work first and made other arrangements to see Keswick through the first week. My eldest son, Gary, said he would be willing to step into the breach. He was assisted by a 'brief' that I prepared giving an hour-by-hour breakdown of all that had to be done in the days of preparation and during the first week of the convention. He did a magnificent job and thoroughly commended himself to the chairman and the council of the convention. As for me, I had total confidence in his abilities, and was able to give my full attention to the congress work.

By now the face-to-face interview with Billy Graham in Nice had taken place, and I was learning how to fit in the Keswick work with the work of the BGEA; 1983/84 were years of preparation for Mission England and we waited with great anticipation and expectation to see what God was going to do as Billy Graham returned once again to this country. The stories of those days have already been told.

CHAPTER SEVENTEEN

THE MISSION TO LONDON

When Mission England ended with the final meetings in Sheffield I was doubtful whether the 'Thin Gold Line' would continue. By now I was very busy working with the Keswick Convention. There were two exceptional features about Keswick at that time. The first was the annual Mabledon Prayer Conference. This two-day gathering brought together all the speakers, council members and trustees to pray for the forthcoming convention in July. A brief time was given to a devotional time and to Bible exposition. But the most time was devoted to several sessions of prayer. Clearly, to me, this was the 'power house' of the convention.

The other feature, at that time, was the fact that we always had a 100 per cent attendance at council and trustee meetings. In many of the committees I had sat upon over the past years, there were always 'apologies for absence'. Not so at the Keswick Convention. Such was the level of commitment that – even if unwell – it seemed that everyone involved regarded these times as total commitment. It was a wonderful encouragement to me as secretary.

It was important because much was going on in the Keswick world. Not least was the decision to build the £1m Convention Centre. Ground was broken in 1986, and the centre was ready and complete for use – together with a brand-new tent – in time for the 1987 convention. It was a wonderful building which opened debt-free thanks to the efforts of Col. Peter Harvey who, with his staff, worked so hard to raise the money required. Amongst the places he visited in the process was San Antonio in Texas. He came back from them with a firm invitation to take the Keswick Convention en bloc to San Antonio – which we did a year later. It was an interesting experience.

Just a year later, in a massive storm at Keswick, our lovely new tent was ripped to shreds by the gale. We had to make emergency arrangements to accommodate the meetings, and a year later a new – and stronger – tent was supplied to us.

Billy Graham continued to visit London from time to time and I was always involved in his plans whenever he was there. Dr Robert Runcie had invited him to attend his enthronement as Archbishop of Canterbury in the cathedral, and he had accepted the invitation. That meant, for me, a journey to Canterbury to find the most suitable place for Mr Graham to stay overnight. Later, with T. W. Wilson in my car and with Mr Graham travelling with Bishop Michael Baughen, we travelled back to Canterbury for the event. Bishop Robert Runcie always had had a high regard for Mr Graham. What Mr Graham had not realised was that he would be in the archbishop's procession. Fortunately he had brought his academic robes with him from America, so he was suitably attired.

T. W. Wilson, Russ Busby (the long-standing Team photographer) and I, along with some others, all watched the ceremony on television in Russ Busby's hotel room. It was an impressive occasion. If we couldn't be there in person it was the next best thing. We felt highly privileged that Billy Graham was able to take part in such a prestigious way. We watched as the future archbishop turned aside to greet him and to shake him by the hand.

After the ceremony we drove back to London where he and Mrs Graham had an invitation once again to have lunch with Her Majesty the Queen. When he returned to America Mr Graham left his academic robes in my care for him to use on another visit to Britain. The temptation to try them on was too great for me and for a fleeting moment, while I was photographed, I was academically qualified!

In January 1989 Billy and Ruth Graham were invited to stay for a weekend at Sandringham House with Her Majesty the Queen. The occasion was her invitation to Billy Graham to preach at the Royal Chapel on Sandringham Estate on the Sunday. I drove them there on Saturday afternoon. T. W. Wilson rode with me and enjoyed the experience of being 'waved through' the gates of Sandringham Estate!

On Sunday there was no room in the chapel for the 20 or so Team members and friends so the service was relayed into the rectory next door. We were invited to stay for lunch afterwards. Dr Walter Smyth made it clear to all of us that after lunch we should leave to return to our hotel immediately. He told us that Mr and Mrs Graham would be brought from Sandringham House to spend some quality time with the Revd Gerry Murphy and his wife Joy. He wanted them to have that time on their own with the Grahams. However, both Gerry and Joy had been long-standing friends of both TW and me and, after lunch she asked us to stay on for tea. We politely declined, in view of Dr Smyth's insistence.

We were all in the car waiting to go back to the hotel when Joy Murphy came out and spoke to Walter Smyth through the window of the car. 'We wanted TW and Maurice to stay for tea, but they tell us you have told them not to. Can I get you to let them stay?' Walter Smyth capitulated immediately and told the two of us to get out of the car: 'Don't keep the lady waiting!' he said. We had a lovely time, and met several of the equerries who had come with the Grahams from Sandringham House. When we got back to the hotel, the atmosphere was distinctly 'frosty'! Dr Smyth had not liked this reversal to his decision.

The next morning, Monday, Dr Smyth and I drove to Sandringham House to collect the Grahams. When we arrived we were met by the Queen's Page, Paul Whyrew, who was a member of the church that Marilyn and I attended at Frinton. As soon as he saw us he invited the two of us into the 'footmen's room' for coffee. Then, when the time came to leave, he took Dr Smyth and me through the inner recesses of Sandringham House where, in the drawing room, we were met by Billy and Ruth Graham as they came downstairs with an equerry. Suddenly the 'frosty' atmosphere disappeared and all was right with Dr Smyth once again!

As we got into the car a footman came out and gave me a cardboard box. 'Here are two pheasants from the Royal Estate for Mr and Mrs Graham,' he said. I put them in the car boot and, all the way back to London, Billy Graham worried about what to do with those pheasants. I suggested that, when he got to the hotel, he should give them to the chef and ask for them to be properly dressed for cooking and then served to Ruth and to him in his room. T. W. Wilson took the box in and, ten minutes later he was back – with the box! 'Hey Maurice!' he said. 'Billy thinks these pheasants are historic. He thinks they should be stuffed!'

I took them back to the office and asked Michael Sage, one of my staff, to organise this. Two weeks later he brought into my office a beautiful 3-D diorama, made by the taxidermist. It was of two stuffed pheasants breasting their way through a corn field, set in a background of a blue sky. At the bottom was a small brass plate which said 'Pheasants from the Royal Estate, Sandringham. Presented to Dr and Mrs Billy Graham by her Majesty the Queen, 16 January 1984'. I asked where this magnificent work had been done and I was told that the Natural History Museum had agreed to do it at no cost when they heard who it was for.

Much of my time was taken up with work for the forthcoming International Congress of Itinerant Evangelists (ICIE). At one stage it looked as though the organising office would be in London but ultimately it was set up in Amsterdam. Marilyn and I went there on a regular basis to help them set it up. The congress itself was held in 1983 and was a huge success. Many thousands of applicants applied and only a limited number of them could be accepted. As a result, Mr Graham decided to have another congress three years later. It was to be twice as big as the 1983 congress but still at the Rai Centre in Amsterdam. My participation was the same as before. It was very hard and demanding work – but so satisfying to see all these young evangelists, from all over the world, enthusiastic and ready for training and action.

Early in 1987 the first of three major shocks came to us. First, at a board meeting in our offices, Dr Walter Smyth told us that the American board had decided that we would have to close down our offices in Camden Town. At the same time he said that

Billy Graham was burdened about 'reaching the whole world for Christ'. At this stage he didn't know exactly how, but he had decided to establish a Headquarters for International Ministry in London. A team from the USA had been over to research locations and they had found an ideal building in Harrow, Middlesex. Bob Williams was appointed as the international coordinator for Mission World (as it was called) and I think the fact that his former Mission England offices had been at David Rennie's business premises in Harrow, had made him realise that this was a good location.

Walter Smyth went on to say that there was an area on the ground floor of the new offices which would ideally suit us. He said that I was to make plans immediately, to move the entire offices to the new Harrow building. Three days later Liz Fane and I went to measure up the new offices – which we discovered were *very* small – and four weeks later we moved in. After our careful measuring, we knew exactly where the essential items would fit in (bearing in mind that we also had the Keswick staff to cope with), and it was a tight squeeze.

We explained that if you wanted to work on our staff, you first needed to have your hips measured to see if you would fit in! But we survived! One thing was clear, there just was not enough room for all the staff we had. Three were involved in the Keswick work and we only had room for three more. So, one by one, we said a tearful farewell to those who had served us so faithfully over many years. Liz Fane was the first to go and, by the end of two more months, there were just three of us left (plus the three for Keswick).

Then on 29 July 1987 came the second shock. I was called into David Rennie's office in Harrow. He found it very hard to tell me that his instructions from Walter Smyth were that I should retire on 31 October 1987. There was nothing 'on the horizon' then and Dr Smyth didn't feel that the association would be justified in retaining me on a full-time basis. He said that I would be 'retained' as a consultant and would remain on the BGEA Board.

Then he went on to tell me that Mission World would not now be happening. The Harrow office would be closed down in October (which coincided with my retirement) and all the American staff would return to the USA. This would mean that our office space would no longer be available to us. This put me in a quandary because Mr Graham had assured me that the Keswick work could be run from our offices, and my contract with Keswick provided for that. So, in desperation, I telephoned Mr Graham to ask what I should do. He was, as always, extremely generous. He told me to find small, but adequate, offices and that the BGEA would pay the rent for five years. And so they did! In fact, Mr Graham sent me a copy of a letter he had written to John Corts, who by now had succeeded George Wilson as the business manager of the association. In it he said:

> In view of my conversation yesterday with Maurice Rowlandson I want you to know his advice and counsel are absolutely invaluable to me. I asked him what he was going to do, and he said he would be moving out of the Harrow office at the end of this month and was going to get a little hideaway for the office of the Keswick Convention. As you know he is the secretary and they have practically no money. He thinks he will be giving almost his full time to Mission England once Blair gets there. I asked him how much it would cost. He said seven thousand pounds a year.
>
> I made a commitment that we would pick up the entire amount as a gift to Keswick.

Later when Billy Graham heard that I was to retire he wrote to me:

> Beloved friend, whether you are involved in what you called 'periphery' service or not, you will always be a part of us! Even though we are making major changes, quite a number of retirements, closing of offices, etc., we have been for so many years a 'family'. Even when a family member no longer lives at home, they are still a member of the family with whom to keep in touch. That's the way I feel. You and Marilyn and the family mean so much to Ruth and me and the rest of the Team. We will look forward to times of fellowship together in the years ahead. Once again, we can never thank you enough for the tremendous job you have done down through so many years, and I know the Lord will continue to use and bless your ministry.

So our third major shock was the need to move out of the eight-month-old offices we had moved into, and again we faced the need to find new offices. I have said it before, and I can say it again because it is so true: the Lord knows the need, and the

Lord provides. Just across the road from the Harrow offices was a small suite of offices, just big enough for us. We still needed to tell the staff we would have to measure their hips to see if they would fit in! We moved into those new offices on 4 November and again it was a tight squeeze. Although I had six staff remaining, only three were in at any one time, so we were able to get by. Three weeks later the BGEA Board gave a retirement party for me at St Paul's, Robert Adam Street, when a large number of relatives, friends and staff came to bid me farewell. Amongst those who came was our old friend and colleague, Harvey Thomas. He told us that he had just been appointed as the organiser of Margaret Thatcher's election campaign. He lost no time in making his Christian witness known, and he did such a good job that he remained in association for the entire time of her premiership. When she retired, she asked the Queen to make Harvey a CBE (Commander of the British Empire) an honour well deserved.

A month later, the American Board of the BGEA also gave a dinner to mark my retirement. Several of my colleagues from the USA had flown over to be with us, and it was a great surprise. I had not known it was going to happen.

Meanwhile, in another sphere, Prebendary Richard Bewes (a member of the BGEA Board) had been in lengthy correspondence with Billy Graham. He wrote, on 22 April 1987, to say:

> I am sending you a signed invitation from a great many of us in the churches of central London. Well over five hundred have signed and I have discussed the possibility with the Bishop of London, as well as with the Archbishop of Canterbury. He has written you a private letter in support of this invitation. Gavin Reid is bringing this invitation to you by hand and we prayerfully trust that the Lord will lay it on the hearts of yourself and your Board to respond positively.

With that letter he sent a 12-page bound book containing all the signatures of those who supported this move. It was an impressive list. A week later Billy Graham telephoned me to tell me that he had responded to Richard Bewes and that the answer was 'yes' for a Mission to London in 1989.

On 2 December 1988, yet another call came for me to visit David Rennie in his office. He had surprising news! He asked me to come back on to the salaried staff for the period of the Mission to London. He said that I would have two responsibilities: first to supervise the Livelink closed circuit television programme, and second (during the mission itself) to run the Team office. These two responsibilities were 'right up my street'. I accepted the challenge on the spot and three days later started working at the Mission to London office in St Paul's Church, Robert Adam Street.

I had a small 'team' working with me on the Livelink programme. Barry Roberts was the coordinator and he had Nigel Crow helping him. I was assigned Alison Carr as my secretary. She was to remain – off and on – in that position until 1997. Our target was 200 Livelink relays and we exceeded that number considerably. The Livelink programme would be transmitted from the Earls Court arena during the third phase of the mission.

Before the mission actually started there was to be a cricket match on the Saturday at Lord's cricket ground. It occurred to me that it would make a relaxing 'day out' for some of the members of the Billy Graham Team: I booked a box at Lord's and Marilyn and I took 16 of them to watch cricket for the day. I made sure that they were well catered for and I wrote a page of information about the game which I entitled, 'An American's Guide to the Game of Cricket'.*

It was, indeed, a wonderful day and the Americans enjoyed it so much that some of them went back to see another match the following week! During the afternoon Liz Fane had said that some Team members wanted to take Marilyn and me to 'Tea at the Ritz' after the match. We had never done that before and it was quite an experience for us. On the way there I stopped at the office to see if there were any important messages. There was – one! It was from Canon Treadgold, the Queen's Chaplain at the Chapel Royal in Windsor Great Park. He asked me if those who were coming with Mr Graham on Sunday would accept an invitation to have drinks with the Queen Mother after the service.

---

* See Appendix B in *Life with Billy*

We would be going to the Royal Lodge! On their behalf I accepted.

I returned to the Ritz to pass on the exciting news. I had to tell them that the ladies would have to wear gloves and hats – which, late on a Saturday afternoon, raised some problems! Where better to pass on the news however, than at the Ritz.

The canon told me that the invitation to Mr and Mrs Graham and me also included the five passengers in our second car. In that car would be Dr T. W. Wilson and Mary Helen his wife; also Blair Carlson and Elizabeth his wife. That left one place to be filled. We decided that it should go to one of the senior staff members and their names were put 'into a hat'. Ingrid Holdsworth was the fortunate person whose name was drawn. She had been working with the counselling and follow-up planning team. She was overwhelmed when she was given the news.

On Sunday, after the service at the Chapel Royal, the Queen Mother with the Queen and Prince Philip mingled with the congregation as they left the service. Canon Treadgold briefed me about our visit to the Royal Lodge. He said it would be a very informal occasion. He suggested that we should allow 'the Royals' a few minutes to walk back to the Royal Lodge before going across to join them. When we got there we were welcomed in by an equerry and were taken through to meet the Queen, Prince Philip, the Queen Mother, Sir William Heseltine, Gerald Ward and about half-a-dozen other friends of the Royal Family.

All the guests quickly made us feel at home and they all spoke to everybody. The Queen herself chatted to Ingrid for quite a long time. I found myself in conversation with the Queen Mother. After ten minutes it was hard to think of things to talk to her about. There was nothing we had in common. Then I noticed two of the corgi dogs sitting under the table. I remarked to her how lovely it was to see the corgis in real life! I said that we often saw their pictures on television or in the newspapers. 'Yes' she replied 'but there are only two of them today. Usually there are three but the third one's gone off to get married!'

When we left the Royal Lodge, Mr and Mrs Graham were taken in the Queen's car back to Windsor Castle for lunch. Later I went there to collect the Grahams. Eventually they came out accompanied by an equerry and Prince Philip. As I looked up, the Queen and the Queen Mother were standing at a staircase window waving them off. As we ourselves drove off through the gates there was a large crowd waiting to give us a farewell wave – although I suspect that they little knew who were in the car!

Phase one of the Mission to London would be at the West Ham Football Club Stadium at Upton Park. We had a problem there which was not an unusual problem for the Billy Graham Team. All the tickets were free and did not stipulate any specific seat. In America, around a quarter to a third of the free tickets were never used. Therefore the mission committee always issued rather more tickets than the seating capacity of the venue. Mostly that meant that the tickets which *were* used just about filled the stadium. But to an Englishman something received free meant that he was likely to use it. So the situation could arise when far more people turned up than those for whom we had seats. West Ham was no exception! I was despatched to deal with the problem of people outside with tickets but no seats. It was almost like facing a lynching mob! 'I've got a ticket' they all said, and I had to pacify them until we could find a solution.

While I faced the mob outside several of my American colleagues were in consultation with the West Ham United authorities. Eventually they negotiated permission to allow us to let people use the turf. So I changed from being the *bête noir* to becoming the champion of the enormous crowd!

Amongst them, unbeknown to me, was a young man who was the exceptional bass guitarist of McKenna's Gold – a popular band of the late 1980s. His name was Alex Bowler and he had been persuaded to come by a friend. Five years later I heard his story – the details of which must await their proper place in this story.

The second phase of the Mission to London was at the Crystal Palace Stadium. We had news that there was to be a major transport strike on the Wednesday of that week and that was the very day when we were to start at the Crystal Palace. This led to a great discussion in the committee whether or not we should cancel. The outcome was that we decided to continue without any change to our programme. One attraction was that the singer Cliff Richard was expected to take part that evening. We hoped and prayed – and believed – that that factor would help to encourage the crowds to come. And they did. We had close on 30,000 there that first night. It was one of the biggest crowds for the whole of the Mission to London.

The penultimate phase of the mission took place over six days in the Earls Court Arena. In effect, the arena became a vast 'studio' as more than 250 closed circuit television programmes were relayed from the meetings across the British Isles and overseas. Each night the arena was filled for what, in effect, became the last series of meetings that Billy Graham would ever hold in England.

At Earls Court, Billy Graham gave me the task of greeting the many VIPs who had responded to our invitation to attend the meetings. Some of them he wanted to meet personally and he would ask me to bring them to his room. This involved fetching them from the VIP lounge at the far end of the building and taking them along the corridors to his room behind the platform. Two people who attended one night were the Archbishop of Canterbury (Dr Robert Runcie) and Cardinal Hume of the Roman Catholic Church. Billy Graham said that he would like to see them together and he sent me to get them. I apologised to both of them for the many double doors which lie between the VIP room and Mr Graham's room. At each pair of doors either the Archbishop or the Cardinal would stand back and ask the other to go first! Eventually we reached the final pair of doors and I told them so, whereupon Cardinal Hume turned to Robert Runcie and asked, 'Your Grace: is this an Anglican door or a Catholic door?' Before he could answer a member of the Earls Court staff appeared and, while he held open one door, I held the other open and they went through the doorway together – whereupon the Archbishop remarked, 'That's how it should be!'

The closing meeting was held at the Wembley Stadium. It was very wet throughout the entire meeting. The rain may have been bad, but the thunder and lightning that accompanied it was worse. The Revd Gavin Reid (who had been chairman of Mission England five years earlier) was just about to talk about the offering. He came to the microphone and, at the instant he said, 'Now

I want to talk to you about money,' there was a gigantic explosion. The lightning seemed to attack the very microphone itself. All the lights went out and the sound was interrupted for a few moments. When the sound came back on, a rather shocked Gavin Reid continued speaking.

As for Billy Graham, he preached in a raincoat, and stood beneath an umbrella. Nevertheless he preached as powerfully as ever. As soon as he gave his time-honoured 'invitation' – 'I'm going to ask you to get up out of your seats and to come and stand at the front' – thousands responded from every area of the great complex. Rain or not, they streamed forward from their places to stand on the turf in front of the platform. I always believed that many of those who came forward that day had been touched by a message earlier in the week. That day, at Wembley, they came with the express intention of going forward.

One last story: throughout the busy period 1988–90 I had three different secretaries working for me at the same time! Susie Sanguinetti was acting as my personal assistant (PA) at the Mission to London office. Alexandra Davison was my PA at the North London Theatre Trust and I now had Liz Fane working with me as my PA for the Billy Graham Evangelistic Association. None of them had ever met any of the others and I thought it was high time that they should get together. So I arranged to take the three of them to lunch one day and we met at a French Restaurant just off Baker Street.

It was a pleasant lunchtime as the three girls shared with each other the intricacies of their work. It was fascinating to see how differently each of them approached their work. Liz was very competent and took a lot of the burden off my shoulders. Susie was the fastest and most accurate secretary I had ever had and Alexandra was entirely dependent upon her own initiative as she did her work for me at the North London Theatre Trust. They all said that they thoroughly enjoyed their work – and that was a great comfort.

Then we got around to talking about how each of them had become Christians. The answers were quite unbelievable. Each of them at different times had worked in Paris for a while and all three of them had found Christ as their Saviour and Lord when they had attended St Michael's, one of the two English churches in Paris! With that bond between them, they made a wonderful team who, from then on, tended to keep in touch.

The 1989 Mission to London was to be Mr Graham's last mission on English soil. It was the conclusion of a ministry which stretched from the late 1940s through to 1989. Scotland was to come of course, and I had not realised that my tenure of office would be extended through that period too.

CHAPTER EIGHTEEN

MISSION TO SCOTLAND

I PREPARED to sink back into oblivion when, out of the blue, came the invitation to be deeply involved in the Mission to Scotland. It would be held in three centres – Edinburgh, Aberdeen and Glasgow.

Mr Graham re-enforced the invitation to me in his letter of 6 June 1990. He said:

> This probably finds you at a very busy time with Keswick and all. I hope that you are keeping up with the events in Scotland. It looks as though we will be going there, God willing, next year, and I certainly would want your advice and counsel at every twist and turn of the road.

My first task, as usual, was to investigate suitable accommodation for the Team members and for Mr Graham himself. The usual criteria applied and I needed to look into things like security; room service; late meals; extra telephones and suitable nearby rooms for his secretarial team. As far as the Team was concerned, it needed to be accommodated not too far from the mission location, but they too needed the facility for late meals. We also needed a few rooms for office use – not least the Team office which was to be my responsibility once again.

Between the end of the Mission to London and the start of the Mission to Scotland in 1991, I travelled up to Scotland several times – always in advance of the arrival of the American Team members. Once they arrived they would take over the day-to-day planning from me. At any rate there was practically no gap between the ending of my involvement with the Mission to London, and with the Mission to Scotland.

I went to Edinburgh about seven days before the mission started and discovered that, once again I was to be in charge of the Team office – a complex activity which involved keeping all the members of the Team informed about all activities; acting as Team banker; taking responsibility for accommodation, transport and the general welfare of the Team. The number varied from time to time but there were, on average, about 30–40 team members with their wives and some American friends.

I had asked Liz Fane to help me once again, but this time she was too committed to come. Marilyn and I talked about who else might be available and suddenly Marilyn remembered Amanda Bragg. She was an interesting – and very competent – young lady who had come with us on one of our Holy Land tours. She was not a Christian, but had been encouraged to come with us by a Christian friend who told her: 'It would not be too holy for you!' In fact, she fitted in very well and attended all our evening Bible talks. Because of the reduction in our staff numbers in London, I had no one who could come and help me at the Keswick Convention in July, so I told the Holy Land tour group that if they knew anybody who might like to help, to let me know. To my surprise Amanda volunteered. I warned her that Keswick would be very different to the Holy Land tour, and that it was 'meetings all the time'. That didn't put her off, however, and she came and did a very good job. I don't think she came to any of the meetings, but the talks were relayed to the room in which she worked.

A year later the same situation arose and I had a telephone call from Amanda asking if I needed help at Keswick once again. I did, and she came and once more did an excellent job. So it was not altogether surprising that her name came up to help in Scotland.

As soon as I telephoned her she was very enthusiastic to come. I warned her that, unlike Keswick, she would be involved in all the mission meetings because my responsibilities needed her full participation. She came and, once again, was a great help to me.

One of the friends of the Billy Graham Team was an elderly gentleman called Pek Gunn. In his younger days he had organised special trains to take parties to wherever there was to be a Billy Graham Crusade. He was, he told me constantly, 'a train man'. He had also organised a 'Tennessee Breakfast' in every city to which he took a train party. We had had one in the Hilton Hotel in London – southern-style and with unfamiliar grits and cornbread!

Now, fully retired, he was so loved by the Billy Graham Team that they were glad to have him with them. He was a great poet, and turned almost every event into a lovely and moving poem. He drove with me out to Edinburgh airport on the day that Marilyn arrived to join me. As she got into the car, he read a lovely poem of welcome to her. She was deeply touched and very thrilled with his contribution.

At times he was a bit of a liability to us. His ancestors had come from Wick in the northernmost part of Scotland and he wanted to visit the town. We managed to find a bus going from Edinburgh to Wick and we put him on it. Later in the day we wanted to use one of the mission's cars but we couldn't find the key anywhere. We looked everywhere and asked everybody. No one had seen it or touched it. Then the phone rang. It was Pek on the other end phoning from Wick: 'Are you missing some car keys?' he asked. Then he told us that he had picked them up by mistake and he had found them in his pocket. We had one less car to use that night!

On our last day in Aberdeen this 85-plus old man sidled up to me in the Team room and touched me on the arm. 'Maureece,' he said, 'you know I am an ol' train man, and I love the trains. I'd love to take the train from here to Glasgow. Would that be alright?' I told him that it would be perfectly alright. Then he went on to ask, 'Would it be alright if I asked young 'Manda to come with me and look after me?' Once more I told him that it would be alright. Then came the punch line: 'You see, Maureece, I asked because I just didn't want folks talkin'.'

The last night in Glasgow was a very emotive one. It was, quite certainly, the last time Billy Graham would preach at a crusade or mission in the UK. I stood in the middle of Celtic Stadium and said to myself, 'Drink this in, Maurice! You'll never see the like of it again.'

It was something of a surprise, however, when Billy Graham invited both Amanda and me to sit on the platform on that last night. He wanted to thank us for our work and could most easily do so if we were sitting behind him. I think Amanda was even more surprised than I was. After the meeting, as we walked back across the turf, she turned to me and said, 'I almost went forward tonight.' I told her that I wished she had for it would have been the culmination of her time working with me.

As Scotland ended, so did my 'recall' to serve with the BGEA. The Board gave me (my second!) 'retirement dinner' as this term of service came to an end.

'Retirement' was really in the air at this time. I had a phone call from Philip Hacking who was the chairman of the Keswick Convention. He asked me to take the train up to Sheffield for a session with him. After a few introductory comments he then told me that he felt the time had come to move the Keswick office to our lovely new Convention Centre in Keswick. He asked me if Marilyn and I would be prepared to move to the Lake District. I had no hesitation in declining the offer and he replied that, perhaps, I should take early retirement after the convention of 1992. I agreed with him but first set out several arguments that I felt militated against moving the office to Keswick. Nonetheless they went ahead and appointed a successor who took over from me after the 1992 convention. He only lasted a few years before my protégé Mark Smith was appointed as the new secretary. He soon found that all the arguments I had put forward were justified, and he moved the office back to the south of England.

So, as far as the BGEA was concerned, I was now back in my 'consultancy' role and remained as a member of the board – until 1998 that is!

CHAPTER NINETEEN

EUROPE93 AND THE GLOBAL MISSION

I HAD another phone call from David Rennie on 12 February 1992. He said that he had had a message from Billy Graham that I was to be reappointed to the Team again to organise the British support for Europe93 – a major outreach to the whole of Western Europe. David Rennie added that Billy Graham wanted to ask me to establish a small office to handle this responsibility and to 'pull out all of the stops' to make it a success.

I thought to myself – the 'Thin Gold Line' is still continuing – and once more I found myself within the orbit of the Billy Graham Team and I thanked the Lord that He was still able to use me in this work.

Because of faxes, e-mails, computer links and other modern technology, I saw no point in a Central London office, so I looked around Frinton to see what I could find. Very quickly the Lord led us to a lovely small suite of offices in the centre of Frinton and I negotiated a short lease to use them.

David Rennie had told me to engage adequate staff to do the job properly, and to make sure that the office was equipped with all the latest gadgetry. I immediately contacted Alison Carr, who had been my PA during the Livelink Mission. She was in a temporary job and was thrilled to come back into the orbit of Billy Graham Missions. She, along with Becky Corton as a junior typist, completed my complement of staff. We set about getting the equipment we needed. As soon as everything was in place we held an Open Day to dedicate the premises and ourselves to this new ministry that the Lord had given to us. A great many people came to support us that day – from all over the country – as well as from Frinton itself.

Europe93 was to be the last event organised by Bob Williams in America before he went to be with the Lord from major physical problems which had afflicted him. For the Europe93 and the Global Mission he organised three training conferences. The first of these was in Budapest, Hungary, in July 1992. Representatives came from all over Europe to learn how best they could contribute to the success of the mission. We learned that the mission would be conducted from Essen in Germany, and would be carried across the European continent by satellite. In effect it became a prototype for the Global Mission to follow two years later.

The training conference in Hungary was followed by a conference for the UK representatives in Coventry. Bob Williams asked me to organise it for all the British participants. It was a wonderful event which really set the delegates 'on fire' and returned them to their locations throughout the United Kingdom, ready to put into practice what they had learned.

I ran into a major dilemma one Friday in May 1993 when I had a letter from Franklin Graham – Billy Graham's eldest son – to ask me if I would carry on the same work for him that I had done for his father. In many ways I would have liked to do that, because I saw it as a continuance of the 'Thin Gold Line'.

On the Sunday I took the letter with me to church and showed it to my 'mentor' David Rennie. He read it through and strongly advised me to decline. He felt that my loyalties were to Billy Graham, and that it could raise a problem if I had split loyalties. 'No man can serve two masters,' he said! The following week my associate John Corts, in Minneapolis, confirmed that this was his feeling too. It was hard to go home and write the 'No' reply, but I felt confident that there were those who knew the situation better than I did, and I rested on their advice.

A week later, David Rennie told me that I was to go to Minneapolis for a conference with Bob Williams and other international representatives. David said that he would be coming too and that he felt it was an important conference.

And so it turned out to be. Bob Williams conducted three major sessions – the last with Franklin Graham present. In the first session Bob shared with all of us his experiences with Franklin Graham in Australia. He told us that he had radically changed his mind about Franklin, and that he was amazed at the excellence both of the meetings and the preaching. He said: 'Franklin is a good preacher – in many ways he is better than his father!' He told us that, in conversation with him, Franklin had shared some of his ideas and vision for the future.

In the second session, Bob explained that there was a complete U-turn in the thinking of the organisation. Up until now we had all clearly understood that when Billy Graham went to Glory, the organisation would be wound up and closed down. Now, however, he said that Franklin had become painfully aware of the immense resources that the BGEA had for evangelism. He had told Bob Williams that, in his opinion, it would be wasting the resources that God had given us, if we closed the association down. Rather, said Bob Williams, Franklin feels we should capitalise on our assets and promote and use them for the Glory of God. Far from closing down, the BGEA would be expanding and each of us would have a part in this greater ministry.

The third session was given largely over to prayer. Franklin was with us and he emphasised that he had this vision of bigger and greater ministries using our resources in the years ahead. He then urged that we get down to prayer. He looked around the 25 or so of us in the room and said, 'You are all totally committed. As we get to prayer, I expect every one of you to take part.' With that, we turned around to kneel at our chairs, and two hours later we rose from a productive and wonderful prayer time.

I began to wonder if my 'no' letter had been premature, but David Rennie assured me that I had done the right thing – in spite of all that we had heard in Minneapolis.

As the successful Europe93 concluded, Billy Graham unveiled his plans for a worldwide satellite ministry to be known as 'the Global Mission'. It would originate from San Juan, in Puerto Rico and, like Europe93, it would be carried by satellite across the world.

Before I became really involved in that project, there was to be a meeting which might well have significance for many years to come. I had a phone call early in July 1994. It was from an Alex Bowler – bass guitarist of the pop group McKenna's Gold. He wanted to meet me to discuss his 'call' to become an evangelist. He told me that this had happened at the Crystal Palace Mission in 1989 (a story I have referred to earlier). Now Alex recounts his experience:

> When Billy Graham gave his invitation to come to the front, I immediately walked down the steps, and there I stood, near the front of the great crowd. As I stood there, I knew that I was a lost sinner who needed to repent. Strange thinking for a rock musician! I remember hanging my head down as I realised the purity of Jesus and the depth of darkness in my own life. I just wanted to give my whole life to Jesus Christ.
>
> Other people were still streaming forward and Billy Graham was scanning the crowd. At one point, it seemed, he was staring at me. As he did so he pointed directly at me and declared 'God may be calling you to be an evangelist!' At that moment God spoke in my heart and it was very real to me.

His reason to contact me had been a development of that 'call' in which he wanted my advice. He continued:

> I have been invited to join the Evangelisation Society, to be their evangelist in the south-west of England.

He knew he had much to learn and he was prepared to be open to the leading of the Spirit of God in his life. I asked myself, 'Is he an evangelist? Is his call real?' I had allowed two hours of my time on the day we met. I had judged that that would sufficient. In the event, it was not! I had to leave for another appointment with a specialist in Harley Street. When the two hours were up I gave Alex a choice. 'We can either say farewell here and now, or you can ride with me in the car to my next appointment.' He chose to ride along.

On arrival at Harley Street a parking meter was soon found and another choice confronted Alex. 'You can either sit here in the car or you can, if you wish, come and sit in the waiting room at the specialist's.' Alex chose the second option, and together we walked up the street to the consulting rooms. As it happened the specialist was ready immediately so I left Alex in the waiting room with some fifteen other people and I disappeared upstairs for my consultation. Returning to the waiting room half an hour later I found that Alex had the whole roomful talking about Christ and he was handing them tracts! 'Now *that* is an evangelist,' I said to myself.

He went to work with the Evangelisation Society, and subsequently, when their ministry came to an end, he formed the 'Alex Bowler Evangelistic Association'. Working through that, he has been invited, as a member of the Luis Palau team, to preach the Gospel in Eastern Europe. He has also conducted several missions in the heart of Africa. Here at home he has been involved in tent missions, and in open-air work. God is using him in a remarkable way – and it all started as a result of a God-inspired 'throwaway line' that Billy Graham used from the platform at Crystal Palace.

Just before we got into gear with the planning for the Global Mission, we had news of the death of Billie Barrows – the wife of the beloved Cliff Barrows. David Rennie phoned me up and told me to go to America to represent London at the funeral. I flew to Greenville, South Carolina, where many of the Team were gathered to pay their respects. It was only a short visit, but I appreciated David's invitation to go.

My marching orders for the Global Mission in the UK were explicit. I was to engender enthusiasm and interest across the whole UK, and encourage local groups to get involved. Our plan was to utilise major locations where the satellite programme could be received, and to run each centre as a 'mini-crusade' (or mission) with trained counsellors and every aspect of a Billy Graham meeting included. Many centres organised their local choirs and there were centres across the entire UK.

In London we took two major decisions. One was to place an announcement on one of the massive coloured and moving signs in Piccadilly Circus. In this we were encouraged by Mark Greene who was with the London Bible College. He and I worked closely together in formulating the publicity for the Global Mission and he was a tower of strength to me. Our communication was mostly by telephone. The ministry was the important thing and our telephone calls rarely lasted more than a minute and a half. He said what he had to say: I said what I had to say – and the work got done, speedily and efficiently. There was one occasion when Mark phoned me up about something, and it took a rather long telephone call. Mark was heard to remark afterwards, 'It's a miracle! I've had Maurice on the phone for more than two minutes!'

It was through his good offices that we got a very advantageous price to use a massive electric moving sign in Piccadilly Circus. It was a high profile location and carried a compelling message.

The other major decision we took was to have a Central London location in the Shaftesbury Theatre. It was an adventurous decision – but a highly successful one. We had four nights there – the first night was filled for a Christian Workers' Conference – ostensibly to brief counsellors and other participants. The next three nights of the Global Mission we carried the programme live from San Juan. The programme was so good that it felt as if we were amongst the audience in the stadium there. The Shaftesbury Theatre was well-filled every night, and there was a good response at the time of Mr Graham's appeal.

The aftermath of the Global Mission meant some continuing work for the office at Frinton. All the follow-up was done from there. But, as that began to run out, I wondered about the future of our set-up. Surprisingly, there were multitudinous small jobs for the BGEA which kept us all occupied until June 1997. Once more on 5 March 1997 I had the proverbial call from David Rennie. This time he asked me to come to Jean Wilson's office in Buckhurst Hill where he, together with Jerry Miller (Billy Graham's representative), Blair Carlson and Mark Smith would have some important information for me! Two days later we met and I was to learn that the BGEA now wished me to retire completely. In recognition of all my service Billy Graham wished them to make some generous concessions to me, not least was to allow me to retain the office for another year, and to bequeath to me all the equipment which we had assembled. They told me that they had appointed David Vardy as my successor and I could think of no better choice. He would have been my candidate for the work.

During this period there was a Minister's Conference in Stirling, Scotland, Franklin Graham's 'Festival' in Johannesburg and investigation throughout Wales to see if Franklin could conduct his festivals there.

I had very little to do in Stirling, except for 'carrying the Billy Graham flag'. David Vardy was anxious that I should be there for that purpose. However, in Johannesburg I was asked to organise the travel for a party of five Christian leaders from different parts of the UK whom I would accompany to South Africa. The purpose was to allow them to see a Franklin Graham Festival in action, and to determine whether or not a similar event could be held in their areas. More than 10 years later not one of the areas represented had gone ahead with any plans.

Finally the investigation in Wales was with Dr Walter Smyth and Blair Carlson. Once again it was to research possibilities for Franklin Graham to visit the principality. Whilst we made some useful contacts, nothing was firmed up as a result of that visit.

Nevertheless, the Board entertained Marilyn and me to my 'third' retirement dinner! Quite an experience.

These and other activities kept the office busy until the final closure date on 30 June 1998. It was a sad day because it marked my last full-time service with the Billy Graham Evangelistic Association, and almost the end of the 'Thin Gold Line'.

I have always said, 'What hope have I got to retire, when my boss is still going strong?' So even although my daily work was over, and my participation on the board had ended, I was comforted by the fact that David Vardy was in charge of things.

Secondly, I was very pleased to know that the new chairman of the BGEA was to be Mark Smith. On 21 September 1983 I had brought him into the orbit of the association by inviting him to join the board. He had acquitted himself well, and it was entirely appropriate that he should succeed David Rennie as chairman.

CHAPTER TWENTY

A KNIGHTHOOD AND THE LAST CRUSADE

FOR ME a rather dotted 'Thin Gold Line' followed my full retirement and the closing of the Frinton office. I was not sure what future ministry there would be – but David Rennie was still looking out for me – until, that is, he passed away in February 2001. It was like losing an elder brother. All through the years he had looked out for ways in which I could be used in the Lord's service. We had first met during the Tom Rees days when we were both members of the Hildenborough Singers. He was just a month or two older than me, so we had much in common.

It was through David Rennie that so many openings in the Billy Graham work had been offered to me. He was my mentor in so many ways. He was always deeply interested in me and my family, and at the time of his funeral, I had many things to give thanks for. But I missed him enormously.

So I wondered, three months later, what would happen when I received the news that T. W. Wilson had passed away. Everything that David Rennie was to me in Britain, T. W. Wilson had been to me in America. He always seemed to have me in his sights, and I appreciated his friendship, advice and, from time to time, his caution. Now he too was gone. In times gone by this would have produced a telephone call from David Rennie to tell me to go to Montreat (North Carolina) for the funeral. Would anyone be watching out for me now in this new situation?

David Vardy came up trumps. The same day that the news came through of TW's passing, David was on the phone and he told me to get a ticket to go to Montreat to attend the funeral. I was off the next day! It was, in fact, my 500th flight, so it was a rather special one for me.

John and Ann Akers met me on arrival at Asheville airport, and they looked after me for the whole day. John Corts, and many other Team members had, naturally, come to the funeral. The service was taken by TW's pastor who had been deeply challenged at the time of Spre-e73 – mostly through the witness and ministry of the dear old British Evangelist, Lindsay Glegg. It was a lovely service in which Bev Shea sang, and Billy Graham spoke. At the 'wake' afterwards it was just like a mini-team meeting once again as we all greeted one another like long lost brothers.

John Corts drove me back to Charlotte afterwards and we were able to have a good talk about future ministry in the UK. He said that he knew that Billy Graham still had plans for the UK, and that he would be expecting me to carry them out. As it happened, Billy Graham's enthusiasm for coming to Britain was greater than his strength, because the coming never happened. Through the intervening years however, we were often in touch. One of my functions was to keep him informed of any stories relating to his friends in the UK.

Then on 20 November 2001 I received a telephone call from Stephanie Wills, Billy Graham's secretary, to say that Marilyn and I would be receiving an invitation from the American Embassy to attend a 'black tie' dinner at the British Embassy in Washington. The occasion was 'to mark the presentation of an honorary knighthood bestowed by Her Majesty the Queen on Dr William Graham'! What excitement – and what a wonderful opportunity!

I went and booked our airline tickets and we flew to Washington on 5 December. Stephanie had made arrangements for us to stay at the J. W. Marriott Hotel (just across from the White House). We had hardly arrived and checked into our room, when she phoned to say that Billy and Ruth Graham would like to see us and invited us to come up right away. We were met by Maurey Scobee and joined Richard and Liz Bewes, John and Ann Pollock and Jean Wilson who had all come over on another airline. After an hour or so with Billy and Ruth, we returned to our room – suffering jet lag – and went straight to bed.

We had to 'kill time' the next day, so we spent some time shopping in Washington. Larry Ross called me and asked me to tell him what it meant to receive a knighthood! He wanted to be able to explain it adequately to the American newspapers! Then I received an e-mail from the Revd C. Alan Stephens in England, to say that the announcement of Mr Graham's Knighthood had appeared in *The Times* that day.

It took some time to get dressed for the occasion but eventually we met everybody else who had been invited in a special bus which took us directly to the British embassy. Most of Billy and Ruth's children and grandchildren were on the bus, and it was an exciting day for them.

Sir Christopher Meyer, the British ambassador, and his wife met and greeted us at the door, and we were ushered into the drawing room for pre-dinner drinks. The embassy dining room was a picture with beautiful flowers and all the best cutlery and crockery that the embassy possessed. It was a memorable occasion.

The ambassador had done his homework well and he made an excellent speech outlining all that Mr Graham had done in the United Kingdom. This is an extract of what he said:

> In 1946, he endured the darkest days of post-war British cooking. During a three-week visit, which took Dr Graham and his Youth for Christ colleagues the length of Britain, we were unable to find a single egg to offer them.
>
> Undeterred, in 1954, Dr Graham was back again, only to find that a member of parliament had tabled a motion in the House of Commons to prevent him entering the country. When he and Mrs Graham did finally land in England, they were greeted with newspaper comments urging the Bishop of Barking to 'call Billy Graham to repentance before he has the effrontery to start converting us'. 'Apologise, Billy – or stay away', said the headline in the *Daily Herald*, a now defunct British newspaper. I hope we can do a little better tonight.
>
> Dr Graham has made an incalculable contribution to civic and religious life over sixty years. He came to a clear sense of calling to the work of an evangelist as a young man. For more than six

> decades since, he has pursued his calling with a straightforward passion and faithfulness. Along the way he has left us an extraordinary legacy.
>
> Billy Graham has preached the Gospel to more people in live audiences than anyone else in history. His ministry has been truly international. Millions of people throughout the world have found his message inspirational. Lives have been deeply touched and changed. In the furthest corners of the world, Billy Graham has blazed a remarkable trail of Christian commitment, marked by tolerance and respect for others.
>
> Such is Dr Graham's high reputation that he is often called a senior ambassador of Christ. As an ambassador of a mere temporal power, it is for me a special privilege to preside over this ceremony this evening.
>
> It is in recognition of the valuable services rendered to civic and religious life, that I am commanded by Her Majesty the Queen, in accordance with the powers vested in me as her Ambassador, to confer on Dr Billy Graham, the Insignia of Honorary Knight Commander of the Most Excellent Order of the British Empire.

Then, with a great flourish, he endowed Mr Graham with his knighthood, placing the ribbon and medal over his head and around his neck. 'Sir Billy Graham' in effect, but, as an Amercan citizen, it was only an honorary title so he would not use the 'Sir', but would be entitled to put the letters KBE after his name.

Mr Graham then responded in his usual competent and compelling way by saying:

> This has been one of the most unforgettable events of our lives. Thank you for your thoughtfulness in including my family.
>
> I'm also delighted that some of our board of directors are here and especially I would like to recognise my long-time friend, Sir David Frost. We've known each other for most of our lives.
>
> I especially want to ask you, sir, to convey to Her Majesty the Queen, my deepest gratitude for the high honour she has graciously bestowed upon me this evening. I accept it with humility and unworthiness and I take it as a symbol of the common historical ties that have bound our two nations together in war and in peace.
>
> I read a quote that appeared in the *Daily News* in 1903 about Queen Victoria. After hearing Dean Farrer preach a sermon about Christ's return to earth, Queen Victoria said, 'Oh how I wish that the Lord might come during my lifetime.' When the dean asked

her why, she replied, 'I should like to lay my crown at His feet.' And that's the way I feel tonight about any honours that may come to me. I'd like to lay them at His feet and plan to do it some day and at my age it won't be too long.

In the same way, I want to give God all the glory and all the praise for what has been accomplished in my life and those of my family and associates that are here tonight. I, too, look forward to the day when I can see Jesus face to face and lay at His feet any honour I've ever received because He deserves it all.

We stand tonight beside this Christmas tree and I thought about Jesus at Bethlehem as a little baby, growing up to go all the way through the life that He lived, the things He taught, the death He died, the fact that He rose from the dead. It reminds me of the great love that He has for all people. He not only loves the Western world, but He loves all people no matter what their ethnic or religious background is. He is a God of love.

Again, Your Excellency, thank you for this delightful and memorable occasion.

Then, as he ended his speech, he walked across to his wheelchair-bound wife, and gave her a kiss and a hug. The ceremony ended with a further reception in the drawing room. Amongst those we were happy to meet was their youngest son Ned, of whom we had been guardians for the year that he was at Felsted School. Altogether it was an event which will live in our memories for a long time. We flew back to England the next day.

We had the opportunity to visit Minneapolis again in January 2004. I knew that the BGEA offices had moved from there to Charlotte and there was a strong possibility that our old buildings in Minneapolis might be pulled down. I really wanted to see them once again before that happened. So we took advantage of a 'special offer' flight to America. Our visit there was just prior to the annual conference of the National Religious Broadcasters in Charlotte, North Carolina. I realised that, if we attended that, it would also give me the opportunity to see the new BGEA offices in Charlotte.

In the event it turned out to be a 'black' visit. Seven days after we arrived in Minneapolis we received an e-mail to say that our eldest son, Gary, had been rushed into hospital with the possibility of cancer of the colon. It was a worrying time. Because we were on 'special offer' tickets we could not fly home without paying the full cost of the fare. That was something that we could not afford so we prayerfully waited to hear of developments.

From his earliest days, Gary had had a passion for young people and evangelism. He was deeply involved in our church and regularly organised special events for the youth of the church. These included *Armory* – a daily 7am talk on the Bible during the school holidays. It was led by Billy Strachan. It was always well attended in spite of the early hour. Then he organised training events for *Attic* – the evening club – to teach person-to-person evangelism. His practical out-working of this was to open a late-night coffee bar in a vacant shop in Edgware. It was called The Drain, and he had me sitting over a bathtub as the water gurgled down the drain to record the 'theme music' for the entrance lobby! He also worked with Larry Norman, the American Christian 'folk' singer, and with the band Liberation Suite (also from America). Finally he organised a tent mission in Edgware with the support of the young people from several local churches. His heart was in evangelism.

So it was not altogether surprising when, after ten years as a teacher, and Head of the RE department, he followed in my footsteps and went to work with Justin Rees (son of Tom Rees) at Hildenborough Hall. It was during the London Mission, 'New Heart for the Nation', that he received his 'call' to full-time ministry as an Anglican vicar. In the three churches he served (St James Muswell Hill as curate, Emmanuel Church Northwood as assistant rector, and then rector of St Leonard's Chesham Bois), his caring heart made him a leader whose advice and counsel was sought after.

Now he was laid aside with this cancer and it was a tough period for us during our remaining days in America. As soon as we got back we went to see him and found him very weak after a major operation. At first he seemed to be recovering well and our last happy memory of him was when he took us to tea at Arundel during his time in a convalescent home. But, sadly, the cancer came back and he contracted the dreaded hospital disease MRSA; on 21 June 2004 he went to be with the Lord.

The following day we received a moving letter of concolence from Billy Graham:

> Just heard that your beloved son, Gary, has been called to Heaven. Our tears become telescopes to see the joy that awaits all of us.
>
> You and Marilyn have been two of the most faithful friends we have ever had. You will both be constantly in our prayers.
>
> Billy

It was hard on his family as well as on us. It seemed hard to understand why the Lord should take someone who had such an effective ministry. But we learned to realise that His ways are past finding out. Gary's life had made an indelible impact upon his various congregations. But we missed him enormously.

Our great encouragement, however, came through the two thanksgiving services – one for our family and friends, and one for the people of St Leonard's Chesham Bois – when more than 1000 people came to pay tribute to our lovely son.

A long time before, in 1952, the great Brethren Bible teacher, Montague Goodman, saw us at a meeting in Westminster Central Hall. Gary and Cherylyn had recently been born and he asked us 'Are you happy with the samples?' We assured him we were. 'Then don't stop there!' he urged. A few years later Julian and Jacqueline were born. With the first two now in Heaven, how thankful we are that we took Montague Goodman's advice and 'didn't stop there'! Because of that we still have our two wonderful younger children – and six grandchildren in addition to Gary's two boys.

In May 2005, a year after Gary had passed on, an e-mail came to say that Mr Graham would be conducting a three-day crusade in New York. It was anticipated that it would be his last-ever crusade. It was an occasion when, in years gone by, I would have received a phone call from David Rennie telling me to go to New York. However, he was no longer there. Unfortunately David Vardy had resigned from the BGEA in 2003, so no help would be forthcoming from him and I was left with nobody who might suggest going to New York. But I desperately wanted to be there.

In a moment of inspiration I thought of John and Ann Akers. John had been a close colleague of Mr Graham's for many years.

He lived close by to him, and he was someone who both knew me, and knew of my years of service to the BGEA. So I decided to write to him and tell him how much I would like to come to New York. That was in early May and by the end of May there had been no reply from him.

Then on 1 June, when we were with our friends Brian and Elizabeth King-Fisher I had a reply: We had been to the Bath and West show on a very rainy day and to dry out and warm up we stopped at a farm shop in Beckington; I took my mobile phone in with me and we had just got our coffee when my phone rang and there was Stephanie Wills to say that the American office would be sending me airline tickets to New York; arrangements had been made for me to stay at the 'Team' hotel – the Marriott at La Guardia airport. I flew to New York on 22 June 2005 and had two days there before the crusade started on 24 June. Most of the Team were staying at the hotel and, as usual, there was a Team breakfast and an hour-long devotional and briefing meeting each morning. It was wonderful to be back in the atmosphere of the Billy Graham Team. All of them were so friendly, that it was like being back amongst members of the family. It was what Billy Graham had said to me in his letter many years ago.

The crusade was the same as – yet profoundly different from – any earlier crusade that I had experienced. It was 'upgraded' for a new generation and the music was louder and more modern. Dan Wooding said: 'The frail and ailing 87-year-old Billy Graham was joined on stage by his long-time crusade associates Cliff Barrows, now 83 and going blind, and George Beverly Shea, now 97. It was a flashback that many will remember for the rest of their lives.'

Yet we still sang the same old hymns, and there was still a solo by that 97-year-old George Beverly Shea – still singing as strongly as ever – just before Billy Graham spoke.

The mayor of New York was on the platform and he brought a greeting. Mr Graham also introduced the former President Clinton who was at the meeting and was sitting on the platform. Mr Graham said that, in his opinion, Mr Clinton was a new man who now had a faith and trust in God. In fact, added Mr Graham, 'he should become an evangelist – and leave his wife to run the country!' It was a remark which brought considerable amusement to the assembled crowd!

Mr Graham was more brief than in earlier years, yet he had lost none of the fire in his preaching. He preached for commitment, and when he gave the same time-honoured 'invitation', people streamed to the front. As soon as he had concluded his main message, Franklin, his son, slipped in behind him to place a special chair for him to sit on as he watched the crowds stream to the front. It was a recognisable end to a normal Crusade meeting.

Not so on the Saturday when, in line with the Team's practice over many years now, the meeting was dedicated and geared to 'Generation X' – the thousands of young people who came to the crusade meeting. Flushing Meadow was packed to capacity with teenagers of clearly a wide variety of ethnic backgrounds. They jigged up and down to the beat music from several different Christian bands but, at the moment Mr Graham came to the microphone, they quietened down and listened with rapt attention. In his appeal at the end of his address, Billy Graham strove to make it as difficult as possible for them to come to the front yet, nonetheless, many thousands came and were dealt with by counsellors in many languages. All across the front of the platform were the enormous signs indicating where each language group was located. It was impressive.

Sunday was an afternoon meeting – in 90 degrees of heat! It was so hot that I was not sure whether I would last the meeting, sitting under the direct rays of the sun. It was a blessing therefore, when Stephanie Wills came and found me and invited me to sit in the shade with other Team members behind the platform. Richard and Liz Bewes were there also for they had been able to include the New York Crusade in the American schedule which they were completing at that time. That time in New York was to be the last time I would see Liz Bewes because shortly after her return to Britain she was taken ill and went to be with the Lord.

Tex Reardon, a long-standing Team member, was sent to find the three of us and to invite us to go with him to meet Billy Graham in his hotel room after the meeting. It was a great privilege to have – what might easily be – the last-ever opportunity to sit down with him. He had received a pressing invitation from James

Barrett, a London businessman, to return to London for a Crusade. Mr Graham wanted to receive our advice whether or not it was an invitation that we should encourage him to accept.

It was with heavy sadness in our hearts that, in our wisdom, we had to advise against his coming. We based our advice on three main factors.

First, when we heard that he was thinking of accepting in either October or November 2005, we considered that the time was far too short to enable us to do justice to the task of preparation. But he could not come at a later date.

Second, we didn't know of any suitable location where such a mission could be held. None of the usual venues were available and the best we knew of was the London Arena. It was without any seating and the logistic problems would have been enormous.

Third, we no longer had the database that we would have had in earlier years. We needed a vast list of contacts and a major mailing list. Neither of these had remained available since the London office had closed in 1987 when all our records were sent to either Minneapolis or the Billy Graham archives in Wheaton, Illinois. It would have been very hard for us to engender the support that would be needed for a successful mission.

It was with great reluctance therefore that we had to advise against his coming. Nevertheless we encouraged him to come in November and meet with his friends. It might also be possible for him to 'hand on the torch' by speaking at two or three Ministers' Meetings in some central location. We left that thought with him.

It was a wonderful 'wrap up' for me as I saw the 'Thin Gold Line' stretch through this event – and now I waited to see where it would lead next.

Shortly afterwards I had – what could easily be – the last letter I would ever have from him. He said:

> Thank you for being willing to come over to my hotel after the closing meeting on Sunday, in order to meet with me and Richard and Liz Bewes about the invitation I had received to London.
>
> After talking with you I feel I do not have the necessary vision, burden, and clearance from the Lord to come back to London at this time. I am deeply grateful for the invitation and the confidence that James Barrett's committee in London places in me, but

do not feel in my heart that I can accept. I will continue to think and pray about the possibility of addressing clergy, or even a dinner for some old friends – this appeals much more to me, given my physical situation.

As well as our discussions about the future, I also enjoyed reminiscing about some of the past experiences. It is hard to forget that you came to Northwestern Schools many years ago when I was president, and since then we have been tied together in ministry – not only in the UK but throughout the world.

I hope you had a comfortable flight home on Monday. Please give my warmest Christian affection to Marilyn.

CHAPTER TWENTY-ONE

WRAPPING UP THE DIARY

THE 'THIN GOLD LINE' that started in March 1948 came to an end in 2005 with the 'last' Billy Graham Crusade in New York. Throughout that time there had been a traceable evidence of God's Hand at work in my life. Within this story I have told many of the incidents and anecdotes that have meant much to me both in my work with Billy Graham, and in my own personal life. Yet the stories already told do not give the whole picture.

There are many stories which refer to matters which concerned my family and me. For example, I have told the story of Cherylyn's death in 1972. Our younger son, Julian, was about to start a new school that very morning and he set off from home with his school briefcase covered with 'Jesus' stickers. Two days before, on the Saturday, he had been at the Festival of Light rally in Trafalgar Square. It had been a thrilling time for him. As a testimony to his faith he had collected these stickers which had been widely distributed. On the way home on the tube, he and another 13-year-old friend had witnessed to a 'gentleman of the road' and he had professed faith in Christ. The boys were so excited. I said to Julian, 'Remember Julian, you have been on the mountain top. But afterwards always comes the valley.'

It was a natural thing to him to continue his witnessing as he went to his new school. I warned him about the possibility of teasing and persecution if he made such an overt stand for Christ on his first day. But he was adamant: that was what Jesus would want him to do! When he came home from school that day we had to tell him that his elder sister had been killed. He said, 'Dad, I didn't know the valley would be that deep!' But his faith survived and saw him through that terrible time.

My diary, which I started on 1 January 1944, has been continued ever since – and still continues – without ever missing a day. It contains a multitude of other experiences many of which, inevitably, involved Billy Graham.

There were other activities too, for instance my association with the Arthur Ransome Society – a group of people who owed something to the writer of *Swallows and Amazons.* It changed me, a boy who at seven years of age hated the water, into someone for whom 'being on the water' became a spare-time obsession. I spent every available minute in one way or another on the various ships that I had owned. Indeed I have not given much space to tell of the many stories from my sailing hobby. Arthur Ransome was not renowned for his interest in spiritual things, and he would have been very surprised to know that his writings inspired evangelistic opportunities – like, of course, the Venturers Cruise. It 'grew out' of the stories in the Ransome books and the cruise deserved a chapter of its own – and got it!

My 27 years sailing off the east coast of Essex in my wonderful Norfolk *Coypu* dinghy was my greatest form of relaxation – yet I never escaped from the aegis of the Christian work I was doing. Nearly always I had a Christian friend (or friends) sailing with me and our conversation was mostly about the various works that God had given us to do. The *Coypu* was replaced later on by a 28-foot Jaguar yacht which meant more space – so even more Christian friends came with me. In turn the Jaguar gave way to an 18-foot Cornish shrimper. The shrimper was about the largest vessel I could handle on my own – an important consideration because Marilyn never liked being on the water and she rarely came with me. I always said, 'I'll go off sailing and leave Marilyn to what she loves to do – her knitting or crochet!' But the *Coypu* was always my 'first love' after Marilyn! Neither can I leave out my 19 trips to the Caribbean, leading Christian groups to sail on the magnificent *Mandalay* – a sailing vessel 236 feet long, with a complement of 72 passengers looked after by a crew of 28. The ten I took with me were a quiet witness for Christ amongst the other 62 passengers.

One thing I discovered amongst the – mostly – American passengers on the *Mandalay* was the difference in talking to them about Billy Graham. In England, as soon as his name was mentioned it was often the end of the conversation. With the Americans on the *Mandalay* it was exactly the opposite. They held him in such high regard, and had such a respect for him, that any mention of his name opened up a lively and interesting conversation.

Canon Michael Saward had come with me on one of these trips. At the time he was Canon Treasurer of St Paul's Cathedral in London. He knew of my reticence to say that I worked for Billy Graham. One day, after a trip ashore in the small ship's boat, he came back aboard and said, 'Maurice, I'm afraid I've blown your cover!' He then told me that there had been a couple of American girls on the boat with him and, in conversation, they had mentioned that the Alpha course had been done in their church in Colorado. It became clear that they were both keen Christians and, inadvertently, he had 'slipped in' my connection with Billy Graham. As a result a whole new area of conversation opened up aboard, and we had some good times of fellowship with them. One of them, Nancy Lindblade, had two daughters and we got talking about the Venturers Cruise. To cut a long story short, those two girls came all the way from Colorado to join the cruise the following year. One of them declared it to be 'a stinkingly awesome experience'! She returned again from Colorado the following year.

Our friends, Nigel and Helen Cooke (whom we first met during our days at Hildenborough Hall) founded an international organisation which Nigel called the Christian European Visual Media Association (CEVMA for short). As soon as we heard about it we wanted to be involved in order to provide some input from the film work of the Billy Graham Evangelistic Association. We went to the first conference in Wetzlar, Germany, in 1981 and have rarely missed a conference since. We found it to be one of the most effective conferences that we ever attended and the spirit of Christian fellowship with participants from all over the world made it very special.

I also need to tell of my 20 plus years as chairman of Trans World Radio in the UK. They were not easy years as we were attempting to bring Christian broadcasting into a nation which prohibited the ownership of Christian radio stations. So we broadcast from Monte Carlo, but the administrative offices were in the UK. The part I played in TWR reflected my own personal interest in Christian radio broadcasting – starting, I suppose, from my involvement in the two Christian radio stations in Minneapolis. From 1988 onwards I was remotely involved in the broadcast of a weekly programme on KTIS, the Christian Radio Station in Minneapolis. My involvement was little more than giving encouragement to Paul Ramseyer who was the executive producer of the programme. From September 1988 he continually sent me cassette tapes of the programme. It was a very light-hearted programme in which the format allowed Christian people to stand back and see how they looked to others. It gently poked fun at some of the things they said and did – yet never with any offence.

Each programme included superb musical items. One of these was a song by guest soloist Johnny Hall whose wife had just had a baby boy. He put into song his thoughts that 'somewhere in the world today' is a baby girl who will grow up and, one day, will become the wife of his baby son. The song prayed that God would protect both babies and bring them together when they grew up, and in His good time. There were other guest participants, and, always, a remarkable closing segment by the host of the programme Richard K. Alison. The most memorable of those presentations by him was just a few weeks before he died from cancer. He asked the question 'Why' (does God allow this thing to happen)? He answered it with a beautiful talk on walking daily and faithfully, with God. Then he closed the segment by singing 'I will trust you, God' and a few weeks later he was in Glory himself.

Every one of these activities and many more gave the opportunity to witness for the Lord. It mattered not which group I was with, they soon discovered my faith and learned what I did. It was inevitable – and profitable for the Lord. Every activity was part of the overall story which helped to make me a 'rounded person'. I was able to look at the world in which I lived, and realise that there were a whole lot of people out there who needed to find the Lord.

The reader will remember George Wilson's original instructions to me: 'You are employed for 365 days a year and 24 hours a day. Any time left over is your own!' Later on, of course, I discovered that this really meant that when the association, or Billy Graham himself, wanted me, then that took priority over everything else. Everything in which I was involved always took second place. I have to say, I loved it! A vocation such as this was a wonderful experience. I rejoiced that God had both called me to this work and allowed me to do it. Looking back, I hope I served Him well.

Now that I have come to the end of the 'Thin Gold Line' it is time to place it back into His hands. He has led me all the way and He has brought me to this point. Have I ever regretted it? No! A thousand times no! As I write this I am more than 81 years of age – yet, like Abraham, my eye is not (too) dim, my mind is still (reasonably) clear. My energy seems unabated (although the knees are a bit weak) and my desire to serve is undiminished. There may be times even yet when I shall be summoned back to do some particular work for Mr Graham or for the association. I have always said, 'What hope have I got of retiring when my boss is still going strong?'

Like Billy Graham, I now look forward to that great and glorious day when the trumpet will sound, and there will be a shout from Heaven to declare, '*Enough!*' and He will return to give us all new bodies and to take us to be with Him. I scarcely think my 'Thin Gold Line' will have any shine to it when it is put against the Glories of Heaven where, after all, the paving stones themselves will be of gold (Revelations 21:21). So I'm not really worried about where the 'Thin Gold Line' will end up when we get to Heaven. All I know about that is that the Lamb will be there and the Glory of God will outshine anything else I ever knew.

I cannot end a book like this without asking if that is also your hope. I would not be true to my lifetime commitment to evangelism if I didn't end by urging you to be sure of your forgiveness. Tom Rees made it quite clear at the very beginning of the story that I was called to be an 'administrator' to make it possible for him (and others like him) to do their job well. So I have tried to honour that calling and to do those things that enable evangelism to be effective, clear, simple and challenging. But that does not mean that I am not personally burdened that you too should have a living faith. I have to ask the question, 'Have you placed your faith in the Lord Jesus Christ?' As I bring this book to a conclusion it is my prayer that you may do so.

How can you do this? Three things are involved. First, a realisation that there are things that are wrong in our lives, which the Bible calls 'sin'. We need to repent to God for those things and to ask His forgiveness. Second, we need to believe that our sins were taken away through the shed blood of Christ on the Cross. By dying there – Himself a sinless One – He was able to pay the price and penalty of sin that God demands. Third, we need to come to Him and accept Him as our Saviour. We need to make Him the Lord of our lives and ask Him to help us overcome the temptation to sin. You need to commit your life to Him. This is a short prayer that could help you to do this:

> Cleanse me from my sin and put Your power within, Lord. Take me as I am and make me all Your own. Keep me day by day Lord, and help me to live for You every moment of every day. For the sake of Jesus Christ Your Son. Amen

These three steps and a prayer like that are the beginning of a fuller life. His Holy Spirit then lives within you and makes your life complete. This means that everything you do in your life is done with the consciousness that He is with you.

From the story you have read you will realise that being a Christian has not in any way inhibited my life. Rather it has enhanced it beyond all measure. God has allowed me to take Him with me into every activity of life. That has given life an exciting dimension – something I wouldn't have changed for any reason whatsoever.

Finally, Billy Graham always encourages those who become Christians to do three things. First, it is important to read the Bible and to pray to God. Prayer is the breath of life for those who believe. Reading the Bible is the food and drink that is needed for a healthy spiritual life.

Second, it is important to get into the life of a good and Bible-teaching church. Cliff Richard was once asked if it was necessary to go to church to become a Christian. 'No!' he replied. 'You can become a Christian without ever going to church.' Then he added, 'But I will say this. After you become a Christian you may find that you would like to be with other like-minded people. And it is most possible that you will find those people in church!' Then he added, 'You'll also learn lots of things to help you to live a Christian life.' As prayer is breath, and reading the Bible is food and drink, so going to church is exercise that you need for a healthy spiritual body.

Third, you need to tell someone else what has happened to you. It will do three things. It will strengthen you as you share your faith. It will encourage other people who are already Christians and it may result in the person you tell becoming a Christian themselves. That is called 'witnessing' and is the way you have 'spiritual babies' as a Christian.

If you need further help in understanding how to take these steps, one of the offices of the Billy Graham Evangelistic Association will be happy to help – or you can find the outline of 'Steps to Peace with God' on this website:

http://www.billygraham.org/SH_StepsToPeace.asp

or by mail:

Billy Graham Evangelistic Association (UK)
PO Box 2032
Woodford Green
Essex IG9 5AP
Phone: 020 8559 0342
(from whom copies of 'The Missing Piece' can be obtained – see page 171.)

Billy Graham Evangelistic Association (USA)
1 Billy Graham Parkway
Charlotte, NC 28201 USA
Phone: (704) 401-2432

Also: Worldwide offices in Australia, Canada, France, Germany, New Zealand and Spain.

Also see: www.billygraham.org

APPENDIX

BILLY GRAHAM'S 23 CRUSADES AND MISSIONS IN THE UNITED KINGDOM FROM 1954–1991

(Note: Mr Graham paid several visits to the UK from 1946 onwards. From October 1946 to March 1947 he lived in the UK – staying mostly in private homes and visiting many local churches. To qualify as a 'Crusade' implies an organising committee: participation of the American Team, training of counsellors and follow-up, and a sequential series of meetings of two days or more.)

1954 March – May. The Greater London Crusade in the Harringay Arena (including closing meetings in White City Stadium and the Wembley Stadium)

1955 Kelvin Hall, Glasgow. Including more than 2000 landline relays across the UK

1955 The Wembley Crusade

1961 Maine Road Stadium, Manchester

1966 Earls Court Crusade

1967 Earls Court closed circuit TV Crusade

1973 Spre-e73 at Earls Court. (Closing meeting at Wembley Stadium)

1980 Oxford University Mission

1980 Cambridge University Mission

1982 Blackpool mini-Crusade in the Winter Gardens

1984 Mission England – Bristol

1984 Mission England – Sunderland

1984 Mission England – Norwich

1984 Mission England – Liverpool

1984 Mission England – Birmingham

1984 Mission England – Ipswich

1985 Mission England – Sheffield

1989 Mission to London – West Ham Stadium

1989 Mission to London – Crystal Palace

1989 Mission to London – Earls Court. (Closing meeting at Wembley Stadium)

1990 Mission to Scotland – Edinburgh

1991 Mission to Scotland – Aberdeen

1991 Mission to Scotland – Glasgow

COPYRIGHT ACKNOWLEDGEMENTS

The Publishers wish to thank all those who have given their permission to reproduce copyright material in this publication.

Prologue	Page 14: Smith, Gypsy, *The Beauty of Jesus* (Epworth Press, 1933) 109
Chapter 1	Page 33: May, John, *The Norfolk Broads Holiday Book and Pocket Pilot* (Hulton Press, 1952) 134ff
Chapter 4	Page 64: Constance Wells writing in *East Essex Times and Gazette*, Friday, 30 September 1949
Chapter 8	Page 109: NOTE – *Souls in Conflict*, *Oil Town USA*, *Touch of Brass* and all other Billy Graham films referred to in this book are produced and distributed by World Wide Pictures
Chapter 12	Page 153: Toby Travis writing in *The Magic Circular*, February 2006
Chapter 14	Page 183: Coomes, Anne, *Festo Kivengere* (Monarch, 1990) 364-70
Chapter 15	Page 205: Williams, Derek, *One in a Million* (Word UK, 1984) 159

Every effort has been made to trace the owners of copyright material and we hope that no copyright has been infringed. Pardon is sought and apology made if the contrary be the case, and a correction will be made in any reprint of this book.

BIBLIOGRAPHY

BGEA, *On the Other Side*, Scripture Union (1968)

Colquhoun, Frank, *The Harringay Story*, Hodder & Stoughton (1955)

Cook, Dr C. T., *London Hears Billy Graham: The Harringay Story*, Marshall, Morgan & Scott (1954)

Coomes, Anne, *Festo Kivengere*, Monarch (1990)

Coomes, David, *Spre-e73*, Coverdale House (1973)

Graham, Billy, *Just as I Am*, Harper/Zondervan (1997)

— *Peace with God*, Doubleday & Word (1953)

— *The Secret of Happiness*, Doubleday & Word (1955)

Haraszti, Dr Alexander, *I Am but One . . .* [video], Fórum Film Alapítvány, Budapest (2001)

Martin, William, *A Prophet with Honour*, William Morrow & Co (1966)

May, John, *The Norfolk Broads Holiday Book . . .*, Hulton Press (1952)

Reid, Gavin, *To Canterbury with Love*, Kingsway Publications (2002)

Rowlandson, Maurice, *I'm Going to Ask You . . .*, Hodder & Stoughton (1997)

— *Life at the Keswick Convention*, O.M. Publishing Co (1997)

— *Life with Billy*, Hodder & Stoughton (1992)

— *Life with the Venturers*, Dudley Stationery (1994)

Smith, Gypsy, *The Beauty of Jesus*, Epworth Press (1932)
Williams, Derek, *One in a Million*, Word UK (1984)

The reader may also like to consult the following:

Drummond, Lewis A., *Evangelist*, Word (2001)
Pollock, John C., *Billy Graham*, Harper & Row (1979)

INDEX OF PEOPLE